Praise for

Marlene Wagman-Geller

Women of Means

"If you've ever wished you had all the money in the world, read Women of Means by Marlene Wagman-Geller. Written in her usual witty prose, these enthralling but petrifying mini-biographies show that when a woman is too wealthy, it can be a curse rather than a blessing."

—**Jill G. Hall,** author of The Silver Shoes and The Black Velvet Coat

"Does money facilitate happiness, fulfillment, the good life? How much time do we all spend wishing we had more of it? These questions and more bubble up from Marlene Wagman-Geller's crisp, exacting prose in her powerful compilation of stories about the richest women in history, Women of Means. Wagman-Geller's stories made me gasp and lodged my chin firmly on my chest as she chronicled the lives of women without a financial care in the world, whose appetites led so often to disaster. And, no, Patrizia, I would rather gleefully ride the bicycle!"

—**R. D. Kardon,** author of *Flygirl*

Great Second Acts

"Others will surprise you as they've all done extraordinary things past the date when women are considered 'young & fresh.' The book is well written and highly entertaining, but it comes with a message: In a society where ageism is rampant, we need to rethink how we view more mature women because they are capable of greatness."

—**Advice Sisters**

"Marlene Wagman-Geller has done it again! She's written another fascinating book filled with interesting facts about women who have done so much to make the world a better place. This time though all the mini-biographies tell stories about females who have had fulfilling productive lives even into their later years. With gratitude, I've found this book to be inspiring and has given me hope and encouragement to continue on my own path as I continue to age."

—**Jill G. Hall**

"These bold women are proof that the rest of your life can be the best of your life."

—**Louise Harmon**, author of *Happiness A to Z*

Women Who Launch

"Want to find courage? Look to those women who changed the game. Women Who Launch shares the stories of the inspiring women behind brands and organizations. You may know their names, but you might not know their stories. This book changes that, and lets you know of the extraordinary women who came before. Learn about women who changed the era, from Estee Lauder to the creator of The Girl Scouts, Juliette Gordon Low."

—**Bliss.com**

"We all need a little inspiration in the world of entrepreneurship, and where better to get it than from reading the stories of women game-changers in the world who built hugely successful companies, organizations and brands, despite all the challenges they faced. This is an insightful read into the women who, in their own way, changed the world they lived in, and blazed a trail for so many other aspirant women entrepreneurs and women change-agents to follow."

—**Lionesses of Africa**

The Secret Lives of

Royal Women

Also by

Marlene Wagman-Geller

*Unabashed Women: The Fascinating Biographies of Bad
Girls, Seductresses, Rebels, and One-of-a-Kind Women*

Fabulous Female Firsts: Because of Them We Can

*Women of Means: Fascinating Biographies of Royals,
Heiresses, Eccentrics, and Other Poor Little Rich Girls*

Great Second Acts: In Praise of Older Women

Women Who Launch: Women Who Shattered Glass Ceilings

Still I Rise: The Persistence of Phenomenal Women

*Behind Every Great Man: The Forgotten Women Behind the
World's Famous and Infamous*

*And the Rest is History: The Famous (and Infamous) First
Meetings of the World's Most Passionate Couples*

*Eureka! The Surprising Stories Behind the Ideas That Shaped
the World*

*Once Again to Zelda: The Stories Behind Literature's Most
Intriguing Dedications*

The Secret Lives of

Royal Women

Fascinating Biographies of Queens, Princesses, Duchesses, and Other Regal Women

MARLENE WAGMAN-GELLER

mango
PUBLISHING

CORAL GABLES

Cover Design: Megan Werner
Cover Photo: Saraid / stock.adobe.com
Layout & Design: Megan Werner

For permission requests, please contact the publisher at:
Mango Publishing Group
2850 S Douglas Road, 4th Floor
Coral Gables, FL 33134 USA
info@mango.bz

For special orders, quantity sales, course adoptions and corporate sales, please email the publisher at sales@mango.bz. For trade and wholesale sales, please contact Ingram Publisher Services at customer.service@ingramcontent.com or +1.800.509.4887.

The Secret Lives of Royal Women: Fascinating Biographies of Queens, Princesses, Duchesses, and Other Regal Women

Library of Congress Cataloging-in-Publication number: 2022939091
ISBN: (p) 978-1-64250-943-4 (e) 978-1-64250-944-1
BISAC category code BIO014000, BIOGRAPHY & AUTOBIOGRAPHY / Royalty

Printed in the United States of America

To my mother Gilda Wagman, to my daughter Jordanna Geller, and to my friend Jamie Lovett

---

"Uneasy lies the head that wears the crown."
—**William Shakespeare**, from *Henry IV*

"Above all things our royalty is to be reverenced, and if you begin to poke about it, you cannot reverence it...Its mystery is its life. We must not let in daylight upon magic."

—**Walter Bagehot**, from *The English Constitution* (1867)

Table of Contents

Foreword

F or anyone in need of a heady dose of schadenfreude, one can keep track of the body count in Shakespeare's tragedies—and even in a couple of his comedies. Macbeth kills the guy who was going to kill King Duncan, and then he kills King Duncan, and then dispatches two drunk attendants whom he *accuses* of killing King Duncan. Then he organizes the killing of his best friend, as well as his enemy's wife and young son, and finally carves up Siward, Junior. Macbeth finally appears on stage as a head that has lost contact with the rest of him. What fun!

But we don't have to turn to the theatre to find treachery and murder; the people sitting in the royal box at the Globe had plenty of that going on well away from the stage. And all too often, those who spilled the most blood—and caused a lot of the spillage—were women who wore crowns. These are the stories that Marlene Wagman-Geller recounts in this collection about royal women throughout history and around the world.

When we were young, many of us learned the bit of doggerel about the fates of Henry VIII's brides—"Divorced, Beheaded, Died, / Divorced, Beheaded, Survived." Catherine, Anne, Jane, the other Anne, the other Catherine, and the *other* other Catherine lived in a world of jewels and axes, of palaces and dungeons. The tale of the first beheaded wife—the first Anne—is told in a straightforward way, but it is obviously told by a woman, and even through the author's objectivity, we can see where her sympathies lie.

The historical ladies Wagman-Geller brings us would make an exhilarating dinner party—with five and a quarter centuries of love and betrayal, of the loss of crowns, and often, heads. We see a much broader look at the stages on which great dramas were played out with real passion and real blood, and with real sovereignty and families to lose. And during a lull in the conversation, we might hear Duchess Cayetana tell of riding her horse into the cathedral or threatening to bury all who opposed her. Or we might hear the soft voice of twelve-year-old future Queen Victoria telling her fellow guests what she already understood at a young age about the weight of a crown: "There is much splendor, and there is much responsibility." There is also much danger and much heartache for those who "know the storm" that the blue bloods weather.

Even monarchs who have thrones, though no swords, have compelling stories. The fairy tale that Princess Diana represented is an example. Wagman-Geller reminds us that Diana had known storms and was ready to embrace the calm when she lost her chance in the Pont de l'Alma tunnel.

And Prince Andrew, the former husband of Diana's sister-in-law Fergie, offers a very contemporary story that is sordid and ugly, but draws comparisons to that of Empress Joséphine, possessed as she was of prodigious carnal talents and "a little black forest." They shock, they entertain; they titillate and infuriate—as royals have done since Henry swapped out Catalina de Aragón for the English Reformation.

Wagman-Geller spills quite a lot of blood on these pages; here there is treachery and betrayal, but passion and loyalty as well. And there are storms that seem, even today, to have assaulted women who wielded the scepter.

Ben Cassel, drama teacher
Yucca Valley, California
January 5, 2022

The Princess Prevails

A nursery rhyme offers the philosophical observation, "What are little girls made of? Sugar and spice and all things nice, that's what little girls are made of." However, there is something else embedded in the DNA of many girls; namely, an obsession with royalty. Mine started when I was a child in 1950s Toronto, Canada, where I devoured every word and looked longingly at each illustration of my book based on the tales by the Brothers Grimm.

The stories of enchantment offered the perfect escape route from reality; how, I wondered, could the exalted few lead such extraordinary lives? The princesses lived in castles, they had treasure chests of jewels, their wardrobes held gowns of gossamer. In contrast, their non-blue-blood counterparts grew up in subdivisions, wore rings compliments of a five-cent toy dispenser, and dressed in clothes that'd had former owners. Who would not want to trade places with those who rode in carriages, had servants to do their bidding, and commanded the best of everything? These golden girls ended up with husbands able to trace their ancestors' lineage for centuries, whose bank accounts had more digits than phone numbers and whose relatives had titles. The rest of us counted ourselves fortunate if we could find a man without a felony or an outstanding warrant, not one familiar with Chapter 13. Moreover, in my dog-eared Brothers Grimm tales, the ladies with the tiaras were also the winners of genetic lotteries. The contrast between those who sat upon a throne and those who did not (merely because of a vagary of fate) was my first brush with the realization that not everyone is dealt equal cards.

Of course, being born royal is not a shield against misfortune. Sleeping Beauty and Snow White fell into preternaturally long slumbers, the result of a poisoned spindle and apple. Nevertheless, their vicissitudes had expiration dates: Prince Charmings came to their rescue. Fall into a sound sleep and be saved? Hell, those scepter-wielding dames sure had it made.

The Disney Corporation hooked a new generation, using princesses to create a merchandising juggernaut. Living in San Diego, where my daughter grew up in the 1990s, the industry was a magnet for wannabe royals: All the little ladies related to a Disney heroine whose idealized image emblazoned their lunch boxes, dresses, and bedding. Indeed, I contributed my fair share to the Princess Industrial Complex, a billion-dollar-plus enterprise. But it is not just little girls who are hardwired for peering through the peepholes of palaces. Ever since Helen of Troy launched a thousand ships, queens have graced countless magazines, stamps, and currency. These ladies have always been fixtures of fascination; Shakespeare devoted whole segments of his folios to their exploits and foibles. As the Bard wrote of Cleopatra, the Queen of the Nile, "Age cannot wither her, nor custom stale / Her infinite variety."

However, is it still relevant to buy into the regal conceit? As adults, we know Prince Charming is not always who he is cracked up to be (Henry VIII, for example, used decapitation in lieu of divorce). Are crowned heads still relevant now that women are striving to shatter glass ceilings rather than salivating for glass slippers? The reality is upper crust watching is at its apogee with no sign of it abating. Proof positive: Seventy-three million tuned in to watch the Netflix series *The Crown.*

The question that lingers: Why are the masses drawn to Her Majesty's magnet? Is it not antiquated to cling to a premise that certain individuals are born to rule? After all, the ideology of the divine right of kings has gone the way of the rotary phone. While there is a battle cry against the patriarchy, why does monarchy, the most elitist of all institutions, get a pass? As even the most casual of history students knows, America fought a war to rid itself of the Brits who taxed our tea; so why are their aristocrats still on our radar? The newly elected George Washington resisted overtures that he be crowned King of the

Thirteen Colonies upon his inauguration. He also rejected the title, "His Highness the President of the United States of America and Protector of Their Liberties." At Washington's request, his men agreed that he would simply be called Mr. President (the two-word title is quite far afield from that of Queen Elizabeth II: Her Most Excellent Majesty Elizabeth the Second, by the Grace of God of the United Kingdom of Great Britain and Northern Ireland and of Her Other Realms and Territories Queen, Head of the Commonwealth, Defender of the Faith). In this more democratic clime, some people argue for what would have been treason to utter a century ago: Royalty needs to pack their scepters in mothballs. Many feel it is time to bid cheerio to the titled few who receive millions in taxpayer dollars in exchange for appearing on the palace balcony for the Trooping of the Colour, cutting ribbons, and waving from vintage Rolls-Royces. An anti-monarchist analogy argues the institution of rule by birthright is akin to the vestigial appendix: no longer needed, dangerous when burst.

And yet, the blue bloods, especially those who formerly ruled from the other side of the pond, remain Pied Pipers luring us with their ever so grandiose ways. In 1860, when Albert Edward, the Prince of Wales, visited the United States on the eve of its civil war, hundreds of thousands of spectators lined up, from Boston to Richmond, to catch a glimpse of one destined to rule. Despite the impending Union-Confederate bloodbath and the fact Wall Street was in a panic, it was the eighteen-year-old prince who appeared several times on the cover of *Harper's Weekly*. The descendants of George III continue to fill the pages of *Vanity Fair*; indeed, the term "vanity fair" can be seen as an apt description of the monarchy—a place characterized by hollow ostentation.

One reason for fealty to the crown is because the royals have larger-than-life existences; they can, therefore, help us to vicariously exchange the black-and-white of everyday existence for a burst of Technicolor. Rather than focusing on the minutia of office politics, the PTA, or bills, through them we can engage in water-cooler convo regarding their jet-setting lifestyles, their fleet of cars, their crown jewels. Would we not have withdrawal pains if we failed to see their outlandish fascinators at the Epsom Derby? We also feel engaged as members of royal families stare out at us from the Internet, magazines, and nightly newscasts, making us feel we have a vested interest in their lives. While we might have no idea as to the identity of our neighbors, most people know Elizabeth Alexandra Mary Windsor, a.k.a. Queen Elizabeth II, her late husband, Prince Philip, her four children, and her corgis. The Windsors serve as a nonfictional *Truman Show*, seeming to exist more for the public's viewing pleasure than as private individuals. The soap opera of the dysfunctional family with posh accents continues to exert a pull on the public just as the wind does one the waves. And the hypnosis holds true whatever one's latitude or longitude.

A further phenomenon that whets the public interest is the lives of the uber rich, the subject of my 2019 book, *Women of Means: Fascinating Biographies of Royals, Heiresses, Eccentrics, and Other Poor Little Rich Girls*. Interest in the top one percent increases when great wealth goes hand in hand with royalty. While the Windsors are the most renowned of the royals, they do not possess the greatest wealth. In 2015, *TIME* Magazine published an article about the world's ten richest hereditary rulers. Heading the list was Bhumibol Adulyadej, King of Thailand, who has a fortune of $30 billion. He is also the possessor of the 545-carat Golden Jubilee, the largest cut and faceted diamond in the world. The second entry was Hassanal Bolkiah, Sultan of Brunei, with a $20 billion bankroll. The King has a penchant for lavish living: he reportedly owns approximately six hundred Rolls-Royces; his residence, Istana Nurul Iman, is the world's largest palace, one that came with a cost of $350 million. The late King of Saudi Arabia, Abdullah bin Abdulaziz Al Saud, left behind a treasury of $18 billion. The statistic is hearty fare for those who borrow from Peter to give to Paul.

Those to the manor born excite interest on a regular basis, especially over a wedding, christening, or funeral. When Prince William married Catherine, they did so while twenty-three million viewers looked on; the world anticipated the birth of Prince George as if it were the second coming. The bereft face of Queen Elizabeth at the funeral church service for her husband tugged at our heartstrings. But what makes the paparazzi go into a feeding frenzy is a scandal royale.

From pre-revolutionary France came a brouhaha involving Marie Antoinette. Marilyn Monroe's lyric "Diamonds are a girl's best friend" did not hold true for this queen, who became embroiled in a publicity disaster over a diamond necklace. The repercussions of the incident helped hasten the death knell for the Bourbon dynasty. Another royal who captured realms of ink was the Duke of Windsor, who abdicated in order to marry his mistress. If repudiating his birthright did not cause enough jaws to drop, a few months later, the couple joined Adolph Hitler in his mountain retreat, where they bonded over tea. More recently, the Firm had to strip Prince Andrew of his royal duties and titles because of his alleged involvement with sex trafficker Jeffrey Epstein, who committed suicide while incarcerated.

An adage by British journalist Walter Bagehot states, "In its mystery is its life. We must not let daylight in upon magic." Familiarity with the famous strips them of their allure, and that is why the Windsors went into a defensive crouch when Oprah announced she would be interviewing Harry and Meghan. Not since Tom Cruise, in an act of Tomfoolery, used Oprah's couch as a bouncy castle to declare his love for Katie Holmes had the talk-show queen aired such a memorable segment. The verbal grenades lobbed against Buckingham Palace made many feel the Firm was a hotbed of racism, a notion that seemed aligned with the imperialist empire which had long championed the notion of "the white man's burden." When the Duchess claimed her in-laws had conversations with Harry in which they inquired about how dark their baby's skin might be, a shocked Oprah responded with the one word, "What?" a reaction that became a social media meme. Patrick Freyne wrote in The Irish Times, "Having a queen as head of state is like having a pirate or a mermaid or an Ewok." After the interview, in response to the outcry that the monarchy was both archaic and racist, Freyne responded, "Well, duh."

The Irish journalist's statement reinforced the notion that it the time had come to stop bowing before those who had not done anything to better humanity. Rather, the only reason royals commanded adulation was because they were the ancestors of someone who, centuries ago, took control through military force. In 1297, François Grimaldi, disguised as a monk, entered a fortress perched on a rock high above the Mediterranean. With a sword hidden in his habit, he overpowered the guards and let in his soldiers, who then murdered the holy men. He set himself up as François I, a king whose descendants still rule the glittering municipality of Monaco. Hereditary titles are the epitome of inequity, a slap in the face to democratic principles. One should bow to Mother Teresa, Nelson Mandela, or Dr. King, not before someone whose genealogy can be traced to a warlord whose creed was "might is right." Prince Harry, in the bombshell tell-all, explained he was walking away from his pedigreed position because he no longer wanted to be a part of a system founded on the bedrock of elitism, one that made his wife a target for trolls (in a nod to irony, the couple used the interview—which garnered millions of spectators—as a plea for privacy).

Given the randy and raucous predilections of the royals, they slake our thirst for pomp and circumstance while satiating our desire for scandal. Besides, paparazzi need the monarchies of the world to provide the never-ending photo ops that set Twitter aflutter. The press knows that the public's thirst will never be filled for blue bloods draped in fabulous attire, on exotic vacations, in over-the-top escapades. For that reason, those who dwell in castles will most likely continue to live at their same ancient addresses. The British national anthem line holds true regarding crowned heads: "Long to reign over us."

In a world where the rug is constantly ripped from under us over headlines that bring heartbreak, the monarchy provides a sense of tradition. The Old and New Testaments and the Quran all reference kings and queens. Royalty has long been part of the world's DNA, dressed in a kaleidoscope of pageantry ranging from that of the pharaohs of Egypt, the emperors of Japan, and the Caesars of Rome to the tsars of

Russia. However, several powerful dynasties once believed impregnable now merely reside in a gilded niche of history: the Bourbons of France, the Romanovs of Russia, the Habsburgs of Austria-Hungary. Winston Churchill, a staunch monarchist, wrote in 1945, "This war would never have come unless, under American and modernizing pressure, we had driven the Habsburgs out of Austria and Hungary and the Hohenzollerns out of Germany. By making these vacuums, we gave the opening for the Hitlerite monster to crawl out of its sewer onto the vacant thrones." The Americans, in a similar belief as to the stabilizing influence of royalty, were behind President Truman's decision to allow Hirohito to remain on Japan's Chrysanthemum Throne.

In a world where epidemics ravage and where every news website reveals further acts of inhumanity, I can surely be forgiven for playing one of my daughter's childhood tapes, an avenue of escapism where the princess always prevails.

CHAPTER 1

The Last Word

— 1501 —

K ings are subject to grand gestures, sometimes of a romantic nature. Legend holds that when Queen Amytis grew homesick for the lush landscape of her native Media, her husband, King Nebuchadnezzar II, commissioned the Hanging Gardens of Babylon in his desert kingdom. When Mumtaz Mahal died giving birth to her fourteenth child with Shah Jahan of India, he immortalized his wife with the world's most magnificent mausoleum. King Edward VIII, urged to give up his mistress, Wallis Simpson, instead relinquished the British throne. Another crowned head changed his country's religion to legalize his obsession.

The most colorful and controversial of Henry VIII's six wives was the daughter of Sir Thomas Boleyn, a prominent courtier, and his highborn wife, Lady Elizabeth Howard. Along with her sister Mary and her brother George, Anne grew up in the imposing Hever Castle in Kent. George and Anne were exceedingly close, while the sisters' relationship was marked by rivalry. The ever-ambitious Thomas used his diplomatic connections to secure his daughters' appointments in the French court, presided over by Henry's sister, who briefly occupied its throne. When Anne's sister Mary returned to England, she served as a maid of honor to Henry's Spanish-born wife, Catherine of Aragon. In her off-hours, Mary also became Henry's mistress; rumor had it she bore him a son. As the merry monarch's romantic relationships came with an expiration date, he pawned her off to William Carey, a younger son without fortune or land.

Another reason Henry severed their sexual strings was because he had become infatuated with Anne, whom he eyed as a future lover. In order to facilitate this end, he sabotaged Anne's romance with Henry Percy, the heir to the vast Northumberland earldom. Although not conventionally attractive, Anne exuded sexuality in spades, a trait for which scepters have oft been tossed aside. The object of Henry's lust had a swarthy complexion and a long nose, and her bosom was "not much raised." In addition, she had a large "wen" (mole) on her neck—the reason she favored necklaces—and a sixth finger on her hand. Determined not to become another abandoned Boleyn, Anne retreated to Hever Castle, where Henry sent her lovesick letters. He wrote he was "Wishing myself (especially of an evening) in my sweetheart's arms whose pretty duckies I trust shortly to kiss." The swain signed off, "Your loyal servant." The first missive came with a gold bracelet that held a picture of the King. Anne's refusal to embark on an affair only fanned the flame of Henry's passion. By sticking to her virginal guns, Anne triggered one of the most monumental events in British history.

The impediment to legitimizing their relationship was Henry's twenty-four-year marriage to Catherine, for whom he no longer felt an attraction. Equally damning, he felt she was to blame for failing to produce the male heir to perpetuate the Tudor dynasty (as Henry felt women did not capable rulers make). Henry's plot to extricate himself from his starter wife led to a series of events dubbed the "King's Great Matter." His justification to dissolve his marriage: His Spanish consort had been his brother Arthur's widow, and therefore, the marriage flew in the face of Leviticus, which forbids the bedding or wedding of a brother's spouse. The king's men, a medieval dream team—Cardinal Wolsey, Archbishop Thomas Cranmer, and Sir Thomas More—badgered Pope Clement VII to grant an annulment. Had it not been for the Pope's refusal, Britons would still be eating fish on Fridays and would be birthing far more children. In a nod to what Henry wants Henry gets, in a time-honored move, he replaced his menopausal spouse with a fertile one; however, in this instance, doing so meant breaking away from the Roman Catholic Church. He converted England to the Protestant religion, giving himself the titles of the Supreme Head of the Church of England and Defender of the Faith. After he had negated his marriage, his daughter, Mary, bore the brunt of illegitimacy. The king's act set the stage for years of bloodshed between the two warring religions.

Free of Catherine, Henry married Anne, showering his ladylove with jewelry such as gold and diamond bracelets, pendants with their intertwined initials, and blood-red rubies. Henry also bestowed upon Anne the title of Marquess of Pembroke, an honor that made her the most prestigious nonroyal woman of his realm. His father-in-law became the Earl of Wiltshire, and he appointed her brother to the Royal Privy Chamber. The coronation of the new queen proved the pinnacle of pageantry: Fifty barges adorned with flowers, streamers, and flags escorted the newly minted royal along the Thames River to the Tower of London, where she awaited the official ceremony. Carried aloft on a litter of gold and white and adorned in a crimson gown encrusted with precious stones, in Westminster Hall, Anne walked over a blue cloth to the Archbishop of Canterbury to receive the crown. If all the splendor was not heady enough, Anne was five months pregnant. The Tudors were gravely disappointed with the arrival of Elizabeth rather than the longed-for male heir.

The Brits did not view Anne as the people's princess; rather, they considered her a harlot who had usurped the rightful queen, and whispers abounded over the "goggle-eyed whore." They also detested her for her role in the country's break from Rome, one that reduced the United Kingdom to a state of civil war. Anxious to stifle hostility against the woman he loved, Henry warned that there was "no head so fine that he would not make it fly." Further trouble infiltrated the castle when Anne suffered miscarriages (one occurred on the day of Catherine's funeral at Peterborough Abbey when the queen gave birth to a stillborn son). Fights between the royal couple erupted, and Henry despaired of ever taming his shrew. With the waning of their sexual and interpersonal chemistry, Henry's wandering eye wandered to a lady-in-waiting. By marrying her lover, Anne had created a vacancy for a new mistress.

Henry and Anne's relationship had commenced with a jewel, and its demise ended with another. Lore holds that Jane Seymour, literally and figuratively a lady-in-waiting, hovered in the wings to supplant Anne. The queen discovered her husband's new flame when she saw Jane wearing a locket with a picture of Henry inside. Once again Henry kept his relationships in the family; just as he had bedded the Boleyn siblings, Jane was related to Anne through their shared great-grandmother. The rivals possessed very different personalities: Anne was outspoken and volatile, while Jane was docile and anxious to please. Their different temperaments were apparent from the mottoes they adopted when they wore the crown. Anne chose the phrase, "*Ainsi sera, groigne qui groigne,*" (That's how it's going to be, however much people might grumble.) Jane chose, "Bound to Obey and Serve." Apparently the possessor of a sadistic streak, to torment her rival, Jane took to opening and closing the locket, a move calculated to enrage the queen.

In a nod to King Henry II's words regarding Thomas Becket, the Archbishop of Canterbury, "Will no one rid me of this troublesome priest?" Henry decided it was time again to discard an inconvenient wife. Henry charged his wife with being unable to control her "carnal lusts," including the offenses of adultery with five men, incest with her brother, and treason against the king. Her large mole and sixth finger were used as signs of witchcraft. Anne ended up in the Tower of London, this time to await her execution rather than her crowning. The trial, in which guilt was a foregone conclusion, resulted in a death sentence for the queen, accused of seducing Henry, along with other lovers, through sorcery. While Anne had been the object of Henry's desires for several years, her reign lasted for only three years, leading to her moniker: Anne of the Thousand Days.

One can only imagine the horror Anne endured in the Tower, separated from her only child, Elizabeth, who would be deemed illegitimate and mocked as the daughter of a witch; shorn of her once magnificent possessions; and facing execution at the hands of her husband. She said of Henry, "The king has been very good to me. He promoted me from a simple maid to a marchioness. Then he raised me to be a queen. Now he will raise me to be a martyr."

The method of death by burning or beheading was at Henry's discretion, and he chose what he felt was the most humane execution. He sent for "the Hangman of Calais," whose swordsmanship ensured it would take only one blow to sever the neck, while an axe often required several blows. On hearing her fate, Anne remarked, "I have heard say the executioner was very good, and I have a little neck." While Henry's decision might seem to have been the most compassionate alternative, it was probably more of a bid at self-aggrandizement. Henry often claimed he was a descendant of King Arthur, and thus the sword was a nod to Excalibur, the symbol of sovereignty in Camelot. Or perhaps Henry still harbored feelings for the wife for whom he had undergone papal excommunication.

On the date of the execution, in the Tower Green, guards opened the gates and a crowd of a thousand (although Henry was not present) gathered to watch the dispatching of their former queen, who still wore a royal garb of black damask over white ermine. On the scaffold, Anne did not protest her innocence; nor did she rail against the man who had split Christian Europe apart to make her his bride and who had condemned to death her hapless brother. Her praise for the architect of her murder was a final ploy to her protect her young daughter, "For a gentler nor a more merciful prince was there never: and he was ever a good, a gentle and sovereign lord."

After the Hangman of Calais finished his historic gesture, Anne's eyes and lips still moved as her head landed on the straw. True to form, Anne had the last word.

CHAPTER 2

A Moment of Time

— 1533 —

The Mother Goose nursery rhyme, "Sing a Song of Sixpence," holds the words, "The king was in the counting-house / Counting out his money / The queen was in her parlor / Eating bread and honey." The children's verse was far different from the nonfictional reign of a queen who steadfastly refused to let a king control her money, her country, or her heart.

In the opening of his novel, *Anna Karenina*, Russian novelist Leo Tolstoy wrote, "All happy families are alike; each unhappy family is unhappy in its own way." Elizabeth Tudor's family was dysfunctional: At age three, her father, King Henry VIII—a red-haired, rotund rotter—had ordered her mother Anne Boleyn's beheading on a trumped-up charge of adultery. In later life, Elizabeth wore a 1575 mother-of-pearl locket-ring that opened to reveal Elizabeth's portrait paired with Anne's. Henry's proclamation that his marriage had not been legally binding conferred upon his daughter the stigma of illegitimacy. Eleven days after disposing of his inconvenient wife, Henry married Jane Seymour, with whom he had Edward, his son and heir. An unwelcome reminder of Anne, Elizabeth lived in a different castle from her father. Nevertheless, the king allowed her an education usually conferred only upon males, and distinguished scholars provided lessons in languages, history, and the classics. Impressed with his student, scholar Roger Ascham declared, "Her mind has no womanly weakness."

After ordering wife number five, Catherine Howard, to the chopping block, Katharine Parr became Henry's sixth spouse; she brought Elizabeth into the royal residence and proved a loving stepmother. The lecherous king died in 1547, a fact that must have brought sighs of relief from single ladies desirous of keeping their heads. Mourning for her husband was short-lived, as six weeks after becoming a widow Katharine Parr married Edward's uncle, Thomas Seymour, Queen Jane's brother. Thomas became interested in the fourteen-year-old Elizabeth—and not in a paternal fashion. He showed up in her bedroom for friendly romps, and on one occasion slashed her dress with his sword. When Katharine died giving birth, Thomas approached Elizabeth with an offer of marriage that she deftly waved aside. His unwelcome attentions ended with his execution for treason against King Edward. Anxious to play down her association with her stepfather, Elizabeth dressed in plain clothes and carried a Protestant prayer book rather than the banned rosary that her half-sister Mary embraced.

At age twenty, Elizabeth was once more in a precarious situation after Edward's death at age fifteen (most likely from tuberculosis). When Queen Mary announced her intention to marry King Philip of Spain, Protestants grew alarmed that her future children would supplant Elizabeth in the royal succession, forever cementing Catholicism into the royal family and the nation. Sir Thomas Wyatt organized a rebellion to dethrone the queen that ended with his death. In the belief that her sister had been part of the rebellion, Mary ordered Elizabeth's imprisonment in the Tower of London, a customary last stop before execution. After two months, Mary approved of Elizabeth's release, perhaps in fear of a Protestant rebellion and perhaps because Wyatt had exonerated Elizabeth while on the scaffold. Able to walk the quivering political tightrope, Elizabeth managed to survive the bloody reigns of her Protestant half-brother and her Roman Catholic half-sister.

In 1558, when Mary died of cancer, the bells of London pealed with the news of Elizabeth's coronation. She declared of her new role, "This is the doing of the Lord, and it is marvelous in our eyes." The twenty-five-year-old queen slipped the coronation ring on her finger and announced she was marrying England. A brilliant self-promoter, she made the occasion the pinnacle of pageantry. As she walked down the aisle of Westminster Abbey, people tore up pieces of the carpet as souvenirs. Elizabeth always dressed for excess, and she glittered with jewels and power gowns designed to bedazzle. While her power and wealth might have made her an object of envy, Elizabeth understood the weight of the crown. She was the queen of an island nation wracked by warring religious factions. Under her direction, the Church of England restored the country to Protestantism, yet the queen allowed Catholics freedom of worship, thereby avoiding the religious strife that had proliferated under Bloody Mary's tenure.

Another issue confronting Elizabeth was the intense pressure to marry, as many found it abhorrent that a queen should reign without a king. When Parliament insisted she secure a spouse in order to secure the Tudor succession and to forge strategic alliances against Catholic Spain and the Pope, Elizabeth, every inch Henry's daughter, responded, "A strange thing that the foot should direct the head in so weighty a cause." The royal families of Spain, France, Sweden, and the Holy Roman Empire, casting a covetous eye on England and the titian-haired beauty of its ruler, sent out their ambassadors with proposals, including one from King Philip II, her former brother-in-law. Over the course of her lifetime, Elizabeth frequently feigned interest in obtaining a spouse, but it was merely a ploy to make her refusal to share her throne less obvious. Her single status led to her moniker "the Virgin Queen," a title that led to the naming of Virginia and the Virgin Islands and introduced the name Virginia. Popular poetry of the day celebrated the queen as Diana, the chaste goddess of the hunt. Elizabeth told her government, "This shall be for me sufficient, that a marble stone shall declare that a Queen, having reigned such a time, lived and died a virgin."

If ever Elizabeth was in love or had an affair, it was with the married Robert Dudley, Earl of Leicester ("my sweet Robin"), whom she appointed Master of the Horse, and thus the only man in England officially allowed to touch the queen. A Spanish ambassador reported that "Her Majesty visits him in his chamber day and night." A divorce could have been arranged had Lady Dudley not died from a broken neck after tumbling down a flight of stairs. Although her death could have been the result of an accident or a suicide, rumors of murder kiboshed a royal wedding, as did the execution of Dudley's father as a traitor. Elizabeth's philosophy was that the perils of matrimony outweighed its benefits: "Beggar woman and single far rather than Queen and married."

Although King Philip II had been her brother-in-law and suitor, in 1588, he assembled warships—the Spanish Armada—in order to conquer England and to return the country to the pope. In order to support her troops assembled at Tilbury, Elizabeth, dressed in a white gown and a silver breastplate, delivered a morale-boosting speech, declaring, "I know I have the body of a weak and feeble woman, but I have the heart and stomach of a king, and of a king of England, too." The defeat of the Armada was the apogee of Elizabeth's reign, and her public persona portrayed her as Gloriana, heroine of England.

Under the reign of the Virgin Queen, Britain enjoyed nearly a half-century of political stability and was transformed into a world power, a formidable foe to foreign powers. She encouraged explorers like Sir Walter Raleigh to expand her commercial and colonial empire. The queen spawned the notion of a British empire whose sun was never to set, and she chartered seven companies, including East India, to plunder in the guise of trade.

This peaceful interlude ushered in a golden age of the arts. Unlike her successor who shut down the theaters, Elizabeth was a patron of William Shakespeare, and the text of his original play *Love's Labour's Lost* is inscribed with the words, "as it was presented before Her Highness last Christmas." So great was the queen's appreciation of Falstaff in *Henry IV* that she ordered a play devoted to the portly knight. Compliantly, Shakespeare wrote *The Merry Wives of Windsor*. The monumental stature of the monarch became apparent when the surveyor Christopher Saxton published his 1579 atlas of Britain with an engraving of the queen on her throne filling the title page. Elizabeth was the embodiment of England. In her emotional "Golden Speech" to parliament at age sixty-eight, she stated, "Though God hath raised me high, yet this I count the glory of my crown—that I have reigned with your loves."

In her later years, the heroically flawed Elizabeth, then known as Good Queen Bess, did her utmost to defeat the ravages of age. In a ploy to cling to this mortal coil, she sent her adviser, sorcerer John Dee, on a 1,500-mile quest with a flask of her urine to see German alchemist Leonard Thurneysser, in an effort to forestall the inevitable. She took to concealing her receding hair with red wigs and ever more elaborate clothes (her wardrobe held nineteen hundred elaborate gowns). To camouflage her pockmarked face—the result of a bout of smallpox at age twenty-nine—Elizabeth applied pasty white makeup, and her smile revealed rotted teeth. However, the queen did not let go of her grip on her kingdom. When Robert Devereux, the stepson of Robert Dudley, tried to organize a revolt, he met his end through beheading. The queen's postmortem comment was, "I warned him that he should not touch my scepter." Nevertheless, even after a half-century of her rule as the head of England, a visitor to Hampton Court caught sight of the queen dancing in front of a mirror. Oblivious to the fact she was not alone, Elizabeth stomped her feet and tossed her head as if in defiance to the specter of death. However, in 1603, after the passing of her longtime friend, the Countess of Nottingham, Elizabeth sank into a depression, hardly sleeping or eating. Increasingly infirm with rheumatism, the queen made a futile bargain with the Grim Reaper: "All my possessions for a moment of time."

CHAPTER 3

"Fortune's Fool!"

— 1537 —

In 2022, Queen Elizabeth II will become the first British monarch to mark seventy years on the throne, an event that will be commemorated with a Platinum Jubilee. In contrast, one crowned head ruled for even less time than Anne Boleyn, the Queen of one thousand days.

Charles Dickens regarded Lady Jane Grey as a martyr; Jane Austen thought of her as a prig. Nevertheless, whatever one's view of the teenaged queen, like King Lear, she was "more sinned against than sinning." Jane—probably so named after King Henry's VIII wife, Jane Seymour—was born in the family's estate in Leicestershire, Bradgate Park, the same year as Edward Tudor, the son and heir of her great-uncle, King Henry VIII. Her lineage was likewise impressive: Jane was the first surviving child of Henry Grey, the Marquess of Dorset, who later became the Duke of Suffolk. Her mother, Frances, was the daughter of Mary Tudor, Henry VIII's younger sister who had spent a brief stint as the Queen of France.

Frances and Henry were deeply disappointed that Jane had not been the son they desired and then were further put out with the arrival of her sisters, Lady Mary and Lady Catherine. The Greys were also irritated with Jane, who did not share their passion for hunting and horses. Instead, she found refuge in education, immersing herself in French, Italian, Latin, Greek, and Hebrew. When the duke and duchess were out on a hunt, Jane's tutor discovered her reading Plato. In response as to why she had not joined in her family's pursuit, she replied, "I wish all their sport in the park is but a shadow to that pleasure that I find in Plato. Alas, they never felt what true pleasure meant." However, her greatest passion was for the new religion that her uncle, Henry VIII, had established after severing ties with the Roman Catholic Church. Aggravated with her daughter's studies and scriptures, Frances—the Mommy Dearest of the 1550s—meted out daily physical abuse such as ear-boxes and pinches. On one occasion, Jane revealed her torment when she confided in her tutor, "I will tell you a truth which perchance you will marvel at...whether I speak, keep silence, sit, stand, or go, eat, drink, be merry or sad, I must do it as perfectly as God made the world, or I am so sharply taunted, yea, and presented with pinches and nips, that I think myself in Hell..."

Yet her childhood contained pockets of happiness. A common practice in the Tudor era was for aristocratic children to spend time in other households, especially when the foster family was of a higher status. Thus, at age nine, Jane went to live with King Henry VIII's widow, his sixth wife, Katherine Parr, and her husband, Thomas Seymour. In her new household, she played cards with King Henry's son, the future King Edward; indeed, her parents harbored hopes that Jane would one day be his wife. During this time, Jane enjoyed a respite from the hell of Bradgate Park. However, with Katherine's death two years later during labor, Jane made her reluctant way back home.

Alas, lady luck was to further desert Lady Grey. At age fifteen, when King Edward was dying from tuberculosis, John Dudley, the Earl of Northumberland, who was the regent of the boy-king, persuaded Edward to sign a Device for Succession that named Jane as his successor, an act that bypassed his half-sisters, Mary and Elizabeth. The document stated the princesses were not in line for the throne because of their illegitimate births. The self-effacing teenager fainted when informed she was to be the queen. Her mother slapped her back into consciousness, at which time Jane reluctantly accepted her fate, to the relief of the Privy

Councilors who knelt before her to swear allegiance. Jane later recalled of the momentous event, "Declaring to them my insufficiency, I greatly bewailed myself for the death of so noble a prince, and at the same time, turned myself to God, humbly praying and beseeching him that if what was given to me was rightly and lawfully mine, his divine Majesty would grant me such grace and spirit that I might govern it to his glory and service and to the advantage of this realm."

The reason why Northumberland had plotted to place Lady Jane Grey on the throne was she had become his daughter-in-law after he had arranged her marriage to his seventeen-year-old son, Lord Guildford. The couple had taken their vows alongside her sister, Catherine, and her sister-in-law at a triple ceremony at Durham House. Although Jane had been opposed to the arranged marriage, Frances had persuaded her with some choice "nips and bobs." By dint of his Machiavellian machinations, the Earl had positioned himself as England's de facto ruler.

On the day of her coronation, Jane and Guildford entered the Tower of London by Lion Gate, an entrance so named after a former royal menagerie. Jane wore a green velvet dress embroidered with gold, with a long train carried by her mother. Her head covering was heavily bedecked with jewels, and on her neck, she wore a chin clout (a scarf) of black velvet decorated with gold, pearls, rubies, and diamonds. She walked under a canopy, accompanied by Guildford, outfitted in white and gold.

The first crack in Northumberland's plan to become the power behind the throne was Jane's decision to do God's bidding rather than blindly going along with her father-in-law's demands. An example of her strength of will was her refusal to make Guildford king. Although history is unclear about how Jane felt about the husband who had been forced upon her, the conjecture is that the girl who had been derived of love throughout her life grew fond of her spouse.

Another flaw in the Earl's calculation was he had not bargained on opposition from Mary, who, cut from the same cloth as her father, did not take kindly to the theft of her birthright. The Privy Council, as well as the Archbishop of Canterbury, had similarly underestimated the threat of the Catholic princess and wrote Jane that in order to dispel opposition, she should be "quiet and obedient." Factions formed in favor of Mary, who gathered her troops in Norfolk. When Northumberland left London to capture her from her stronghold of Framlingham Castle, the Privy Council switched sides and proclaimed Mary the new queen. In a move calculated to save his own skin, Henry signed the proclamation before fleeing. Seeing in which direction the political wind was blowing, the Earl's supporters dispersed.

After nine days, Jane ceded the throne to her cousin. Mary's men arrested Jane and her husband and charged them with high treason. Of her father-in-law, Jane stated, "He hath brought me and my stock in most miserable calamity and misery by his exceeding ambition." Once again bearing the title Lady Grey, Jane and her husband landed in the Tower of London, William the Conqueror's twelfth-century fortress where two of Henry's VIII's discarded wives had met their gruesome ends. Frances, true to form, never contacted her doomed daughter, though she did plead for her husband's pardon.

On trial, as evidence of Jane's guilt, there was a document that bore the words, "Jane the Quene." The court decreed that Jane be either burned or beheaded; Mary chose neither option, aware that her cousin had been a mere pawn in a power game. She allowed her prisoner to be attended by three gentlewomen and the privilege of walking in the Queen's Garden. Her mercy did not extend to Northumberland, whose scheming ended with his execution.

Jane might have lived, although in captivity, had her father and uncle not participated in the Wyatt Rebellion, brought about by Mary's decision to marry Philip, the King of Spain. Mary's advisers took the uprising as a sign that Jane remained a rallying figure for Protestants, a fact that sealed the teenager's fate. Even after hearing of her sentence that demanded the ultimate price, Jane did not hear from her mother, who was having an affair with a servant fifteen years her junior. The day before her death, she wrote her younger sister a farewell letter, penned on a page of a Greek New Testament Bible, "Consider that I shall be delivered of this corruption." Henry had meddled for his last time as the crown decreed his death.

In 1554, on her way to the chopping block at the Tower Green, the hapless girl spied the body of its recently dispatched victim, her nineteen-year-old husband, whose body lay on a stretcher, his severed head ensconced between his thighs. Although abandoned by her family and supporters, Jane derived comfort from the faith that had always been her pillar. She recited Psalms 51:8, "Let the bones you have crushed rejoice," and then begged her executioner, "I pray you dispatch me quickly." After tying a blindfold over her eyes, unable to find the block where she was to kneel, she revealed her turmoil, "What shall I do? Where is it?"

Jane's remains ended up next to Anne Boleyn's in an unmarked grave in St. Peter ad Vincula by the Tower. The former Queen Jane became a Protestant martyr who has long aroused empathy. Almost three hundred years after her decapitation, Charles Dickens wrote that the English axe "never struck so cruel and so vile a blow." The Tower's ever-present ravens, that as a rule feast on rabbits, showed as much compassion as the queen had displayed toward her cousin. The last prayer the condemned uttered was, "Lord, into thy hands I commend my spirit." However, the words of Romeo—who also lost his life in his teens—could well have been Jane's own: "O, I am fortune's fool!"

♟

CHAPTER 4

"In My End"

— 1542 —

"**C**at fight," a sexist term without a male equivalent, implies women's interactions involve the sharpening of nails, a fact some males find titillating. One high-profile female-against-female feud involved two British duchesses and engendered endless speculation as to who made who cry. Their alleged spat would pale in comparison to the tensions between two Renaissance frenemies over the rule of a royal roost.

While some princes spend decades waiting to assume the throne (such as Charles, the Prince of Wales, who is still cooling his heels in his seventies), when King James V died from a fever, the Scottish crown passed to Mary, his six-day-old daughter. As a female head of state might not be accepted by the war-like Scots, five years later, Mary of Guise sent her daughter to safety with her French family, power players in the court of King Henry II. Preferring power over blood, the non-maternal mother did not accompany her child, remaining in Scotland so she could rule as regent. The young Queen, more Francophile than Scot, grew up to be a five-foot eleven-inch beauty with titian hair and amber eyes. The court referred to her as "*la plus parfait*," "the most perfect."

Throughout her childhood, Mary's companion was the Dauphin (the future Francis II), whom she wed when they were teenagers. The marriage made her the possessor of the Scottish and French thrones; however, it was her claim to a third that would result in the shadow that stalked her life. Always sickly—the reason why their marriage was likely not consummated—Francis passed away from an ear affliction two years later.

Mary left her luxurious life as the dowager Queen of France and returned to Scotland, a daunting prospect for a Roman Catholic in a predominately Protestant country; she vowed to implement religious tolerance. The Scottish lords, to their great displeasure, discovered the Frenchified young woman was not a marionette whose strings they could manipulate. James, her half-brother, organized a coup to topple her from the throne; Mary issued him a pardon. Beset by enemies, Mary lamented, "I am their queen, and so they call me, but they use me not so."

In Victor Hugo's *Les Misérables*, Inspector Javert is the implacable nemesis of Jean Valjean; the foe who darkened Mary's days was her non-kissing cousin, Elizabeth I of Britain. Had circumstances been different, given their commonalities, they could have been friends. The queens reigned over a patriarchal society and encountered detractors such as John Knox, the Calvinist preacher who wrote *The First Blast of the Trumpet Against the Monstrous Regiment of Women*. A shared relative was Henry VIII, the king with the penchant for divorces and decapitations, and both their crowns sat atop flaming red hair. The cousins were also fastidious regarding their complexions. In order to cover up her smallpox scars, Elizabeth favored white chalk-like makeup made of vinegar and lead, while Mary's cosmetic consisted of white wine. The blue bloods dressed for excess; the British monarch took four hours a day to ready her wardrobe. Understanding that their subjects expected pomp, Mary traveled in a flotilla of twelve ships; one carried her four adored ladies-in-waiting (all named Mary). Another ship held her maids, grooms, cooks, and servants. The remaining ships bore the Queen's possessions such as her extensive array of gowns, jewelry, pets, and furniture (including forty-five beds).

Although Mary possessed several sterling traits, she shared the fatal flaw of ambition with famed fellow Scottish royal Macbeth. Not content with wielding the scepter of Scotland, Mary also coveted the English throne. Her justification: Henry VIII had divorced his first wife to wed Anne Boleyn, Elizabeth's mother, a union not sanctified by the pope, and thus their illegitimate daughter was merely a pretender to the throne. Roman Catholics shared her opinion, and as Elizabeth's fears for her crown grew, so did her animosity for her cousin. Although their paths were strewn with landmines, for the sake of an alliance between their two kingdoms, they maintained a cordial relationship. In a letter to Elizabeth, Mary wrote, "In one isle, of one language, the nearest kinswomen that each other had." In a return missive, Elizabeth signed her letter, "a dear sister and a faithful friend."

Religion was not the only factor that set the two powerhouses apart. Elizabeth, determined to reign as queen bee, became known as the Virgin Queen due to her single status. She believed that as soon as the ink dried on the marriage contract, royal consorts tended to usurp power. Instead, she embarked on covert love affairs. In contrast, Mary's heart ruled her head, and she longed for the physical and romantic intimacy that as a devout Catholic, she could only achieve through church sanctioned unions. As she told Elizabeth's ambassador prior to her 1565 wedding to her cousin, Henry Stuart, Lord Darnley, "Not to marry, you know it cannot be for me." Besotted, Mary described Henry as "the lustiest and best proportioned man." Tragically, Henry's physical proportion did not equate to his moral ones, as he possessed a violent temper and indulged in alcohol and adultery. Although the couple had decided to reign as equals, Henry demanded that his wife serve as his subordinate. British ambassador Thomas Randolph stated, "I know for certain that this Queen repenteth her marriage: that she hateth him and all his kin." One of Henry's conquests was Mary's Italian secretary, David Rizzio. Believing the court's rumor that Rizzio had shared Mary's bed, in a fit of jealousy over his wife's supposed infidelity, Henry and several armed noblemen stabbed him fifty-six times. The six-month pregnant Mary watched the horror unfold as guns aimed at her prevented her from summoning help. Later that year, Mary gave birth to James, the heir to the Scottish and British thrones. She chose Elizabeth I as her son's godmother. Upon the death of his mother and godmother, James assumed both their thrones.

As the birth of James had secured the royal succession, some men felt Henry had outlived his usefulness. Accordingly, they planted gunpowder in his Edinburgh home, where Henry was convalescing from an illness. Dressed in his nightshirt, Henry managed to escape into an orchard, evading the blast, though he could not escape strangulation. James Hepburn, the Earl of Bothwell, Mary's closest confidant, stood trial for the murder. Although he was acquitted, many were convinced that Bothwell and Mary were complicit in the crime.

Shortly afterwards, on her way to Edinburgh, the queen encountered Bothwell, accompanied by 800 men, who warned her of unrest in the city and offered her protection. Protection amounted to abduction as Bothwell kept Mary as his hostage and forced himself upon her. Pregnant and unwilling to give birth outside wedlock, Mary agreed to his demand of marriage. The diplomat, Nicholas Throckmorton, described him, "He was a vainglorious, rash, and hazardous young man." As with his predecessor, Bothwell had a penchant for violence. In his wife's presence, he beat one of her servants to death. He also had a proclivity for power. Mary later wrote of her third husband, "We cannot dissemble that he has used us otherwise than we would have wished or yet have deserved at his hand." She ended up miscarrying, purportedly twins. The Scots did not take kindly to their queen remarrying mere months after she had become a widow. As a result, John Knox pronounced her promiscuous. Rebellious Scottish nobles captured the newlyweds at the Battle of Carberry Hill; the victors exiled Bothwell, imprisoned the queen in the island of Loch Leven, and forced her to abdicate her throne in favor of her one-year-old-son.

Bothwell fled to Denmark, where he died behind bars eleven years later. Supporters restored Mary to power; however, upon their defeat, the deposed queen fled to England to plead for mercy. Astonished that her enemy had landed in her domain, Elizabeth did not meet with her—the cousins never had a face-to-face encounter—and refused to help Mary recapture her lost kingdom. Instead, although Elizabeth lacked jurisdiction over the foreign royal, she placed Mary under house arrest for eighteen years. During captivity in her gilded cage of a castle, Elizabeth allowed Mary clothes and furniture from Paris and the company of her pets. Devoid of purpose and passion, Mary wasted away. Ill and despondent, the former queen lamented, "I am no longer who I once was."

Fearing a Catholic uprising was brewing to free Mary and steal her crown, Elizabeth wrote a last letter to her rival ruler, "It ages me to bear such a burden, ordering to death the only other woman who knows what it means to rule as a queen in this land."

In 1587, in the Great Hall of Fotheringhay Castle, Mary knelt and thanked her executioner with the words, "You will do me much good in withdrawing me from this world, out of which I am very glad to go." With regal bearing, Mary approached the makeshift scaffold and cast off her black gown to reveal a red dress underneath—the shade of martyrdom. After several attempts to sever the queen's head, the hooded axman held it aloft, a warning to anyone thinking of locking horns with Elizabeth Tudor. As the spectators recoiled in shock, the hangman dropped his gory souvenir; he was left holding a red wig. Geddon, Mary's Skye terrier, emerged from where it had been hiding in her dress and refused to leave her side. The words Mary had once embroidered on her pillow explained why she did not fear death: "In my end is my beginning."

CHAPTER 5

"Semiramis
of the North"

— 1729 —

Individuals trapped in an unhappy reality frequently long for a *tabula rasa*, a "clean slate," for a chance at reinvention. While many attempt escape from a life where there seems to be no exit, few fared as well as the woman whose metamorphosis made her a world-renowned empress.

In his play *Twelfth Night*, William Shakespeare wrote, "Some are born great, some achieve greatness, and some have greatness thrust upon them." The lines from the play apply to Princess Sophia Augusta Frederica (historically known as Catherine), in Stettin, Prussia, currently Poland. She was the daughter of an embittered, pushy, sixteen-year-old mother, Johanna. Eighteen months later, a son arrived who passed away at age twelve. Catherine's father was a German soldier, Prince Christian August of Anhalt-Zerbst, whose regiment referred to him as "that idiot Zerbst." Despite his title, the family was impoverished.

The princess had greatness thrust upon her at age fourteen when Empress Elizabeth, daughter of Peter the Great, went on a quest to find a wife for her nephew, the future Emperor Peter III (her designated successor, as she was childless). Karl Peter Ulrich of Holstein-Gottorp had grown up in Germany, as his father was a German prince; upon the early deaths of his parents, his care had passed to his sadistic tutor, who contributed to his lifelong psychological issues. Peter was far from pleased when his aunt plucked him from his native Holstein and transplanted him to Saint Petersburg.

Johanna dangled her daughter as a potential imperial bride, a fact that did not delight young Catherine, who had already met Peter—her second cousin—when she was ten and he was a year older. She recalled he was a buffoon with bulging eyes, a weak chin, and lank hair who enjoyed torturing his pets. The empress was taken with Catherine, seeing in the spirited girl a version of herself. She also admired the teenager's beauty; a gown preserved in the Kremlin Armory is testimony to her waspish waist. Believing anything better than living with her domineering mother in straitened circumstances, Catherine acquiesced to the betrothal. Determined to start afresh, Catherine traded her Lutheran faith for Eastern Orthodoxy, exchanged her German language for Russian, and shed the name Sophia for Ykaterina in honor of Elizabeth's mother, whose name was anglicized as Catherine. Post marriage, she became the Grand Duchess Catherine Alekseyevna.

Life in the imperial court, however, did not prove the longed-for panacea. The mother of the bride became pregnant by one of the court's couriers. Moreover, Catherine's relationship with Peter was a match made in hell. The seventeen-year-old groom, adept only in alcoholism, was obsessed with dressing his servants in military uniforms for indoor parades. For their wedding night, Catherine wore a pink nightie made in Paris; Peter was only interested in playing with his toy soldiers, which he took to bed. In her memoirs, Catherine wrote of her unconsummated union, "Matters remained in this state without the slightest change during the following nine years." The first time her husband mentioned the word love it was to inform Catherine he had fallen for one of her ladies-in-waiting. The lack of an heir threatened the Romanov dynasty, and military officer Sergei Saltykov assumed horizontal husband duty. Empress Elizabeth, thrilled with the birth of Paul, took charge of the nursery, a pattern repeated with Catherine's three other children. Emotionally adrift, Catherine wrote, "The trouble is that my heart is loath to remain even one hour without love."

Catherine achieved greatness at the passing of Empress Elizabeth, which turned her husband into Tsar Peter III. Not a subscriber to the idea that "less is more," for her coronation, the tsarina commissioned an imperial crown of unimaginable bling. Designed to represent two hemispheres, the crown held 5,000 diamonds (nineteen of which weighed over five carats) bordered with thirty-seven pearls.

Peter was not made of the stuff of his famous Romanov forebearers. Military mishaps—playing with toy soldiers did not make for adequate preparation—led to his plummeting popularity, as did his allegiance to Germany over Russia. When Catherine learned that her husband was plotting against her, she enlisted the help of her lover, Grigory Orlov, and staged a counterattack. Dressed in a guardsman uniform with a sword at her side, astride a white stallion, the tsarina led 14,000 soldiers to arrest her husband and force his abdication. The bloodless transition of power led Frederick the Great of Prussia to remark, "Peter allowed himself to be dethroned like a child being sent to bed." Eight days later, the dethroned tsar died in prison in Ropsha Palace near Saint Petersburg, likely at the hand of Grigory's brother, Alexei. The official cause of death was hemorrhoidal colic, which most viewed as a euphemism for murder. Catherine was in Grigory's debt both for handing her the throne and because he was adept in the boudoir. After she tired of him, in a desperate attempt to regain her affection, Grigory gifted her an almost 200-carat diamond from India that had once been used as an eye of an idol in an ancient Brahmin Temple. The present did not regain the royal favor, but it did become the centerpiece of the Romanov crown jewels.

Catherine turned her empire into a world power and ushered in the golden age of Russian history. During the long years of her loveless marriage, Catherine had immersed herself in the works of enlightenment philosophers and had carried on a correspondence with Voltaire, in which he at times signed his letters "the old hermit." Under the influence of liberal ideals, the tsarina instituted the first state-funded school for females, humanized the penal system, and founded orphanages. She was also the first European monarch to decree civil equality for Jews. Her massive country expanded with her annexation of the Crimea, Poland, the Ukraine, and Lithuania. The empress erected the Hermitage near the Winter Palace to house paintings she had acquired by Rembrandt, Rubens, and Van Dyck. She also used the museum as a venue for intimate parties where she mandated that "one must never groan over one's own problems or inflict boredom on others." Through the infusion of culture and reform, Catherine altered the European perspective of her nation as one that consisted of snow, wolves, and vodka. And in one instance, she proved herself even more advanced. Under the threat of a smallpox epidemic, Catherine set an example by becoming one of the first to receive an inoculation that other rulers shunned as far too dangerous.

Although intellectually opposed to serfdom, when Yemelyan Pugachev, an illiterate Cossack, fought to alleviate their oppression, she ordered his execution. After the French Revolution, Catherine held ever tighter to her bejeweled scepter, fearful that Russia might also be ripe to become a constitutional republic. Although she was perceived as one of the greatest of monarchs, what she accomplished was at the cost of the peasants who comprised half the country's population, and their status diminished under her leadership. Equally manipulative with her family, Catherine had a contentious relationship with her son, Paul, fearing he would make a bid for the throne when he came of age. However, the empress held onto her scepter with a grip of steel, and he only assumed the throne as Paul I upon her death. As with his grandfather, he met his end through assassination.

Although Catherine the Great, Empress and Autocrat of all the Russias, also known as Rossiya-Matushka, "mother of Russia," built her empire into a world power and created one of the world's greatest art museums, her prevailing image is of a royal nymphomaniac who died having intercourse with a horse. A joke circulated that that the busiest thoroughfare in Saint Petersburg was Catherine's Canal. In actuality, the only mention she made of a horse in her memoirs was when at age thirteen, lying in bed with a pillow between her legs, she imagined herself astride a stallion that she rode "until I was quite worn out." Despite her reputation for bedding innumerable men, Catherine had twelve lovers and was at heart a monogamist. During her marriage, she confided in her memoir, "Had it been my fate to have a husband whom I could love, I would never have changed toward him." When tired of her paramours, generous gifts followed. One received a thousand indentured servants; another lover, Stanislaw, was made the King of Poland. Her heart's most significant other was Gregory Potemkin. The tsarina described him as "one of the greatest, most bizarre, and most entertaining eccentrics of the iron age." He was also the possessor of "elephantine sexual equipment." In a letter to Potemkin, she wrote after a fight, "Precious darling, I took a cord with a stone and tied it around the neck of all our quarrels, and then I tossed it into a hole in the ice." At his passing, Catherine wrote a friend, "You cannot imagine how broken I am." The tsarina's rule lasted for thirty-four years until she had a stroke, went into a coma, and died at age sixty-seven.

Upon viewing the prism of Catherine's life, divergent images appear: the good, the bad, and the sexual. Voltaire's take was to dub her after the legendary Queen of Babylon, a woman who succeeded in an age when men traditionally held the reins of power, "Semiramis (the Shining Star) of the North."

⚜

CHAPTER 6

"A Far Better Rest"

— 1755 —

Those who wear the tiara capture the popular imagination, as queens exist in an emerald city of gowns, palaces, and jewels, oh my! And when a royal alters the course of world history, the dust never settles on their stories.

Except for the general from Corsica, Napoleon Bonaparte, no other outsider outstayed his or her French welcome more than a particular Viennese princess. The lady whose life turned fractured fairy tale was the Habsburg princess, Maria Antonia Josepha Joanna, remembered by her French name, Marie Antoinette. Her mother—the eighteenth-century "momager"—was the Empress Maria Theresa, who regarded her sixteen children as pawns on the European chessboard. At age ten, Maria Theresa pledged Marie Antoinette to the eleven-year-old grandson of French monarch Louis XV, in order to cement the alliance of the Habsburg and Bourbon dynasties. Marie Antoinette, the seventh and youngest archduchess, served as the chosen one since her older sisters had already been the brides of other European rulers or had perished from smallpox.

At age fourteen, Marie Antoinette experienced the trauma of leaving her cosseted cocoon for a court hostile to Austria, France's traditional enemy for centuries. Maria Theresa's parting words were, "Do so much good to the French people that they can say that I have sent them an angel." In a display of the might and majesty of her empire, Austria sent off its princess with a procession of fifty-seven coaches, 376 horses, 132 dignitaries, and an assortment of doctors, hairdressers, cooks, bakers, blacksmiths, and a dressmaker. Upon her arrival, the French forced Marie Antoinette to relinquish her nationality along with her personal possessions—including her beloved pug, Mops. The archetypal poor little girl's destiny was to be prisoner as much as she was princess.

Louis Auguste de Bourbon and his child bride married two days after their first meeting in the chapel at the Palace of Versailles. Four years later, before Louis's grandfather succumbed to smallpox, he pronounced, *"Après moi, le déluge"*—"After me, the deluge." The Dauphin became King Louis XVI in a coronation at the cathedral in Reims. His newly appointed queen wrote to her mother, "Protect us, Lord, we are too young to reign!" In addition to the weight of her crown, there was trouble in the boudoir. The socially inept, heavyset groom was not to deflower his wife—or not, at least, to finish the job—until seven years later. The lack of intimacy distressed Marie Antoinette, who dropped hints about "living in intimacy," a tenet of their vows. Maria Theresa, after encouraging her daughter to "lavish more caresses" on her husband, dispatched her son, Emperor Joseph of Austria, to "stir up this indolent spouse." Once Louis got the hang of it, he fathered Marie Therese, Louis Joseph, Louis-Charles, and Sophie. A doting mother, Marie Antoinette's most treasured moments were spent with her children at Petit Trianon, a château on the royal grounds that had been built by Louis XV for his mistress, Madame de Pompadour. Unlike most members of the court, who always viewed the foreign royal as "L'Autrichienne" (an insulting play on the French words for Austrian and for a female dog), the Princesse de Lamballe befriended the queen.

While Maria Theresa was a workaholic consumed with matters of state, Marie Antoinette sought diversion in opera, theater, and gambling. As she admitted to her trusted adviser, Austrian ambassador Florimond Claude, comte de Mercy-Argenteau, "I am terrified of being bored." Keeping boredom at bay involved outlandish spending: A pair of her diamond bracelets cost as much as a Paris mansion. Dressed for excess,

Marie Antoinette lavished over $3,000,000 a year on her jewel-encrusted gowns. While Louis never took a mistress, Marie Antoinette dressed like one, something that did not sit well with a country used to the wives of Louis XIV and Louis XV, unobtrusive baby-makers. Informed of her daughter's extravagant lifestyle, Maria Theresa fired off a letter, "You lead a dissipated life. I hope I shall not live to see the disaster that is likely to ensue."

Ensconced in the gilded cage of her palaces in Versailles and the Château de Fontainebleau, Marie Antoinette was oblivious to the plight of the poor. A failed harvest made the price of grain the highest in a century, and the populace were far from impressed that the queen used precious flour in her elaborate pompadours. The rumor mill circulated that in response to the people's demand for bread, she scoffed, "*Qu'ils mangent de la brioche*" "Let them eat cake." France's financial woes led to her nickname, Madame Deficit; the country blamed her for the fact that it was on the brink of bankruptcy. As Maria Theresa had predicted, her daughter was "hurtling toward an abyss." If serving as the bullseye of hate was not difficult enough, Marie Antoinette became a bereaved mother at the death of her nine-year-old son, Louis Joseph, who succumbed to tuberculosis of the spine. The passing of her daughter, Sophie, before her first birthday, had preceded the loss of her son.

The start of the revolution that signaled the death knell of the House of Bourbon was the 1789 storming of the Bastille prison, a symbol of royal tyranny. Marie Antoinette tried to convince her husband to put down the insurrection; however, a French Hamlet, he was too indecisive to act, thereby handing over Paris to the revolutionaries. Honoré-Gabriel Riqueti, comte de Mirabeau, wryly observed that the queen was "the only man at court."

Three months later, a mob of some seven thousand women armed with spikes and sickles marched on Versailles, where they entered the queen's private quarters and vented their fury by smashing her mirrors and ripping her bed to shreds. Outside Marie Antoinette's window, someone waved a spike that held the decapitated head of the

Princesse de Lamballe. The enemies of the crown escorted the family to the Tuileries Palace, where National Guardsmen held them captive. To placate the people, Marie Antoinette took to wearing the patriotic tricolor garb. Count Fersen, a Swedish count purported to be Marie Antoinette's grand passion, arranged their escape in a coach; however, they were recognized in Varennes, and the revolutionaries captured the Bourbons and returned them to Paris, where they were met with a hostile crowd. After a reprieve, the militants imprisoned the royals in the Temple tower, a foreboding fourteenth-century fortress founded by the Knight Templars. In a nod to Nero fiddling while Rome burned, Marie Antoinette continued to wear her stylish outfits while in captivity. For the next two months, the authorities left the family alone; the interlude ended when guards locked up the former king on a different floor and put him on trial. The militant Maximilien Robespierre sealed the dethroned king's fate, saying, "Louis must die so that the country may live." A court condemned Louis to the guillotine, where a mob estimated at 20,000 looked on.

Six months later, the new leaders of France arrived to transfer the widow Capet (Maria Antoinette's new title, so named after the medieval dynasty) to the Conciergerie, located on the River Seine, a dank prison dubbed "death's antechamber." The eight-year-old Louis-Charles (Louis XVII to royalists) clung to her skirts until guards pried him off. His captors plied the child with alcohol between beatings and taught him to sing the "Marseillaise" while forcing him to wear the red hat of a sans-culotte. Two years later, the child passed away, ill and alone, in his dungeon cell.

In *The Tragedy of Macbeth*, Shakespeare wrote of the Thane of Cawdor, "Nothing in his life / Became him like the leaving it." In the same vein, Marie Antoinette's suffering gave her the backbone she had always lacked as the Princess of Austria and as the Queen of France. In a letter, she wrote after her failed escape from detention in Paris, "Tribulation first makes one realize what one is."

At her trial for treason, Marie Antoinette, emaciated and visibly aged, maintained her composure during the thirty-two-hour ordeal. The most shocking accusation against the former royal was when the prosecution presented the trumped-up testimony of Louis-Charles that he had sex with his mother. Outraged, Marie Antoinette responded, "Nature refuses to answer such a charge brought against a mother. I appeal in this matter to all the mothers present in court." The trial was a foregone conclusion, and the new government pronounced a sentence of death. On the eve of execution, Marie Antoinette wrote to her sister-in-law asking her to persuade Louis-Charles to never seek revenge, and ended her letter, "I am calm, as people are whose conscience is clear."

At dawn, Citizen Sanson, the head executioner, cut off her hair, which had turned white with her agony. When a priest told her to have courage, she told him, "Courage? The moment when my ills are going to end is not the moment when courage is going to fail me." A cart carried the condemned woman to the Place de la Révolution; onlookers spit and hurled insults as she drove by, yet she maintained her regal bearing throughout the ordeal of her execution. The words of Charles Dickens in A Tale of Two Cities apply to the last Queen of France: "It is a far better rest that I go to than I have ever known."

CHAPTER 7

Last Words

—— 1763 ——

The British poet, Alfred, Lord Tennyson, wrote, "In the spring a young man's fancy lightly turns to love." A conqueror whose empress conquered his heart proved that in the winter, old men's hearts also may turn to love.

History acknowledges that France's most acclaimed general possessed the ambition of the Scottish general Macbeth. What is less well known is Napoleon Bonaparte also possessed the romantic nature of Romeo, as well as the jealousy of Othello.

Napoleon's destiny, Marie Josèphe Rose Tascher de La Pagerie, proves that one can never foretell where the spotlight of fame will cast its beam. Marie, who history remembers as Joséphine (the name Napoleon preferred), was born to blue-blooded French colonists on the Caribbean Island of Martinique. She recalled growing up "in a paradise of pleasure," where she "splashed in the sea like a dolphin and sucked on sugarcane plucked from the fields." But hurricanes destroyed their crops, and her cash-strapped, gambling addicted father arranged sixteen-year-old Joséphine's marriage to Alexandre François Marie, Viscount of Beauharnais, the son of her aunt's lover. Upon meeting her fiancé, Joséphine was ecstatic: Alexandre was wealthy, well connected at court, and reputed to be one of the best dancers in Paris. Alexandre, less enthused, was not enamored of the plump, unsophisticated girl with the blackened teeth, the result of years of sugar cane consumption.

He preferred his mistress, a married woman eleven years his senior. Nevertheless, Joséphine became his wife, and together they had children Eugène and Hortense. Marital relations deteriorated, and Joséphine, along with her children, moved into the Panthémant Convent in Paris, which housed other inconvenient wives. In a bid at reinvention, Joséphine shed her island provincialism and weight; she also learned to cover her mouth with a handkerchief when she laughed to hide her decayed teeth.

After a two-year visit to Martinique, Joséphine returned to a far different France. Her husband had made a swift rise in the National Assembly, one that the Reign of Terror just as swiftly brought down. The monarchy fell in 1792, and the revolutionaries imprisoned the royalists as enemies of the state, including the Viscount and Viscountess de Beauharnais. They ended up in the rat-infested Carmes Prison; Joséphine's cellmate was Marie Grosholtz, who later achieved acclaim as wax-wunderkind Madame Tussaud. Their guards shaved their hair in preparation for their executions. While incarcerated, Alexandre and Joséphine indulged in amorous pursuits—though not with each other. Before the Terror ended, the guillotine claimed Alexandre, as it did approximately 40,000 others. Joséphine kept her head as three months later the architects of the Terror met their end at the edge of a blade, and the Viscountess walked free.

Ever the opportunist, the widow slept her way to the top of the Parisian social hierarchy. Women wondered what men saw in Joséphine; the answer was she made them imagine horizontal positions. The femme fatale, well versed in the art of seduction, had a fondness for mirrors that multiplied the images of lovemaking, thereby creating the illusion of an orgy. One of her conquests, Paul de Barras, had orchestrated the fall of the revolutionary Maximilien Robespierre. A politician remarked of de Barras that he "had all the vices of a king without having a single one of the virtues." Tiring of Joséphine's out of control spending, Paul introduced his mistress to a Corsican general six years her junior. The man with the diminutive stature held grandiose ambitions and declared that he should be crowned king well before anyone else shared that opinion. Although she had not been the first woman to capture Napoleon's eye, Joséphine was the one who captivated his libido. He was greener in the bedroom than his new lover and declared he was "baffled and excited by her repertoire of techniques," especially moves he referred to as her "zigzags," perhaps akin to the Seinfeldian "swirl." In a letter to his mistress, the smitten general praised her "little black forest. I kiss it a thousand times and wait impatiently for the moment I will be in it. To live within Joséphine is to live in the Elysian Fields." The scent of his woman held Napoleon in thrall; he wrote to Joséphine, "I am coming home. Don't wash."

Less than a year after their first meeting, Joséphine was waiting in the town hall of Paris's second municipal district for her groom. He arrived four hours late because he had been caught up in planning the invasion of Italy. He made it up to her by shaving four years off her age on the marriage certificate, one of the perks of being the Consul. A few months later, Madame Bonaparte confided to a friend, "My husband does not love me; he worships me. I think he will go mad."

When Napoleon left on a military campaign that determined the fate of Europe, Joséphine concentrated on amassing art and a priceless collection of jewelry. She also embarked on an affair with Hippolyte Charles, a handsome, decade-younger officer. When he learned of his wife's extramarital affair, Bonaparte became insanely jealous; but after a heated row, they ended up reconciling. The couple took up residence in the Tuileries; as décor, Napoleon hung Leonardo da Vinci's painting *Mona Lisa* in their bedroom. After it became apparent the general was on the way to becoming the ruler of France, Joséphine's infidelities ended and Bonaparte's began. In 1884, Napoleon and Joséphine stood in Notre Dame Cathedral, where the general became an emperor in a ceremony presided over by Pope Pius VII. She played the part of consort to the hilt and dressed in magnificent gowns: one she had covered entirely in rose petals, another in hundreds of diamond-tipped toucan feathers. The new empress had more ladies-in-waiting than Marie Antoinette. The story of the man from Corsica and the woman from Martinique becoming the crowned heads of France after a revolution had abolished the monarchy could have come from the pen of Victor Hugo.

The serpent in the royal couple's Eden was the lack of an heir, a fact of great consternation to an emperor desperate to secure his dynasty. Initially, they believed the infertility lay with him as Joséphine was already a mother. However, when Napoleon's mistress gave birth to his son, they realized the problem was Joséphine's age and her mistreatment in Carmes Prison. Napoleon decided it was time to bid adieu to the woman he had often described as his lucky talisman. One evening, the palace's staff were jolted awake as a shrill scream emanated from behind a closed door: The emperor had dropped the bombshell that for reasons of state, he required a divorce. Eventually, Joséphine understood that against another woman, she would have been the victor; but against Napoleon's ambition, she did not stand a chance. Devastated, Joséphine sobbed so much at her divorce proceedings that she had trouble reading her prepared statement: "With the permission of my dear and august husband I declare that, no longer preserving any hope of having children to satisfy the political need for an heir in France, I proudly offer him the greatest proof of love and devotion ever given to a husband on this earth."

In an act of *mea culpa*, Napoleon allowed his former consort to keep the honorary title of empress. He also gifted his ex-wife their fifteen-room country refuge, the Château de Malmaison. In her magnificent garden, she cultivated 250 varieties of roses and amassed a menagerie of black swans, emus, and kangaroos. Rather than turning into Charles Dickens's reclusive Miss Havisham, Joséphine entertained on a grand scale, and she doted on her children and grandchildren. In a twist of fate, Napoleon's son died before he could become king. In contrast, two hundred years later, through Eugène and Hortense, whom Napoleon had adopted, Joséphine became the ancestor of the ruling houses of Sweden, Norway, Denmark, Belgium, and Luxembourg.

Napoleon, who had declared, "I must be aligned with sovereigns," married a trophy wife three months later, the great-niece of Marie Antoinette and the Austrian Emperor's eighteen-year-old daughter, Archduchess Marie Louise Habsburg. A year later, the long-awaited son arrived, Napoleon François Charles Joseph, on whom the emperor bestowed the title "King of Rome." What mitigated the joy of the birth of his heir was the winds of war turning against the emperor; his 1812 invasion of Russia proved a debacle. He lamented that his separation from Joséphine had been the turning point in his fortune. Forced to abdicate, he ate the bitter bread of exile in Elba. Marie Louise, who had taken a lover, stayed in France with their son. Fallen from the height of power, for comfort, Napoleon surrounded himself with pictures of Joséphine, the lost love of his life.

Joséphine showed her allegiance when she wrote Napoleon telling him that she would join him in exile, but destiny had another plan. While walking in her garden with Tsar Alexander I, she fell ill, and soon after succumbed to pneumonia.

Upon hearing of Joséphine's death, Napoleon kept to his bed for three days in a darkened room, alone and without food. When he passed away seven years later on the remote island of St. Helena, his last words were, "France, *armée, tête d'armée*, Joséphine."

CHAPTER 8

We Two

—— 1819 ——

A British woman watching Sarah Bernhardt's performance in *Antony and Cleopatra* stated, "How different, how very different, from the home life of our own dear Queen." The comment attested to the high approval rating of Queen Victoria and to the belief she led a life of propriety. In truth, her biography makes contemporary soap opera stars seem staid.

The woman who ruled over an empire on which the sun never set, whose descendants shaped world history, bore a name she made synonymous with the nineteenth century. Princess Victoria Hanover was the daughter of Edward, the Duke of Kent, the fourth son of George III, and the widowed Princess Victoria, the mother of two. The couple had moved from Victoria's native Germany to England, where their home was Kensington Palace, partially designed by Christopher Wren. The Archbishop of Canterbury and the Bishop of London officiated at Victoria's baptism with a gold font borrowed from the Tower of London. Among the guests was her maternal uncle and benefactor, Prince Leopold, the future King of the Belgians.

When little Victoria was eight months old, Edward fell ill and died after doctors bled him six times with leeches. Once more a widow, knowing only a few words of English, the elder Victoria made her daughter the focus of her world. A German tiger mom, her parenting style put the letter S before the word mother. She raised Victoria in a Draconian manner—the Kensington System, wherein she made her daughter share her room, read her diary, and forbade her to walk downstairs unless someone held her hand. Despite the austerity of her youth, the princess possessed a sense of entitlement, as manifested when she informed a girl, "And I may call you Jane, but you must not call me Victoria."

At birth, young Victoria had been fifth in line to the throne; however, various deaths and illegitimate heirs pushed her further along the line of succession. When her governess told the twelve-year-old that one day she might inherit the throne, Victoria responded, "How many a child would boast, but they don't know the difficulty. There is much splendor and there is much responsibility."

Upon the passing of William IV, the Archbishop of Canterbury and the Lord Chamberlain made haste to Kensington Palace and knelt before the newly minted eighteen-year-old queen. She recalled that after hearing the life-changing news, "I cried much on learning it and ever deplored this contingency."

In 1837, a crowd of 4,000 lined the streets of London to catch a glimpse of Victoria as she headed to her coronation at Westminster Abbey. With her newfound status, Victoria demanded the luxury of an hour alone, followed by her decree that her mother be banished to a distant room. The princess reacted to her daughter's behavior by presenting her with an edition of Shakespeare's play *King Lear*. The crown made Victoria one of the wealthiest and most powerful women in the world, but possessing the scepter of monarchy over a global empire carried a heavy load: London suffered from labor unrest, Ireland was undergoing the Potato Famine, war raged in the Crimea—and that was just in the first two decades of her reign.

The image tattooed in world history regarding the empress is of a heavyset dowager whose dour expression echoes her famous phrase, "We are not amused." Legend (though currently discounted) holds she was obsessed with modesty and that her marital advice to her daughters was, "Lie back and think of England." The truth paints a far different portrait.

Along with his royal duties, King Leopold had doubled as matchmaker when he introduced his teenaged niece and nephew to each other: Prince Albert of Germany and Princess Victoria of Britain. Three years later, Albert returned for another visit that proved love at second sight. The adoring Victoria gushed, "My dearest, dearest, dear." As she had become queen, Victoria had to be the one to propose, which she did a few days later.

The wedding captivated the world, partially as royal unions had traditionally been affairs of state rather than of the heart. Charles Dickens, caught up in the frenzy, wrote, "Society is unhinged here by Her Majesty's marriage, and I am sorry to add that I have fallen hopelessly in love with the Queen." When Albert gifted his fiancée an engagement ring—a novel gesture at the time—he ushered in a worldwide ritual. Victoria was likewise a trailblazer when she chose white for her wedding dress as well as those of her twelve bridesmaids. Before she established this trend, brides wore brightly colored gowns that could be worn again for other occasions. She accessorized with Turkish diamond earrings and a sapphire and diamond brooch from her groom; Albert's wedding band bore the date Victoria had proposed. Their subjects lined the streets as the couple rode to their ceremony in a golden carriage bound for the Chapel of St. James's. The nine-foot wedding cake weighed 300 pounds, topped with figures of the bride and groom—a nuptial touch that ushered in another wedding ritual (their figurines were dressed in ancient Greek robes).

Victoria lay back—not only for royal heirs, but because she enjoyed carnality. The queen also initiated the use of chloroform for labor pains in defiance of the belief that the agony of delivery was women's punishment for Original Sin. Delight in receiving the drug for her eighth baby, Leopold, led to his nickname, Anesthesia. After her ninth delivery, physicians advised the thirty-eight-year-old queen against having more children. Victoria responded, "Can I have no more fun in bed?" An 1858 letter to her pregnant daughter illustrated the downside of procreation: "What you say of the pride of giving life to an immortal soul is very fine, my dear, but I own I cannot enter into that; I think much more of our being like a cow or a dog at such moments."

The Queen's daughters became the consorts of various European royals, and her grandchildren were rulers of various countries. Along with properties and titles, Victoria passed along the hemophilia gene that played a role in the destruction of her granddaughter, the Tsarina of Russia, and brought down the curtain on the Romanov reign.

As testimony to Shakespeare's admonition, "Uneasy lies the head that wears the crown," there were eight assassinations attempts on Victoria's life, one when she was pregnant. She endured the loss of three of her children—Princess Alice, Prince Leopold, and Prince Alfred. However, the most devastating blow was the death of her adored Albert, who she had lovingly called "Bertie." In 1861, the man she had deemed "pure perfection" came down with typhoid. As he lay dying, he agreed to her offer of "ein kuss," "one kiss," before he passed away. Beside herself with grief, Victoria preserved his room as a shrine. Albert's final resting place was in the magnificent mausoleum the Queen erected at Frogmore; over the entrance, Victoria had inscribed the words, "Farewell best beloved, here at last I shall rest with thee, with thee in Christ I shall rise again." In his coffin, Victoria placed a "sultry" portrait of herself. For years, Victoria—dubbed the Widow of Windsor—refused to appear in public, and for the rest of her life dressed only in black.

The man who ultimately wrested Victoria from her grief was John Brown (not the one who raided Harper's Ferry). He was her gamekeeper and servant at Balmoral Castle, as well as the Victorian Lady Chatterley's lover with whom she enjoyed a twenty-year relationship. Always in his Majesty's service, he aborted an assassin's attempt on her life. A disapproving public referred to John as the Queen's Stallion and the Empress as Mrs. Brown. Victoria's high regard for John was in evidence when she banished her son, then the Duke of Edinburgh, from Buckingham Palace over his refusal to shake "that servant's hand."

Despite condemnation, John was able to accomplish what all the queen's horses and all the queen's men could not: He put Victoria together again.

Upon her return to public life, Victoria expanded her empire, the world's most powerful one that included 400 million subjects. In 1877, Victoria became Empress of India—a country she referred to as "the jewel in my crown." Victoria's Golden Jubilee feted her fiftieth year on the throne and ushered in celebrations throughout the empire. For the grand occasion, fifty kings and princes, along with the governing heads of Britain's overseas colonies and dominions, paid homage. A decade later, on her Diamond Jubilee, the empress embraced the new technology by sending out a telegram thanking her subjects for their devotion.

In 1901, an era ended with the passing of Queen Victoria. As she lay on her deathbed, she whispered her request that her Pomeranian, Turi, be brought to her bed. Victoria had scrupulously micromanaged her realm and did the same with her funeral. She requested she be buried in a white dress, with her wedding veil placed on her head. Just as Victoria had carried Albert's photograph with her since his passing, she instructed one such be buried, alongside a cast of his hand. She also requested mementoes of John: a lock of his hair rested in her hand, and she wore a ring that had belonged to his mother. Whatever love affairs the queen may have had, her final word was "Bertie." After his passing, she had longingly referred to their relationship as the time of "We two."

CHAPTER 9

Aurora

—— 1837 ——

The Princess of Wales and the Empress of Austria, though they lived a century apart, led parallel lives: both were married off to Europe's most eligible royals, dealt with formidable mothers-in-law, and lived to rue the fact that fairy-tale weddings do not always equate to a happily ever after.

The girl who would become queen of a kingdom that had dominated the map for six centuries was one of the great beauties of her era, so much so that she captured the heart of an emperor. Elisabeth "Sisi" Amalie Eugenie arrived on Christmas Eve; each of the eight children—as well as two illegitimate daughters from her father—were so indulged that each year they received their own Christmas tree. Her enchanted childhood was spent at Possenhofen Castle on Lake Starnberg, outside Munich, where she and her siblings ran wild in the adjacent forest. Her mother, Ludovika, was the daughter of King Maximilian I; the patriarch was a duke from the House of Wittelsbach, the reigning dynasty since 1180. The ruler of the Bavarian kingdom was Sisi's cousin, King Ludwig II, known as "Mad Ludwig." His fairy-tale mountain home, Neuschwanstein, later served as the model for Sleeping Beauty's Castle in Disney theme parks.

Europe in the nineteenth century was the personal chessboard of the Habsburg dynasty, whose members sat on almost every throne of the continent and wielded untold power. In 1853, Ludovika and her sister, Archduchess Sophie, arranged a match between their respective children. Ludovika brought the eighteen-year-old Helene, "Nene," to the scenic resort town of Bad Ischl to meet the world's most eligible bachelor, the newly crowned Emperor Franz Josef. However, when the king saw Sisi, who had tagged along for the trip, he was smitten: her chestnut hair cascaded to her ankles, her features seemed chiseled from a cameo, her waist smaller than that of Scarlett O'Hara. The Archduchess Sophie pointed out that Helene was his intended, and she was aghast when her dutiful "Franzi" declared the younger sister would be his bride. Reluctantly, the royal mother succumbed, at least comforted by the realization the teenager would instill an infusion of popularity into the stodgy regime. Sisi was flattered at being the love interest of one of the world's most powerful men. Nevertheless, doubts about her new role nagged at her elation: "I love the emperor. If only he were not the emperor."

At age sixteen, Sisi was the most envied of women when she became engaged to Europe's most powerful and wealthy king. The royal wedding of 1854 caused a sensation as thousands lined Vienna's streets to catch a glimpse of the princess-bride. In her glass coach, Sisi sobbed with trepidation. As it transpired, she became the people's princess due to her sweet disposition, dedication to charitable causes, and ethereal beauty. Queen Victoria found the empress "even lovelier than she had been led to expect." Yet her diamond and emerald tiara proved an unwelcome burden. Austria was the largest European state except for Russia, and the once carefree Sisi became the empress of her own country, as well as the kingdoms of Hungary, Bohemia, Bavaria, and other regions that together held fifty million subjects.

Terrified of intercourse, Sisi spurned the advances of her groom for three nights. When consummation occurred, the act became the topic of conversation of the palace. The morning after, as with every morning thereafter, the imperial couple had breakfast with Elisabeth's aunt/mother-in-law, who asked intimate questions. People remarked of Sophie that she was "the only man at court."

Franz Joseph worshipped his wife, who declared she made him "as happy as a god," but he was immersed in the gargantuan task of ruling the Habsburg Empire, which was crumbling under the weight of open revolt. He worked on his wedding day, and his wife discovered that with her husband, country came first, his mother second, and his wife, third. And while opposites attract, this did not prove the case with the royal couple. The emperor was dedicated to duty and convention; the empress craved excitement and romance. Elisabeth felt stifled living in a larger-than-life goldfish bowl governed by rigid rules of protocol and referred to the Habsburg Palace as her "prison fortress." A small act of rebellion: Sisi refused to give away her shoes and boots after a single use—a royal ritual—and defiantly wore them for a month.

Motherhood might have proven an outlet, but the Archduchess assumed parenting duties of daughters Sophie and Gisela and the long-awaited son and heir, the crown prince Rudolph. Denied a meaningful role, Sisi spent her time in her private suite, reading the works of Heinrich Heine and penning poetry on a desk that had belonged to a former Habsburg princess, Marie Antoinette. She used the pen name Titania, from the character in Shakespeare's *A Midsummer Night's Dream*. She hardly ate, while exercise became a mainstay of her daily regimen. In her quarters, she installed gymnastic equipment in order to maintain her waspish waist. To keep her flawless complexion, she slept with a mask made of raw veal applied to her skin. Renowned for her floor-length tresses, her hairdresser worked on them for three hours a day, fashioning them into a braided crown. After discovering her husband's infidelities when she came down with a venereal disease, Sisi took to traveling to far-flung countries such as Pompeii, Egypt, and Corfu; on the Greek island, she built a palace she named Achilleion after the mythological Achilles. The disconsolate queen remarked, "Every ship I see sailing away fills me with the greatest desire to be on it." Guilt-ridden over the pain he had inflicted on his wife, Franz Joseph admitted he had "a debt of conscience he never could repay" and showered his consort with gifts, including star-shaped diamonds that she intertwined into her Rapunzel locks. Other trappings of her bottomless wealth were thoroughbred horses and vacations on yachts. Enamored of the sea, she had a tattoo of an anchor on her shoulder that might also have been a nod to the weighty mantle of royalty. Her husband footed all bills, asking only she spend time at his side. However, no matter where the empress traveled, depression and mental instability hovered. As a result, Sisi took an interest in the new innovations in the treatment of the insane. Viennese Sigmund Freud would have been her best choice—and she toyed with the idea of opening her own psychiatric hospital. "Have you not noticed," she once asked, "that in Shakespeare the madmen are the only sensible ones?"

As the years passed, the empress asserted her influence; her most significant political act was to persuade her husband to grant Hungary a constitution that led to the Austrian-Hungarian Empire. The move lessened the couple's issues, and Sisi and Franz Joseph resumed their intimate relationship. Their fourth child, Marie Velerie, was born in Budapest.

There is a saying that it is not good to let too much light into the castle, a truth that applies to the Empress of Austria, who endured crippling misfortunes. Her sister, Duchess Sophie, perished in a fire in Paris; her two-year-old daughter, Sophie, passed away from illness; and her cousin King Ludwig's corpse was found in Lake Starnberg— either from murder or suicide. No stranger to misfortune, Franz Joseph survived an assassination attempt, and his brother, Maximilian I, met his end through a firing squad in Mexico. The most devastating loss was that of thirty-year-old Rudolph, the heir to the throne, who perished in a hunting lodge at Mayerling, a small village southwest of Vienna. Beside his corpse was the naked body of the seventeen-year-old Baroness Maria Vetsera. News spread like the proverbial wildfire that Rudolph had shot his companion and then turned the revolver on himself. The double murder, shrouded in mystery, crushed his mother's already bruised spirit, "Rudolph's bullet killed my faith." The crown prince's passing irrevocably altered the destiny of an ancient empire—and that of the world. Succession ultimately passed to Franz Joseph's nephew, the Archduke Francis Ferdinand, whose assassination in Sarajevo in 1914 led to the outbreak of World War I, the death knell of the Habsburg dynasty.

After the loss of her son, Elisabeth wore black for the rest of her life, refused to be photographed so she would be remembered at the height of her beauty, and traveled incessantly to distance herself from the pain of her past. She sojourned across Europe and North Africa, refusing imperial protection. In 1898, Sisi was in Lake Geneva, where she traveled under an assumed name, with a lady-in-waiting accompanying her. Also in the city was an Italian anarchist, Luigi Lucheni, who had made his way to Switzerland to assassinate Prince Henri of Orléans in order to protest the royals he viewed as bloodsuckers. News of the crowned head in their midst leaked to a newspaper, and unable to attack the French royal, Lucheni turned his sights on the empress. As Sisi was about to board a steamship for Montreux, the assassin lunged at her; the attack led to her death from internal bleeding, ending her forty-four-year reign. Her dying words, "What happened to me?"

A train returned the empress's body to Vienna, and the Austrian-Hungarian Empire plunged into mourning; eighty-two sovereigns followed her funeral cortege to the Capuchin Church, the ancient Imperial Crypt of the Habsburgs. Unlike Sleeping Beauty, who awoke from her slumber, Sisi never attained the fairy-tale heroine's Latin name meaning dawn: Aurora.

CHAPTER 10

"Farewell to Thee"

— 1838 —

Hawaii proves an irresistible magnet for tourists drawn to the azure waves of the Pacific, the pink-hued sunsets, and the exotic-colored flowers. Ironically, the beauty of the island nation led to paradise lost for its first and only queen.

Kamehameha the Great witnessed the arrival of missionaries, whose crusade was to spread Christianity, which they saw as "a mission of progress into a barbarous region." Dressed in tightly buttoned black, the visitors from New England provided a sharp contrast to the barely dressed Polynesians. Appalled at the native women, who wore a cloth around their hips and left their breasts exposed, missionary wives introduced a loose-fitting dress, the muumuu. The foreigners also instituted a ban on the *hula,* a dance they viewed as an unabashed flaunting of sexuality. The Americans were the equivalent of the nineteenth-century British, determined to convert the heathens of Africa, a task they termed "the white man's burden." The descendants of the Presbyterians accumulated great wealth from the abundance of natural resources they found, leading to the saying, "They came to do good—and did well."

When David Kalākaua became king in 1874, the monarchy was dangerously dependent on American businessmen who owned extensive pineapple and sugar plantations. In 1887, the American land barons forced King Kalākaua to sign the Constitution of the Kingdom of Hawaii, known as the Bayonet Constitution since it was signed at gunpoint. The foreigners justified their action with the claim it was needed to protect Hawaii from a corrupt despot. The move greatly curtailed the political power and rights of the island's indigenous population and paved the way for Hawaii losing its sovereign status. The people of the island were never consulted and never voted on the Constitution that impacted their lives and country.

Lili'u Loloku Walania Wewehi Kamaka'eha (her royal name was Liliuokalani) was born in Honolulu to this world of intrigue, the third of ten children and the sister of King Kalākaua. Following the native tradition of *hānai*, two close family friends, Pāki and Konia, adopted the baby. At age two, missionaries baptized Liliuokalani into Christianity and changed her name to Lydia. In 1887, as the Crown Princess, she served as Hawaii's representative at Queen Victoria's Crown Jubilee, where the monarch planted a kiss on her forehead. On her visit to the United States, President Grover Cleveland welcomed her to a state dinner at the White House. Although she moved in rarified circles, Liliuokalani never abandoned her allegiance to her people.

At age twenty-four, Liliuokalani married John Owen Dominis, the American born son of a sea captain, in an Anglican ceremony. His marriage brought him perks such as his post as the governor of Oahu and Maui. The newlyweds settled into the grand Washington Place, a residence owned by John's widowed mother. The marriage was not happy as her mother-in-law always viewed Liliuokalani as an intruder. Although the couple did not have children, John fathered a baby with one of their servants. Longing for motherhood, Liliuokalani adopted his child as well as two others. Despite his infidelities, upon ascending the throne, Liliuokalani granted John the title of Prince Consort. He died several months into her reign; his widow deeply mourned his passing.

When her brother embarked on a world tour, Liliuokalani acted as regent, an event that coincided with a smallpox epidemic that originated with Chinese laborers the plantation owners had imported to work in the sugarcane fields. The native people had no resistance to the disease, and their population greatly diminished. To protect her subjects, Liliuokalani closed the ports, a move that infuriated the wealthy businessmen who believed profits took priority. The monarchy continued, although with greatly reduced power. Upon King Kalākaua's death in 1891, followed by the passing of another brother, Liliuokalani became Hawaii's first queen. She took up residence in the Lolani Palace, that translates to "bird of heaven," the only royal residence in the United States—unless one counts Graceland.

To her great sorrow, the queen was witness to the destruction wrought by foreigners who viewed her beloved homeland as their personal piggybank. With the cultivation of ever-encroaching plantations owned by mainland Americans, fishponds, forests, and rare birds disappeared. Liliuokalani was also vocal in her opposition to the Reciprocity Treaty that had granted commercial concessions to the United States and had ceded the port of Pearl Harbor. Her first order of business was to revoke the Bayonet Constitution, an act calculated to restore full power to the throne. In response, William Randolph Hearst, in his *San Francisco Enquirer*, lampooned her as "a black, pagan queen." However, not all foreigners viewed her with distaste; British author Robert Louis Stevenson was her guest, and they drank Château Lafite together out of crystal goblets imported from Bohemia.

On January 17, 1893, 154 marines, each armed with eighty rounds of ammunition and equipped with a cannon, surrounded the Lolani Palace. The Queen made her way to the balcony to discover the source of the disturbance. Her enemies demanded her immediate abdication and the annexation of Hawaii to the United States of America. Desperate to avoid bloodshed, Queen Liliuokalani surrendered, though she refused to waive her royal rights.

The following morning, as the queen awaited her daily bouquet of red lehua blossoms, soldiers besieged the palace, one they transformed to a barrack. The interlopers lounged in her throne room, sitting beneath crystal chandeliers. The newly established provisional government disbanded the royal household guard and confiscated a million acres of crown lands, worth billions of dollars in today's currency. To escape the nightmare, Liliuokalani decamped to Washington Place. In protest, she wrote notes imploring the intervention of the US, England, Germany, and France. Further indignities followed: An American warship fired a salute, and marines hoisted the American flag. The former queen wrote, "May heaven look down and punish them for their deeds." Three native women offered themselves as sacrifices to appease the gods so that Liliuokalani would reign once more. Members of the Royal Hawaiian Band declared they would rather eat stones than swear allegiance to the imperialists. Rumors that the interlopers were plotting the assassination of Liliuokalani ran rampant.

In 1895, the Hawaiians staged a counterattack to restore their queen to the throne and reclaim their stolen kingdom. Their plan was to distribute weapons at Diamond Head; however, the Americans had planted spies who alerted them to the resurrection. After a week, the provisional government had squashed "the rebels" and had incarcerated 355 men.

The result was a warrant for the woman ruler (her usurpers called her Mrs. Dominis) whom they placed under house arrest in a room in Lolani Palace. From her chamberlain, she discovered the rape of her former residence. An Irish American soldier had found Kalākaua's crown and had pried off its jewels, which he then used as payment in a game of dice. He kept one of the biggest diamonds, which he sent to his sister, not realizing its astronomical worth. Other stolen treasures were glass vases gifted by Queen Victoria, a dress adorned with peacock feathers, and royal staffs covered with albatross plumes. Further horror came when she learned of land baron Sanford Dole's order of the arrest of her household retainers, including her long-employed coachman. Her jailer shared the news that she was to face imminent execution, along with six others, for treason.

The Kingdom of Hawaii's death march ended in 1893 with Liliuokalani's formal forced abdication. As she had already seen too much blood spilt to restore her throne, and as her jailers had told her they would release her allies from prison, she agreed. The first and only queen of Hawaii signed a document that she was abdicating "after free and full consultation with my personal friends, and with my legal advisers." Her shaky signature was indicative of her duress. As per instructions, she signed it "Liliuokalani Dominis." Afterwards, in her former throne room, a military tribunal put her on trial. Fearing the execution of the deposed queen would lead to her martyrdom, the court spared her life.

For eight months, Liliuokalani remained a prisoner; in her confinement, she worked on a quilt on which she embroidered the Kalākaua coat of arms, the Hawaiian flag, and in its center, "Imprisoned at Lolani Palace." Later, guards removed her to Washington Place, where she spent the remainder of her days. Her jaw would have dropped to the floor if she could have known that in 1993, on the hundredth anniversary of the overthrow, President Clinton issued a formal apology to native Hawaiians.

One of the poignant reminders of Hawaii's deposed queen is a lyric she composed that found its way into the film *From Here to Eternity*, Elvis Presley's song, "Blue Hawaii," and Disney's film *Lilo and Stitch*. The words are a paean to the setting of the sun on Liliuokalani's lost kingdom, "*Aloha 'Oe*," "Farewell to Thee."

CHAPTER 11

"Yours, Yours"

— 1872 —

U pon occasion, an individual is the possessor of an extraordinary life résumé, as is the case with a woman who traversed the road from princess to empress to saint. Her story wove a tapestry that bound together the threads of majesty, mayhem, and massacre.

A biblical injunction states, "For unto whomsoever much is given, of him shall be much required," a quotation well applied to Victoria Alix Helena Louise Beatrice (she went by the name Alix) from the Grand Duchy of Hesse of the German Empire. Her pedigree was fourteen-karat; her mother Alice, the daughter of Queen Victoria, had wed a minor royal: Louis IV, the grand Duke of Hesse-Darmstadt. Tragedy descended on the House of Hesse when Alix's brother died from a brain hemorrhage after suffering from a fall from a window. The six-year-old Alix also lost her mother and sister from diphtheria. Queen Victoria arranged for "grandmamma" vacations at Balmoral Castle, and many felt Alix was her favorite. The princess studied philosophy at Heidelberg University; a strong-willed young woman, she defied Queen Victoria's request to marry her first cousin, Prince Albert Victor of Wales.

At age twelve, Alix met the sixteen-year-old Nicholas in Saint Petersburg at the wedding of her sister Elisabeth of Hesse and by Rhine to his uncle, Sergei Alexandrovich, the Grand Duke of Serge. Besotted, Alix carved their names on the window of the Peterhof Palace. The teenaged Nicholas was the scion of the Romanov dynasty: Saint Petersburg bore the name of his ancestor, Peter the Great. In contemporary currency, the Romanov wealth would have ranged from $250 to $300 billion. Nicholas's father, Alexander III, owned the largest yacht in existence, dozens of diamond-encrusted Fabergé eggs, paintings, and palaces. The dynasty held sway over one sixth of the world's land mass and controlled the lives of millions.

After five years, Alix returned to Russia to visit Elisabeth and reconnected with Nicholas; they went ice skating, attended balls, and reignited their earlier spark. Before she returned to Germany, Nicholas hosted a farewell party in Tsarskoye Selo Palace, which boasted 200 rooms on 800 acres that included an artificial lake. Peter the Great had purchased the palace for his wife, and its magnificence put Versailles to shame. Nicholas confided in his diary, "My dream is to someday marry Alix. For a long time, I have resisted my feeling that my dearest dream will come true." Tsar Alexander did not share his son's feelings; as with most Russians, he was anti-German and felt an obscure princess was not a matrimonial prize. An absolute autocrat on the throne and with his family, Alexander had a disconcerting habit of bending iron pokers or cutlery to emphasize a point. The usually compliant Nicholas refused to consider another wife. At age forty-nine, Alexander suddenly became gravely ill, and in the belief that Nicholas would be a more effective ruler with the stability of a spouse, he granted permission for the union. Initially, Alix rejected Nicholas's proposal since she was a devout Lutheran, and as tsarina, she would be required to embrace the Russian Orthodoxy. Placing heart over religion, Alix relented, at which time they both broke down in tears. A week after the funeral was held for Alexander, Nicholas married the newly minted Grand Duchess Alexandra Feodorovna; in private, they referred to one another as Nicky and Alicky. They exchanged vows in the Grand Church of the Winter Palace, where the bride's white dress was so encrusted with jewels that she required assistance to kneel or stand.

Nicholas's popularity plummeted with his country's disastrous defeat in the Russian-Japanese War, along with the Bloody Sunday massacre where imperial troops gunned down unarmed workers. Resistance against the tsar escalated; under duress, he accepted the Duma, an elected parliament founded on a constitution.

Although ineffectual at running a country, Nicholas proved a devoted family man. Insulated in Tsarkoye, the royal couple welcomed a succession of four daughters: the Grand Duchesses Olga, Tatiana, Maria, and Anastasia. In their isolated palace, the four sisters formed an unshakable bond and referred to themselves as the OTMA, an acronym derived from the first letter of their respective names. The tsarina's Mauve Room was her favorite retreat, so named as everything in the room was the shade of a branch of lilac Nicholas had once gifted Alexandra. They were over the moon at the birth of Alexei Nikolaevich, the vortex of his close-knit family. Elation transformed to agony when the infant Tsarevitch bled from his navel: He had inherited his great-grandmother's hemophiliac gene.

As the years went by, with prayer and physicians unable to treat Alexei, the desperate mother turned to the peasant holy man, Grigori Rasputin, rumored to possess healing powers. His mysterious ability to help counter Alexei's bleeding episodes granted him prominence in the royal inner circle. Resentment mounted as "the mad-monk" rampaged throughout the court with the restraint of a raging bull, engaging in drunken escapades with prostitutes. The tsar, powerless when it came to his wife, remarked, "Better ten Rasputins than one of the empress's hysterical fits." The nobles were infuriated that the peasant had usurped their power, and the rest of the country, oblivious to the Crown Prince's condition, were appalled their ruler revered a sinner as a saint.

Nicholas's prestige further eroded during World War I when he left Petrograd to assume command of the army at the front (carrying his wife's photograph in his pocket), thereby leaving Alexandra—and Rasputin—in charge. The situation provoked fury as many felt the German-born tsarina secretly sided with Kaiser Wilhelm II, her second cousin. Postcards proliferated with images of the tsarina and Rasputin in sexual poses. The Russian version of a Greek tragedy continued when the aristocrat Felix Yusupov, along with his coconspirators, arranged the assassination of Rasputin as "an act of patriotism" carried out to save Russia from ruin. Due to his prodigious strength, Rasputin only succumbed after being poisoned, clubbed, shot, and drowned. Nicholas's mother was thrilled at his murder while Alix feared her adored son Alexei had lost his hope of staving off hemophilia.

In 1917, with Russia splitting apart at the seams from loss of life incurred during the war, with strikes resulting from severe food, housing, and fuel shortages, at midnight Tsar Nicholas abdicated his throne on behalf of both himself and Grand Duke Alexei. To compound the humiliation of letting his birthright slip through his fingers, the man who had wielded absolute power was a prisoner at the mercy of vengeful revolutionaries.

After five months of palace arrest in Tsarskoe Selo, the Bolsheviks ordered the Romanovs relocated first to Tobolsk in Siberia, then to the Ipatiev House in Yekaterinburg, in the foothills of the central Urals. While the tsar and the children were polite to their captors, Alexandra treated them with haughty disdain. However, her aloofness might have stemmed from unimaginable grief. Her family, who she loved above all else, was in shambles: her Nicky was inconsolable that he had placed his loved ones in danger; her daughters sported shaved heads, a result of measles; Alexei was confined to a wheelchair. Shrieks in the night from the girls resulted from sexual molestation by their captors. The only light in the literal gloom—the windows of their prison had been painted black—was that the family remained together, and in the prayer the counter-revolutionary White Army would come to their rescue.

On midnight, July 16, 1918, after seventy-eight days of captivity, Yakov Yurovsky, awakened the Romanovs and ordered them to dress in preparation for relocation as the White Army was advancing. Guards escorted them to the cellar of the home where Nicholas sat with his arm around Alexandra, Alexei on his lap. As they waited, a twelve-man execution squad barged into the room, holding revolvers. Yurovsky stated, "Your relations have tried to save you. They have failed, and we must now shoot you." Nicholas rose from his chair to shield his wife and son. The deposed tsar met his end with a bullet to his head. Alexandra started to make the sign of the cross before she fell in a bloodied heap. The terrified OTMA survived the first barrage of bullets as their dresses held precious jewels sewn underneath their garments. Diamond-filled corsets made killing them with bayonets a difficult task.

Indignity continued postmortem: The assassins loaded the corpses (including three servants and the family physician) onto trucks, drove them to an abandoned mine shaft in the forest, hacked the bodies into pieces, and doused them with sulfuric acid before burial in a family grave. With the discovery of their remains, Russia canonized the family as martyrs and laid them to rest amidst great ceremony in the Romanov crypt in Saint Petersburg, eighty years after their assassination.

The love story of Nicky and Alicky had brought ruination to their family and empire, an ironic contrast to the words Alexandra had written in her diary on her wedding night, "At last united, bound for life and when this life is ended, we meet again in the other world and remain together for eternity. Yours, yours."

♕

CHAPTER 12

The Storm

— 1875 —

Crowned heads usually walk the prescribed path of sumptuous palaces, eye-popping jewelry, and envy-worthy travels. One royal woman took this road, but along the way, her life also intertwined with Count Dracula, a Dorothy Parker poem, and a revolution—and that was merely the tip of the proverbial iceberg.

In 1938, Romania's dowager, Queen Marie, lay in state while a quarter million people gathered to pay their final respects. The scene of her funeral was as colorful as her biography: Red flowers surrounded her body, lavender flags wafted from windows. Among the mourners were her children, Romania's King Carol II, Greece's ex-Queen Elizabeth, and Yugoslavia's Queen Mother Marie. The air vibrated with the strains of Wagner's "Götterdämmerung," compliments of the Bucharest Symphony.

Except for Dorothy Parker's 1937 poem, few people are familiar with the former Romanian ruler: "Oh, life is a glorious cycle of song / A medley of extemporanea / And love is a thing that will never go wrong / And I am Marie of Romania." The queen to whom Ms. Parker alluded was Princess Marie Alexandra Victoria (Missy to her family). She was the granddaughter of England's Queen Victoria and of Russia's Czar Alexander II, and as such, her family ruled almost half the world. Her parents were Prince Alfred, Duke of Edinburgh, and Grand Duchess Maria Alexandrovna. Marie and her three siblings spent their childhood in Eastwell Park in Kent, Clarence House in London, and Osborne Cottage on the Isle of Wight. On visits to Windsor Castle, they met with Queen Victoria, who Marie later referred to as her "wonderful little old Grandmamma."

As Marie was ninth in line to the throne, there was little chance she would wield the scepter; instead, the expectation was she would wed a fellow blue blood. The possibility presented itself when George, the Prince of Wales and the future King Edward VII, proposed. However, Marie's mother vetoed his request as her childhood Russian Orthodox religion prohibited marriage between first cousins. Another early suitor was Winston Churchill, although he was not a viable match as he was not the possessor of royal blood.

The Duke and Duchess of Edinburgh had not originally sought an alliance with the Romanian throne. At the time of Marie's birth, the Balkan nation would not become a kingdom for six years; it was only in 1881 that the German Prince Charles of Hohenzolleren-Sigmaringen became its King Carol I. However, when the king's nephew and heir, Ferdinand, was in quest of a wife, Marie's mother agreed to a match even though Ferdinand was a decade older than her seventeen-year-old daughter, Marie had only met him a few times, and he was a Catholic. Along with her trousseau, the teenager might have considered packing a crucifix and garlic. The Gothic writers of the era depicted the forests of the Carpathians as the haunt of vampires that Bram Stoker immortalized four years later in *Dracula*.

In 1893, Ferdinand and Marie wed in a lavish ceremony overlooking the Danube River at Schloss Sigmaringen, the castle that belonged to the groom's father, Prince Leopold. In the presence of assembled royals, Kaiser Wilhelm II signed the marriage contract. The bride's jewelry consisted of a 478.68-carat blue sapphire pendant that matched her sapphire tiara.

The first few months in Budapest were challenging, as Marie was homesick and endured marital and in-law problems. When she discovered she was pregnant, Marie had to petition the court for doctors to administer chloroform to help with the labor as Romanian medics believed that "women must pay in agony for the sins of Eve." The couple went on to have six children, as well as his and hers affairs. Some of Marie's greatest romances were with Barbo Stirbey, head of the Romanian royal household, the American Waldorf Astor, the future husband of Nancy Astor, and Colonel Joseph Boyle, a Canadian soldier of fortune.

At the onset of her reign, Marie was self-engrossed; a member of her family discovered a piece of paper in her palace on which were the words, "Marie of Roumania—one of the most wonderful women in the world. A woman like that is born once in a century." The handwriting belonged to the queen. However, Romania's political turmoil turned the pampered princess into a warrior queen. In her case, the times made the woman.

Her transformation started in the field hospitals of the 1913 Second Balkan War in which thousands of soldiers perished from cholera and typhus. Rather than remain in the refuge of her palace, Marie left to work as a nurse for the Romanian Red Cross on the front, where she dressed in a shapeless, white, nun-like garment. She held the hands of dying men, prayed with them, and handed out sweetened tea, all the while refusing to wear a mask. Covering her face, she explained, would dehumanize the men's final moments. When an aide suggested she at least wear gloves, the Queen retorted, "I really can't ask them to kiss Indian rubber." A prolific wordsmith, she wrote of the war years, "The remembrance I keep of those days is of a suffering so great that it almost blinded me. Yet I was quite calm and continued living and working as though my heart had not been torn from my breast." Photographs of Marie kneeling in mud and feces endeared the British-born royal to the Romanians.

In 1916, the day Romania entered World War I on the side of Britain, France, and Russia, Queen Marie wrote in her diary, "What can a woman do in a modern war? It is no more the time of Joan of Arc?" Within three months, enemy troops had taken over Budapest, necessitating the flight of King Ferdinand and Marie to the north. A year later, despite the opposition of the royal couple, Romania's politicians signed a peace treaty with their former enemies.

In 1919, Marie descended on Paris, where the Allied Powers convened to divvy up empires and redraw the map of Europe. Along with King Albert of Belgium, she arrived in order "to urge the claims of their small countries." Romania's fear was the victorious powers would shrink its borders in retaliation for it having signed a peace treaty with the Germans. She stayed in a suite of twenty rooms at the Ritz, saying, "I feel this is no time to economize;" and not one to pass up French fashion, Marie purchased thirty-one coats, sixty gowns, eighty-three pairs of shoes, twenty-two fur wraps, and twenty-nine hats. The queen's political agenda was her warning that unless her kingdom received fair treatment, it would embrace Bolshevism. Her ploy was well-played: Under the Treaty of Versailles, Romania doubled in size, becoming the fifth largest nation in Europe, with an accompanying rise in population from eight to eighteen million. Deflecting from her success, Marie stated, "One woman's word cannot change the face of such big events." A British official demurred, describing her as "the most astonishing propagandist" he had ever seen. Another observer noted, "I know of no one who went away from Paris with more satisfactory annexations than Marie of Romania."

In tribute to the queen, the citizens of Brasov gifted her Bran Castle, a Transylvanian fortress in the Carpathian Mountains erected by Teutonic knights in 1212. The castle carried a certain cachet, as two centuries later it served as residence of Vlad the Impaler, known as the toothy Dracula.

Although Ferdinand and Marie had assumed the crown in 1914 after the passing of the childless King Carol I, because of World War I, their coronation had been postponed until 1922. The ceremony was held at the cathedral of Alba Iulia, once a Middle Ages fortress. The new queen dazzled in a 478.68-carat Cartier sapphire pendant necklace made the year prior that completed her Russian sapphire tiara. Enthusiastic crowds chanted, "Regina Maria!"

In 1938, Queen Marie passed away in Pelisor Castle; mourners transported her to Bucharest where she lay in state in the Cotroceni Palace's white drawing room. Her interment was at the Curtea de Arges Monastery; however, in accordance with her will, her heart, enshrined in a small, gold box, came to rest in the Stella Maris Chapel in Balchik, in the castle that had been her favorite summer residence. During World War II, when the area became part of Bulgaria, her family relocated her heart to Bran Castle. After the Iron Curtain descended on Romania, the new regime seized Bran and deposited the organ in a storage room in the National Museum of Romanian history. After seventy years, Marie's children arranged for her heart, ensconced in a silver box and attended by eight soldiers on horseback, to be placed behind the couch in Pelisor Castle where she had passed away. The procession from the museum to the castle was accompanied by hundreds of people, including dignitaries, onlookers in traditional attire, and the queen's descendants who had returned to Romania for the occasion. Onlookers waved flags accompanied by the strains of the Romanian and British national anthems.

Had Marie's destiny been to marry King George V, she would have had a far more staid life, one that would no doubt have left her restless. The queen would well have understood Dorothy Parker's words, "They sicken of the calm, who know the storm."

CHAPTER 13

"Bubbikins"

— 1885 —

Princess Diana owned a red sweater with dozens of white sheep and one black on it, perhaps a tongue-in-cheek nod to her status with her in-laws. Another royal who experienced similar alienation was Princess Victoria Alice Elizabeth Julia Marie, known as Alice, born in Windsor Castle in the presence of her great-grandmother, Queen Victoria. The baby was the daughter of Princess Victoria of Hesse and by Rhine and Prince Louis of Battenberg. She was the eldest of four; her siblings became the Queen of Denmark, the Marquess of Milford, and Earl Mountbatten of Burma. Born deaf, she mastered lip-reading in several languages and could tell what the actors were really saying in silent films.

At age seventeen, Alice attended King Edward VII's 1902 London coronation, where she fell "really, deeply in love" with Prince Andrew of Greece and Denmark, the fourth son of King Constantine I. The couple married a year later in Germany; their wedding gifts were valued at $750,000, $23 million in contemporary currency. One of these presents, a diamond tiara, compliments of Tsar Nicholas II and Tarina Alexandra of Russia, would currently carry a price tag of $14 million. The couple lived in Greece's royal palace, where they raised their four daughters and their youngest child, the long-awaited son. Philip was born on a kitchen table in Corfu at Villa Mon Repo, their Greek summer home. When he married the British Princess Elizabeth, he used gems from the tiara as the setting for her engagement ring and bracelet.

During the Balkan War of 1912, Alice volunteered at battlefield hospitals. She wrote to her mother, "God, what things we saw. Shattered arms, legs, and heads—such awful sights." World War I shook the foundation of Alice's world. In 1916, the family had to take refuge in the palace cellars during the French bombardment of Athens. The following year, King Constantine's pro-German alliances in World War I necessitated his abdication. The new military government court-martialed Prince Andrew after the ill-fated Asia Minor Campaign between Greece and Turkey after the Great War. Fearing for their safety, the family fled Greece on the British cruiser, the *HMS Calypso*. The eighteen-month-old Philip made his escape in a makeshift cot made from an orange box. Two of Alice's aunts, Tsarina Alexandra Feodorovna and Grand Duchess Elizabeth Feodorovna, met violent deaths at the hands of the Bolsheviks.

In 1929, Alice's family became increasingly concerned about her mental health; she acted erratically and claimed she had received divine messages. She spoke of conversations with Jesus and confessed they often flirted. At one point, she even hinted that something even more was going between the two of them. After suffering from a nervous breakdown in 1930, she left for treatment at a Berlin clinic; there, Dr. Ernest Simmel diagnosed her as a paranoid schizophrenic. Simmel consulted his colleague, Dr. Sigmund Freud, who concluded that her madness was the result of an aborted love affair and that the Princess's mental health problems were the result of "sexual frustration." His suggestion was to x-ray Alice's ovaries in order to "cool her down—kill her libido" by bringing on menopause. Against her will, the doctors committed her to Kreuzlingen, a sanatorium in Switzerland, where she remained for two years before her transfer to a clinic in Meran, a northern Italian village. Andrew only visited twice as he was otherwise engaged in the south of France, playing card games on yachts with various girlfriends. After her release, Andrew lived on the French

Riviera with his lover, Countess Andrée de La Bigne, while Princess Alice traveled incognito in Europe. Philip saw little of either parent during his childhood and instead bed-surfed with various relatives. At the home of one, he signed the guest book, "Philip...No fixed abode!" For several years, Alice cut all ties with her family; although husband and wife led separate lives, they never divorced. Alice reconnected with her family at the funeral of her daughter, Cecilie, who had perished in a 1937 plane crash over Osten, Belgium, along with her husband and two children. The tragic event entailed a mother and son reunion; also in attendance was Nazi bigwig Hermann Göring.

Partially to cope with the tragic deaths and her other sorrows, Alice found solace in religion. She returned to Greece, donned a gray habit (her uniform for the remainder of her life), and became a member of the Greek Orthodox Church. To fund the convent she established, the Christian Sisterhood of Martha and Mary, she sold her priceless possessions. Her mother was appalled at her daughter's lifestyle and stated, "What can you say of a nun who smokes and plays canasta?"

During World War II, Alice lived in Athens, where she devoted her life to helping the poor. She had long divested herself of any aristocratic trappings and lived in a two-bedroom apartment. Alice hid the Jewish Rachel Cohen and her children in her Athens home, a situation made even more tense when her daughters and their SS officer husbands visited. On another occasion, interviewed by a suspicious member of the Gestapo, she used her deafness as an excuse for not understanding their questions. They dismissed the cigarette smoking, princess nun as a doddering old woman. Because of Alice, the Cohen family survived and today lives in France.

In 1967, after the takeover of the military dictatorship in the Colonels' Coup, Philip invited his mother to live with him in Buckingham Palace. She only accepted when her daughter, Sophie, the Princess George of Hanover, told her that the invitation had also come from her daughter-in-law, Queen Elizabeth II. Her response, "Lilibet said that? Right, we go this afternoon." During her time at the palace, Alice became close to Princess Anne, who called her *Yaya*, the Greek word for grandmother. The Windsors, rather than banishing the older woman to the attic as Mr. Rochester had done to his first wife in the famed Brontë novel, gave her a suite of rooms. An earlier occupant of these accommodations had been the Duchess of Windsor when she had returned to England to attend her husband's funeral, a moment captured in a photograph where she is seen watching the Trooping of the Colour procession, her face wreathed in mourning. Fellow palace residents became used to the anomaly of an older woman dressed in a nun's garb who smoked incessantly. The press was taken with the eccentric blue blood, and Philip dubbed her "the Royal Saint."

Princess Alice's funeral took place at St. George's Chapel in Windsor Castle in 1969, where she had been born eighty-four years before. Intensely private until the end, she destroyed all her papers and only left behind—of her once fabulous treasures—three dressing gowns. She had sold her magnificent collection of jewels and other treasures to benefit the poor. She also left behind a note to her son, with whom she had shared a difficult relationship: "Dearest Philip, be brave, and remember I will never leave you, and you will always find me when you need me most. All my devoted love, your old Mama." In Prince Philip's replies to letters of sympathy at his mother's passing, he replied that hers had been "a life of wars, revolutions, separations, and tragedies." And there had been so much more he could have added.

A decade later, Jerusalem's Yad Vashem gave the royal-turned-nun posthumous recognition when it named Princess Alice Righteous Among the Nations, Israel's highest honor for those who saved Jews during the Holocaust. Prince Philip and his sister accepted the honor on her behalf. In 2010, the British government deemed her a Hero of the Holocaust.

Alice, who always chose to fly under the royal radar, made posthumous headlines. Her wish had been to be buried near her aunt and role model, the martyred Grand Duchess Elizabeth, a Russian Orthodox saint who had also established a convent and helped the poor. The gravesite she had pinned her hope on was outside the church of St. Mary Magdalene in Gethsemane in Jerusalem. Nineteen years after Alice's passing, her eldest daughter, Princess George of Hanover, flew in with her coffin. The princess's body, protected by armed Israeli border police, was to rest in the hallowed grounds of St. Mary Magdalene, granting her final request. The British parliament did not approve of Prince Philip attending the interment due to Israel's human rights offenses against the Palestinians.

In 1994, there was at last redemption between Philip and his "old Mama" that may have laid to rest any residual anger he harbored against the woman who had been more intent on saving the world than being a parent. A relative of the Cohens had suggested that a street in Jerusalem be named after Princess Alice in acknowledgment for her heroic role during the Holocaust. When the British government permitted Philip to pay a visit to his mother's Jerusalem grave, he responded to the Cohens' request: "I suspect that it never occurred to her that her action was in any way special. She was a person with deep religious faith, and she would have considered it to be a totally human action to fellow human beings in distress." The Prince's words represented the reconciliation between Princess Alice, and, to use her term of endearment for Philip when he was little, her "Bubbikins."

CHAPTER 14

The Mill

— 1896 —

U pon occasion, it requires more than a box of Godiva chocolates or a Hallmark card to capture the heart of a ladylove. Richard Wagner composed the "Siegfried Idyll" as a birthday gift for his wife, Cosima. Tsar Alexander III presented jewel-encrusted Fabergé eggs as Easter gifts for his tsarina. Richard Burton wowed Elizabeth Taylor with a sixty-nine-carat pear-shaped diamond. Yet these gestures pale in comparison to what a royal relinquished for his ladylove.

In 1936, King Edward VIII climbed the Gothic stairway of Windsor Castle and delivered perhaps the most renowned radio broadcast of the twentieth century. Edward Albert Christian George Andrew Patrick David (who preferred David) later claimed he had written the speech with only slight help from Winnie, his nickname for Winston Churchill. As he held a microphone, the king declared, "You must believe me when I tell you that I have found it impossible to carry the heavy burden of responsibility and to discharge my duties as king as I wish to do, without the help and support of the woman I love." In his speech, he never mentioned the object of his devotion: Bessie Wallis Warfield Spencer Simpson.

Bessie Wallis was born at Monterey Inn, in the resort village of Blue Ridge Summit, Pennsylvania. Her parents, Teackle Wallis Warfield and Alice—later spelled Alys—had arrived from Baltimore hoping to help her father's ailing health. He died five months after the birth of his daughter; left without an income, Alys took in boarders. Feeling the name Bessie more suitable for a cow than a socialite, the girl went by her middle name.

At age twenty, Wallis married a twenty-seven-year-old naval aviator, Lieutenant Earl Winfield Spencer Jr. When in the throes of alcohol-fueled binges, Earl locked her in her room. When the navy stationed Earl in the Far East, the couple visited Peking brothels where Wallis discovered ancient sex secrets. After their 1921 divorce, she wed Ernest Aldrich Simpson, a Brit living in New York who left his wife for her. The Simpsons moved to England so Ernest could run his family's shipping business.

Wallis met David when his mistress, Lady Thelma Furness, introduced them at her country home in Leicestershire. Wallis recalled that she was immediately smitten with the Prince of Wales's "slightly wind-rumpled hair, the turned-up nose, and a strange, wistful, almost sad look about the eyes when his expression was in repose." The fact David was one of the wealthiest men in the world might have factored into her romantic equation.

In 1934, Lady Furness left for New York to support her twin sister's custody battle over her daughter, Gloria Vanderbilt. Over their luncheon at the Ritz, she requested of Wallis, "Look after the little man. See that he does not get into any mischief." Thelma, who viewed Wallis as unattractive, did not look upon her as a rival.

Mrs. Simpson (as the press dubbed Wallis) became the Prince's ever-present shadow, and a member of a special branch of the police reported that the lady seemed "to have the POW [Prince of Wales] completely under her thumb." The besotted royal declared, "In character, Wallis was, and still remains, complex and elusive, and from the first, I looked upon her as the most independent woman I had ever met. This refreshing trait I was inclined to put down as one of the happiest outcomes of 1776." The prince provided the open sesame to an unbelievable vista of privilege, and she felt she was "Wallis in Wonderland." Queen Mary, not a fan, always referred to Wallis as "that woman."

In the summer of 1934, the Prince took Mrs. Simpson to Biarritz on a yachting trip; Mr. Simpson was absent with leave. In her 1956 memoir, *The Heart Has Its Reasons*, Wallis wrote, "The Prince and I found ourselves sitting alone on deck. Perhaps it was one of these evenings off the Spanish coast that we crossed the line that marks the indefinable boundary between friendship and love. Perhaps it was one evening strolling on the beach at Formentor in Majorca. How can a woman ever really know?" The relationship was not what caused a scandal, mistresses being as old as the monarchy; rather, it was the Prince's publicly flaunting his dalliance with a married woman.

With the passing of King George V, David became King Edward VIII "by the grace of God, of Great Britain, Ireland, and the British Dominions beyond the Seas, King, Defender of the Faith, Emperor of all India." Alarm bells sounded when Wallis sought a divorce, indicating that she and David planned to make their relationship legal. The royal family and the government were adamant: they would never accept a divorcee as queen.

David understood that if he abdicated, he would be forever estranged from his family, who would not forgive the royal scandal. Moreover, he would become an exile, as his abdication would result in the loss of the stipend he needed to support an uber opulent lifestyle. The momentous decision also meant a renunciation of the role of his birthright. The official motto of the Prince of Wales is the German motto *"Ich dien"* ("I serve"), and therefore, his rejection of the crown meant the betrayal of his family, his country, and his church. Wallis, devastated she could never be queen, was content to remain the royal mistress. She explained, "How can a woman be a whole empire to a man?" Queen Mary was in disbelief and stated, "To give up all this for that." Perhaps the reason David did so was because of the rumor that Wallis had "the ability to make a matchstick feel like a cigar." Another theory is David was homosexual, and as king, his secret life would be under a microscope.

To commemorate Wallis's having her lover relinquish the throne of England on her behalf, in 1936 *TIME* made her "Woman of the Year," the first occasion the magazine had ever given its "Man of the Year" title to a woman. The royal who would not be king, the newly titled Duke of Windsor, gave his fiancée an engagement ring with the inscription *WE are ours now* (the *W* stood for Wallis, the *E* for Edward). With the Windsor wealth, the dedicated clotheshorse dressed in Chanel, Givenchy, and Dior, complemented by a king's ransom of jewels. Magazines included her on the list of the ten best-dressed women in the world. Her response to the honor, "I'm nothing to look at. So the only thing that I can do is dress better than anyone else."

In 1937, the couple wed in a borrowed château in Loire Valley, France. The bride wore a floor-length dress by Mainbocher of crepe satin in a shade evoking forget-me-nots that became known as Wallis blue. The newly minted royal later told writer Gore Vidal that the morning after her marriage, she awoke to find her husband "standing by the bed, saying, "And now what should we do?" For their honeymoon, they left for Venice, where they attended a performance of *Romeo and Juliet*. As they entered the theater, the audience rose to its feet and roared, "*Viva l'amore!*" To the world, theirs was a legendary love story, but Wallis once stated, "You have no idea how hard it is to live out a great romance."

In May of that year, David and Wallis listened to the broadcast of the coronation of his younger brother, George VI. Among the king's first acts was to confer on David the title of His Royal Highness the Duke of Windsor; he refused to bestow the honorific of Her Royal Highness on his sister-in-law, who became the Duchess of Windsor. King George viewed his brother and his wife as embarrassments to the crown, not only for their acts that had placed a spotlight on the royals, but also for a damning photograph that showed Adolf Hitler kissing Wallis's hand as David looked on.

The Duke and Duchess's main residence was a mansion in the Bois de Boulogne that they shared with their beloved pugs, who dined from silver bowls, carried the scent of Christian Dior perfume, dressed in mink, wore diamond studded collars, and had gold Cartier leashes. Another estate, the one where Wallis felt most at home, was a converted eighteenth-century mill outside Paris known as Le Moulin de la Tuileries. In their country residence, they entertained celebrity friends such as Elizabeth Taylor, Richard Burton, Marlene Dietrich, and Maria Callas. Amongst her priceless treasures, Wallis had a needlepoint pillow with the words, "One can never be too rich or too thin."

David passed away in 1972, and Queen Elizabeth II allowed Wallis to visit Buckingham Palace for her husband's interment in Frogmore Garden at Windsor Palace. Bereft at her husband's passing, the Duchess's diet consisted mainly of alcohol; in 1973, she broke her hip and became bedridden. In her later years, she lost the ability to speak and her memory worsened, a weakness that her French lawyer, Suzanne Blum, exploited. Abandoned by her in-laws and with no family of her own, Wallis became a prisoner in her own home, often sedated by Blum, who sold jewelry from Wallis's legendary collection. Death at age eighty-nine brought release, and she lay once more beside the man who had given up his empire.

In the Moulin de la Tuileries, the Duchess had these words inscribed on its wall, a nod to the agony hidden under her royal gilt: "I am not the miller's daughter, but I have been through the mill."

CHAPTER 15

A Velvet Glove

— 1900 —

An 1865 poem by William Ross Wallace states, "The hand that rocks the cradle rules the world." Because good ol' mom shapes society, the matriarch of the world's most famous family became a magnet for public scrutiny. Born in the dawn of the twentieth century, the royal remembered as the Queen Mother died a year after it ended.

Lady Elizabeth Angela Marguerite Bowes-Lyon grew up when Britannia ruled the waves. She was the ninth of ten children of Lord Glamis, a nobleman whose family's seat was Glamis Castle in Scotland, the place where Macbeth murdered King Duncan in Shakespeare's play. Another family residence was in the fashionable Knightsbridge section of London. The young Lady Elizabeth had a sunny disposition. Her favorite hobby, she once stated, was "making friends."

In 1911, tragedy intruded when Elizabeth's brother, Alec, died of a brain tumor, the result of a cricket ball landing on his head. World War I erupted on Elizabeth's fourteenth birthday, and her parents patriotically turned their ancestral home into a convalescent hospital for injured officers. Elizabeth did her best to bring cheer to the men, who, in appreciation, referred to her as Princess. To shield her mother from bad news, every morning, Elizabeth waylaid the mailman so she could be the first to check their letters. In 1915, her sibling, Fergus, a captain in the Black Watch, died in the Battle of Loos. After the loss of another son, her mother, Lady Bowes-Lyon, fell into a deep depression that overshadowed her life.

When the war ended, Elizabeth's days consisted of a serious search for a husband. Had she met an ordinary partner, her life would have followed the prescribed path of an upper-class lady: balls, dogs, high tea. Instead, Elizabeth met Prince Albert Frederick Arthur George, nicknamed Bertie, the second son of King George VI and Queen Mary. Along with his elevated status, Bertie carried the burden of crippling shyness, a severe stammer, and life under the shadow of David, his debonair older brother. When Bertie's formidable mother learned of his romantic inclination, she paid a visit to the Bowes-Lyon home and gave her approval. Elizabeth, however, did not. Over time, though, Albert's unwavering devotion eroded Elizabeth's resistance. In 1923, Lady Elizabeth finally accepted the prince's proposal; she later stated, "I felt it my duty to marry Bertie, and fell in love with him afterwards."

Their 1923 wedding was a national extravaganza, and crowds swarmed Westminster Abbey in a ceremony conducted by Randall Davidson, the Archbishop of Canterbury. The Abbey's clergy did not allow the event to be broadcast on radio because of their fear that men in the audience might not remove their hats. Although Elizabeth had initially been a reluctant royal, "afraid never, never again to be free to think, speak, and act as I feel I really ought to," she graciously accepted her role, understanding that with great privilege came great responsibility.

The newly minted Duchess of York and Albert moved into a twenty-five room Piccadilly home replete with twenty-one servants. Their first child was Princess Elizabeth Alexandra Mary, so called after three English queens, followed by Princess Margaret Rose. Besides child-rearing, another duty was to support her husband; while he hated the spotlight, he was obliged to make ever more frequent public appearances as David appeared more interested in his social life than affairs of the crown. Being forced to speak in public was torture for Albert, and encouraged by Elizabeth, he sought treatment for what was called his "affliction." When he was delivering a speech, Elizabeth sat nearby, mouthing the words. His condition improved, to such an extent that his father sent the couple on their first royal engagement for the opening of the Australian parliament. In contrast to Albert's shyness, Elizabeth was gregarious. On one occasion, waiting impatiently for his wife, Albert told her, "If we do not pass on, I shall soon pass out." Her husband was grateful for a partner who gave him the sympathy and support that he had never found in his parents' castles.

Albert and Elizabeth would have been relegated to a forgotten footnote of history had it not been for an affair that sent shock waves throughout England. In 1936, following Silver Jubilee celebrations that touched George V with a strong outpouring of support, the king passed away. David became King Edward VIII; however, the newly minted monarch continued to step out with Wallis Simpson, a twice-divorced American. Unsurprisingly, the prospect of a Queen Wally did not sit well with Queen Mary, the Prime Minister, and Albert. Confronted with the dilemma of relinquishing the crown or the woman he loved, David chose Mrs. Simpson. After the abdication, Albert reigned as King George VI; Elizabeth became the Queen Consort and the last Empress of India, whose new residence was Buckingham Palace.

Shy and self-conscious, Albert dreaded the prospect of living in the world's greatest fishbowl and confided to his cousin, Lord Mountbatten, "Dickie, this is absolutely terrible. I'm quite unprepared for it. David has been trained for this all his life. I've never even seen a state paper." Nevertheless, he rose to the occasion, declaring, "With my wife and helpmeet by my side, I take up the heavy burden which lies before me." His wife Elizabeth, the antithesis of Lady Macbeth, said, "We must make the best of it." Making the best of it included buying Balmoral Castle and Sandringham from the former monarch. Albert also made the provision that in order for David to receive the income that would allow him a kingly lifestyle, neither he nor his wife Wallis would be permitted to return to England without royal consent. David, in the role of deserter, left for exile in France; communications between the brothers resembled those between Cain and Abel. Upright Elizabeth never forgave David or Wallis for besmirching the royal reputation and forcing her husband into the Firm (the family business as it is known to those within it). She viewed David, a Nazi sympathizer who had forfeited his birthright, as a royal turncoat. Elizabeth was instrumental in convincing her husband that while David could continue as his "Royal Highness," his wife should not receive the HRH status she desperately coveted. When the Duke and Duchess of Windsor married, only twelve people attended the Paris ceremony, none of whom were members of David's family. Wallis reciprocated her sister-in-law's animosity, and dubbed her "Cookie," a jab at Elizabeth, who did not share Wallis's abhorrence of carrying excess weight.

In 1939, Bertie and Elizabeth were the guests of President Franklin Delano Roosevelt and First Lady Eleanor at a meal where the Brits first tasted hot dogs. In her memoir, Eleanor described the meeting, where her husband the president said, "My mother does not approve of cocktails and thinks you should have a cup of tea," to which Albert replied, "Neither does my mother." They both had cocktails.

At the outbreak of World War II, the British Cabinet advised Elizabeth to seek refuge in Canada with her daughters. She refused, stating, "The princesses would never leave without me, and I wouldn't leave without the king, and the king will never leave." She remained in London, where she took up target practice at the palace with a revolver, a gift from the new Prime Minister, Winston Churchill. In 1940, while the royal couple was at home, the Luftwaffe bombed Buckingham Palace. Elizabeth endeared herself to her nation with her remark, "It makes me feel I can look the East End in the face," a reference to a working-class area of London that had sustained great damage in the Blitz. Ironically, the greatest tribute to the Queen came from Adolf Hitler. Watching Elizabeth's morale building visits to bomb weary Britons, the Führer deemed her "the most dangerous woman in Europe."

King George's always-fragile health worsened with the stress of the war, the demands of the crown, and his forty-cigarettes-a-day habit, causing him to pass away from lung cancer in 1952. Bowled over with grief, Elizabeth wrote to President Eisenhower, affirming, "One cannot imagine life without him, but one must carry on as he would have wished." *The Times* reported that no monarch in history had ever owed more to his wife. The fifty-one-year-old widow assumed what was to be the longest role of her life: that of Queen Mother. Although she lived a Marie Antoinette lifestyle including betting at the races, shooting pool, and knocking back a pint, she made the world's least ordinary family seem somewhat ordinary. Proof the Queen Mum was no stuffed shirt was evident when she called down from an upper floor of her palace to request help from her household staff, which included several homosexuals, "Are there any old queens down there who'll fetch a gin and tonic for an old queen up here?" The apogee of her later years was on the commemoration of the fiftieth anniversary of V-E Day, when Elizabeth appeared on the balcony of Buckingham Palace as she had a half-century before. She was a Rock of Gibraltar sheathed in pastel silk and crowned with a feathery hat.

At age 101, two months after the death of Princess Margaret in early 2002, the Queen Mum passed away. To the beat of a gun salute from the Royal Artillery, and attended by 1,500 soldiers in scarlet tunics and bearskin hats, 400,000 onlookers paid homage. The coffin traveled on a horse-drawn carriage draped in her personal standard and topped with a diamond-encrusted crown and a wreath of white roses. The bouquet held a card with the words, "In loving memory," and the nickname by which Elizabeth called her daughter, Queen Elizabeth II, "Lilibet." Lord Halifax had captured the Queen Mother's essence when he described her as "a steel hand within a velvet glove."

CHAPTER 16

"More Human"

— 1903 —

O n August 15, 1945, eight days after the first atomic bomb had annihilated tens of thousands of people, Emperor Hirohito delivered a radio broadcast that marked the first time the public had heard his voice. He stated that Japan would have "to endure the unendurable and suffer the unsufferable." The head of that ancient kingdom had accepted the Allied Powers' demand for unconditional surrender. By his action, Hirohito saved his country and the Chrysanthemum Throne (the name of Japan's monarchy). Those who preferred death to the dishonor of surrender committed suicide in front of the palace. At the other end of the spectrum, millions flooded into Manhattan's Times Square, and the iconic photograph of a sailor planting a kiss on a nurse became the symbol of America's elation as the curtain descended on World War II.

For most girls in their early teens, the future is an unchartered territory. Yet this was not the situation for Nagako, the eldest daughter of Prince Kunihiko Kuni, a descendant of a thirteenth-century emperor. As with other daughters of nobility, she attended the elite Joshi Gakushuin School in Tokyo. At age fourteen, Nagako received a summons to visit the imperial palace, where, along with other girls, she took part in a tea ceremony. Hidden from view, Crown Prince Hirohito watched from behind a screen. Counter to tradition, he was to choose his own wife, and he set his sights on Nagako. The prime minister, who was from a rival clan to that of Prince Kuni, was angered at Hirohito's choice and fostered rumors that Nagako had color-blind relatives whose debility would taint future royals' bloodlines. The politician felt her lineage was not impressive enough for that required of the wife of a future emperor, who would be revered as a living god upon his ascension to the throne, in keeping with the prevailing Shinto religion. The sixteen-year-old Hirohito would not be swayed; though Nagako was not the most beautiful of women, he felt she was his destiny. Nagako left school to begin the six-year-training to attain the accomplishments she would need as the royal consort. During this period, the couple only met on nine occasions, always under the eyes of chaperones.

The catastrophic Tokyo earthquake of 1923 delayed their wedding, but on January 26, 1924, Nagako and Hirohito wed in a Shinto ceremony. Two years later, his dissolute father, Emperor Taisho, passed away, and Hirohito ascended to the Chrysanthemum Throne—the world's oldest dynasty, in a ceremony in Kyoto. Whenever the husband and wife traveled through the streets in their Rolls Royce, onlookers bowed their heads, as commoners could not look upon the imperial couple. The Japanese people revered the emperor as the Son of Heaven, the 124th direct descendant of the Sun Goddess.

Content to remain cloistered in her palace, protected by a moat and high walls, Nagako played the piano, violin, and the Japanese harp. She composed thirty-one-syllable poetry, known as *waka*, and painted landscapes and still life scenes. She signed her artwork as Toen or Peach Garden. Hirohito was also content in the royal palace, and yet, deeply devoted to duty, performed all imperial obligations. On the military parade grounds, resplendent in royal uniform, he sat astride his famous white stallion, Shiroyuki ("White Snow.") Nevertheless, Hirohito was more in his element where he was peering into his microscope in the palace laboratory, where he built an eminent reputation in the study of the marine microorganisms known as hydrozoa.

The couple was devoted to one another; she called him *okami*, "honorable master," and he affectionately nicknamed her Naga-Miya, or princess Naga. However, her prime responsibility was to produce a son, an heir to the ancient dynasty. To the couple's deep consternation, after a decade of marriage, Nagako had given birth to four daughters; however, only a male could inherit the throne. Members of the Imperial Household Agency cruelly nicknamed the empress *onna bara*: "girl womb." The military pushed for Hirohito's abdication in favor of his younger brother, the father of sons. Similarly, couriers encouraged Hirohito to bring back the thirty-nine concubines he had dismissed after his marriage; even if a boy were born outside of marriage, he would be eligible to become the next emperor. They also submitted photographs of suitable young women, while the court ladies took to wearing their most alluring dresses and dousing themselves with perfumes. Hirohito refused to partake of the palace-sanctioned promiscuity. In 1933, another royal pregnancy resulted in the birth of Akihito, an event his mother called "the happiest moment in my life." The boom of cannons sounded the joyous news. Another son and daughter followed. Ironically, the deity and his wife had limited power as court officials pulled the strings. When Akihito was three, he went to live with attendants who treated him with great veneration though little warmth, and he endured a lonely childhood. Nagako, who always toed the line of duty, never publicly voiced a complaint about the painful separation.

A Chinese curse states, "May you live in interesting times;" as it transpired, Nagako's life was to become the embodiment of the curse. During World War II, Japan's generals used the emperor as a symbol of propaganda, and he made comments such as, "Your life is as light as a feather, but your life loyalty is as heavy as a mountain." With these phrases Hirohito sent off thousands to fight and die, many on suicide missions. Their dying words were the battle cry "Banzai!"

The degree to which Hirohito bore responsibility for Japan's involvement in the war is mired in the gray area of subjectivity, and little is known about his wife's views of the nightmare years. The only insight she offered was when she described the era as the hardest time of her life. She also stated that her "heart was in pain when she saw the emperor deeply agitated every day during and immediately after World War II."

Nagako put aside her poetry and painting in order to contribute to the war effort. She rolled bandages, knit scarves for the generals, and wrote letters of condolence to bereaved families. The emperor and empress remained in the imperial palace in downtown Tokyo, though they sent their six children (a daughter had died at age two) to the countryside for their protection.

At the close of World War II, Nagako, like the rest of Japan, was reeling from the horrors of Hiroshima and Nagasaki, as well as her country's formal declaration of defeat. She was also terrified that the Allied Powers would execute her husband as one of the architects behind the bombing of Pearl Harbor. To her great relief, General Douglas MacArthur, the American commander of the Allied occupation of Japan, thought it best to keep the emperor on his throne as a unifying force in a devastated and politically unstable country. The formal surrender took place aboard the battleship *Missouri* in Tokyo Bay. The emperor and empress, no longer considered divine, made public appearances where they offered solace in a charred wasteland.

While Nagako proved a devoted wife, spouse, and empress, she was a despotic mother-in-law who was aghast when Akihito wed Michiko Shoda, a commoner. Mother-in-law dearest denigrated the Crown Princess, from her choice of clothing to the manner in which she raised her children. Michiko, a college educated, liberal minded woman, chafed under the attacks. She regarded her chief lady-in-waiting as a spy for Nagako, and with the support of her husband, fought to have her dismissed. But the Imperial Household Agency did not grant their consent. The intrigue took its toll on Michiko, who became increasingly gaunt and withdrawn, possibly as a result of nervous breakdowns, she lost her ability to speak for several months.

In their twilight years, Hirohito and Nagako were content to live in seclusion in their two-story Western-style Fukiage Palace. Constructed in 1961, it stands in the spacious 300-acre grounds of what in feudal times had been the Do castle, the moat-surrounded residence of the Tokugawa shoguns. However, while Japan became an economic powerhouse, the emperor and empress appeared an unassuming elderly couple. Nagako remained the doting wife who placed a bouquet of fresh roses on her husband's desk each morning, a far cry from their days when he was a living god and she his consort.

The empress's first time abroad was on a 1971 European tour where she presented Queen Elizabeth II with one of her original paintings. Though they experienced protests due to the emperor's wartime involvement, Nagako stated that going abroad was "the most enjoyable experience of her life." Four years later, she accompanied her husband on a visit to the United States, where she met President Nixon in Anchorage and shared a handshake with Mickey Mouse at Disneyland.

The empress, after spending eleven years as a widow, passed away in 2000 at age ninety-seven; after a Shinto funeral, she joined her emperor to whom she had been married for sixty-five years in the imperial mausoleum. Flags flew at half-mast, and the lights were turned off in Tokyo Tower, a replica of the Eiffel Tower.

Never one to wear her heart on her sleeve, history would have gained a peephole into her ziplocked heart had Nagako revealed her response to Hirohito's question to his wife after the Allies had stripped him of his divine status, "Do I look more human to you now?"

CHAPTER 17

"So Boring"

— 1906 —

"**G**od Save the Queen," the British National Anthem first performed in 1745 employs the lyric, "Send her victorious / Happy and glorious / Long to reign over us..." In contrast, one European crowned head reigned for only twenty-seven days as "The May Queen."

The Moirae, the mythological weaving sisters, spun a tapestry that fated a European princess to reign in an ephemeral web. Marie-José Charlotte Sophie Amélie Henriette Gabrielle of Saxony-Coburg was born in the imperial villa near Ostend, Belgium, the only daughter of Albert and his wife, Elisabeth of Bavaria. From her mother's side, Marie-José was related to Empress Sisi of Austria; she had two brothers, Charles and Leopold. Marie-José found the court stifling. Lady Curzon, a friend from England, recalled of a visit, "The royal children were never allowed to utter a word at meals unless they were addressed by one of their parents."

In 1909, Albert succeeded his uncle, King Leopold II, notorious for his ruthless exploitation of the Congo. Five years later, with the German invasion of Belgium during World War I, the family left Brussels and settled in La Penne, where King Albert I became the rallying point of his country's resistance. Queen Elisabeth abandoned her passion for music and devoted herself to nursing wounded soldiers. The royal couple sent their children to safety in England, where they first stayed with Lord and Lady Curzon. On occasional visits to spend time with her parents at the Western Front, Marie-José met French Prime Minister Georges Clemenceau, the Prince of Wales, and the violinist Eugène Ysaÿe. With the return of peace, Marie-José resumed her blue-blood role. For her first ball in 1924, she received a diamond tiara and antique pearl necklace once owned by Stephanie, Grand Duchess of Baden, the first of her many priceless gems.

With a nod to uniting their Roman Catholic kingdoms, the Belgian and Italian sovereigns planned a dynastic marriage between Princess Marie-José and Umberto, Prince of Piedmont. To prepare for her future role, Marie-José attended the College of the Santissima Annunziata, a convent school outside Florence. The Belgian royals visited King Vittorio Emanuele III and Queen Elena at Battaglia, their residence near Padua, in order to introduce their children. Both thirteen years old, Umberto was taken with Marie-José's beauty; six years later, the crown prince arrived in Belgium to formalize their engagement. The following day, a student named Fernando de Rosa, infuriated that the Italian monarchy was colluding with the dictator Benito Mussolini, attempted to assassinate Umberto, who had just laid a wreath on the Tomb of the Unknown Soldier. (Although de Rosa managed to get within a dozen feet of Umberto, the one shot the would-be assassin fired missed, and then the revolver jammed, giving Belgian security police a chance to apprehend the miscreant.)

The royals married in 1930 in Rome's Pauline Chapel at the Quirinal Palace in one of the grandest gatherings of European royalty ever experienced. The guests, many of whom were former monarchs, led the bride's father to remark, "There are many unemployed in our trade." The Duke of York, later King George VI, felt slighted when the King of Italy sent Marie-José's brother, Prince Charles of Belgium, in to dinner ahead of him. He reported to his father, "There's one thing, Papa, I'll never go to Rome again!" Marie-José refused to sign her name on the wedding register as Maria Giuseppina, a move expressly against Mussolini's wishes that she sign her name in the Italian fashion. Her anti-fascist stance led to her being nicknamed the "rebel queen."

Following their nuptials, Umberto and Marie-José had a state audience with Pope Pius XI.

Upon their return from their honeymoon at San Rossore, the couple settled at the Royal Palace in Turin. Unlike her parents, who had adored one another, Marie-José later revealed that her marriage was never happy. She loved music and spontaneity while her husband was formal and dedicated to the military traditions of the House of Savoy. Annoyed at Umberto's deference to protocol, she stated, "It seemed as if we were in China, with all that bowing." In 1934, with Umberto's promotion to general, they relocated to Naples to an estate they renamed Villa Maria Pia after the birth of their daughter. Three years later, succession was assured with the arrival of Victor Emmanuel, the Prince of Naples, followed by Maria Gabriella and Maria-Beatrice. Parenthood did not erase their incompatibility, and Marie-José confided to journalist Indro Montanelli in 1940, "You know, I don't have much to do with the House of Savoy. It's not a family, it's a Frigidaire."

Upon the outbreak or war, Marie-José was horrified that her royal relatives had become allies of Germany. Following her mother's example, Marie-José served for a time with the Red Cross, and she accompanied the army on its invasion of Abyssinia (later Ethiopia). Ignoring her father-in-law, who demanded that "she keep her nose out of family politics," under the guise of an archaeological trip to Pompeii, Marie-José held a clandestine meeting with a diplomat at the Vatican, fellow anti-fascist Monsignor Giovanni Battista Montini, the future Pope Paul VI. Determined to release her adopted country from the yoke of tyranny, Marie-José supplied the Italian Resistance with funds and weapons. When the princess saw Allied bombers over Rome, she wrote of them as "white liberating birds."

Rumor has it that although Marie-José was repulsed by Mussolini as Il Duce, she was attracted to him and they engaged in a sexual relationship. In a 1993 interview, when asked about the affair, Marie-José replied, "He was a lion. I, too, am a lion. And we both feared one another."

Although the princess may have been simultaneously attracted to and repelled by Mussolini, she was unequivocal about her hatred of the Führer. In 1940, Marie-José traveled to Hitler's Alpine mountain retreat, Berchtesgaden, on behalf of Belgium, annexed by the Nazis in 1940. Over tea, she pled for food for her starving countrymen and for more humane treatment for her brother, King Leopold III, imprisoned in Laeken, who had assumed the throne after his father's death in a climbing accident. The answer to all her requests: *"Nein."* However, struck with Marie-José's Nordic appearance, Hitler complimented her eyes, which he described as "the color of the German sky." She recalled that Hitler ate chocolate throughout their meeting. Marie-José added that if she had brought a gun, "she would have had the strength to use it." The king, angry with his daughter-in-law, banished her to Sant'Anna di Valdieri. After Mussolini's defeat in 1943, Umberto, Marie-José, and their children fled Rome for Switzerland. She reportedly told friends that she regretted not having joined Italian partisans who fought to oust the swastika.

After the war, King Vittorio Emanuele's subjects could not forgive him for sleeping with the enemy or for fleeing the country during Italy's lowest ebb. In a bid to save his throne, he abdicated in favor of his son and took refuge in Egypt, the guest of King Farouk. Umberto II and Queen Marie-José assumed the throne on May 9, 1946. Twenty-seven days later, Italy voted in favor of becoming a republic: 12.7 million to 10.7 million. Thus, the May King (so called as he assumed the throne in that month) was the last of the line in a dynastic chain that stretched back to the Middle Ages. A devastated Umberto stated that he would accept the decision rather than risk a civil war.

A further kidney-punch to the House of Savoy was the new constitution, which decreed that Umberto, his Queen, son Prince Victor Emmanuel, and any further male descendants were barred from ever again setting foot in Italy. The refugee royals left for Portugal's "Gold Coast," where they joined dozens of dethroned royalty and blue bloods who found sanctuary in Cascais. Exile did not bring Umberto and Marie-

José closer; in 1947, she left for Switzerland. Her new residence was the eighteenth-century Château de Merlinge near Geneva, where members of the exiled dynasty spent their exile. She spent her time writing and working on instituting the *Fondation du prix de composition musicale Reine Marie-José*, a body that still awards prizes to talented musicians. In the 1980s, the former Queen was on the move again, this time to Mexico, to live with her youngest daughter, Princess Maria-Beatrice, and her grandchildren. However, North America did not prove her final destination, and she returned to Europe, where she stayed with her other children in either France or Switzerland. The Italian government allowed her a bittersweet visit in 1988, in part because of the support she had given to the opponents of Mussolini. Although Umberto had never been able to return to his native land, upon his 1983 passing, he bequeathed the Shroud of Turin to Pope John Paul II.

Although the royal couple had not lived together for the latter part of their lives, when Marie-José passed away from lung cancer in 2001 at age ninety-four, her final resting place was beside Umberto, in France's Hautecombe Abbey, where they joined other rulers of the House of Savoy. Although the last King of Italy felt his birthright had been stolen, the loss of her royal status did not bring Marie-José the same heartache. As she had once remarked, "Being queen is so boring."

♕

CHAPTER 18

The Sharpest of Thorns

— 1915 —

When one conjures the image of European royalty, what comes to mind are the Habsburgs of Austria-Hungary, the Bourbons of France, the Windsors of England. Yet one small nation also boasted a crowned head, one whose life as queen could have sprung from a film noir.

Countess Geraldine hailed from aristocratic roots: Her family could trace their descent back to the conquest of her native Hungary in 894 AD. Her paternal grandfather served as the Grand Marshal of the Habsburg Court. She was one of three children of the impoverished Count Gyula (Julius) Apponyi de Nagy-Appony and Gladys Virginia Steuart, the daughter of the American consul in Antwerp. Her mother was also a descendant of the Mormon leader Brigham Young, and President Richard Nixon was her eighth cousin. The land-rich, cash-strapped count owned an enormous country castle and a townhouse in Budapest (in what was then part of the Austrian-Hungarian empire). The couple raised their three children Geraldine, Virginia, and Gyula on their ancestral estate, located on the perimeter of a vast forest at Nagy-Appony, a property that had been in the count's family since 1280. With the collapse of the Austrian-Hungarian Empire, the Apponys embarked on a peripatetic odyssey: the Wienerwald in Austria and a family château in Czechoslovakia. They returned to their homeland in 1921. After her husband's 1924 death, Gladys, along with her children, moved to Menton, in the south of France, to live near her widowed mother. With Gladys's second marriage to a French officer, she enrolled her daughters in the Sacred Heart School at Pressbaum, near Vienna, and the girls spent their vacations at Zebegny with their aunt, Countess Fanny Karolyi.

Because World War I had eroded the family's finances, as a young woman, Geraldine was grateful that her uncle, the director of the Hungarian National Museum in Budapest, found her a job as a clerk selling postcards in its gift shop. Despite her straitened circumstances, Geraldine's lineage and beauty made her a highly sought-after debutante. In 1935, she took part in a charity performance of *La Bohème* where the press displayed her photograph taken at a ball with the caption "The White Rose of Hungary."

Albania, the birthplace of Anjezë Gonxhe Bojaxhiu, better known as Mother Teresa, was also home to Ahmet Bey Zogu, who had advanced from tribal chief to prime minister to president to Albania's first royal, King Zog I. The newly minted crowned head, referred to as the Balkan Napoleon, had his share of trouble. He had barely escaped an assassination attempt in 1931 as he exited the Vienna Opera House. His mother kept watch over the royal kitchen to ensure her son's food did not contain poison. Zog, anxious for an heir to ensure his dynasty, remembered the beauty of central European women from his years as a young officer in the imperial Austrian army and decided one would be his future consort. To this end, his six sisters left for Vienna and Budapest in search of a suitable bride. His favorite sister, Senije, felt she had found Zog's perfect match and sent him Geraldine's photo. The Muslim monarch was smitten with the beauty of the Roman Catholic countess.

An official from Albania, General Cyczy, visited the Appony family to invite Geraldine to visit the king. In response, her friend Countess Katherine Teleki left for Tirana, the Albanian capital, to thank the king and to "have a good look around." When the countess gave her approval, King Zog invited Geraldine to his palace; she brought along a family friend, Baroness Ruling, as her chaperone. There she met the man, twenty years her senior, who had survived a score of assassination attempts, pulled all-nighters at the poker table, and smoked 150 cigarettes a day. Shortly after her arrival, she attended the king's New Year's Eve ball, along with 3,000 other guests. Entering the royal residence, she walked past walls covered with ancient costumes, crossed swords, and hundreds of candles. In the great hall, King Zog handed her a glass of champagne while a cannon boomed. Enthralled, he courted her with priceless gifts, and his vice president presented her with a velvet pocketbook that contained $500,000; Geraldine promptly presented it to the National Albanian Charities. Geraldine claimed she had fallen for Zog and pronounced her suitor a man of "maturity and authority." The next day, she received one hundred red roses along with her breakfast tray. After ten days, when Geraldine accepted King Zog's proposal, he gave her the title of Princess of Albania. Their courtship took place to the accompaniment of Leber waltzes and native folk music. The discordant element: Mussolini, hell-bent on annexing Albania in order to transform it into a fascist colony, did his best to undermine Geraldine since he wanted an Italian on its throne. However, King Zog and his people would not be swayed in their steadfast devotion to Geraldine.

The couple married in 1938; with her coronation, Geraldine became Albania's first queen and the only member of European royalty with American blood. The lavish ceremony took place in Tirana; Geraldine wore a white satin pearl and diamante wedding dress her fiancé had ordered from the House of Worth in Paris, and her veil trailed from a diadem of orange blossoms. She had six bridesmaids, and the wedding cake, which the bride sliced with her husband's saber, was ten feet wide. Mussolini's son-in-law, Count Galeazzo Ciano, served as a witness. Fifty thousand children in native costumes applauded, and even enemy clans shared wine. The gifts were over the top: a scarlet Mercedes from Hitler (the only replica of his own car), four Lipizzaner horses from Admiral Horthy, the regent of Hungary, a bronze equestrian statue of a dragoon from King Victor Emmanuel III of Italy, and a rare cabinet from Franco. Mussolini, miffed at the king's choice of consort, sent copper pots. At age twenty-two, Geraldine Margit Virginia Olga Maria Apponyi de Nagy-Appony became the second youngest queen in the world; only King Farouk of Egypt's wife, Queen Farida, was younger. Queen Geraldine established the Albanian Red Cross and wrote that the scale of the mountain forests made those of Switzerland seem small. Nevertheless, a shadow hovered; *The New York Herald Tribune* observed that Queen Geraldine "seems to be marrying the Roman-Berlin axis as well as her king." It concluded that she was "certainly marrying Mussolini's foreign policy."

The roar of cannons heralded the birth of their son, Prince Leka, but soon the air filled with a different form of artillery. The fairy tale came with an expiration date as a year later, a 40,000 strong Italian army invaded, and King Victor Emmanuel III assumed the Albanian crown. Queen Geraldine, along with her two-day-old baby, fled in a car that traveled over torturous mountain roads to Florina, Greece. The king and 115 members of his court, as well as an arsenal of weapons, followed. Exile was made easier as Zog had also made off with Albania's gold reserve. With the imminent invasion of Greece, the wandering of the Albanian royals began: Turkey, Romania, Poland, Belgium, and France. Ian Fleming, author of *James Bond* who served with British Naval Intelligence, spirited them out of Paris just before the arrival of the Nazis. He arranged their evacuation on a ship to England with the blessing of King George VII.

King Zog rented an entire floor of The Ritz in London. Although Geraldine spoke flawless English—as a polyglot also versed in French, German, Hungarian, and Albanian—she was unhappy as her six sisters-in-law, who had also fled Albania, demanded too much of her husband's attention. Their next destination was a villa in Alexandria where Geraldine spent her happiest years in the company of the exiled Queen Giovanna of Italy. With Nasser's toppling of Farouk's throne— Geraldine watched as he boarded his yacht—they departed for Cannes, France. Zog toyed with immigrating to the United States, and in 1951, he purchased a sixty-room mansion on a ninety-five-acre estate in Syosset,

Long Island, though they never set foot on the estate. King Zog, after a decade of declining health, passed away in 1961.

The Albanian National Assembly in exile, meeting in the Hotel Bristol in Paris, declared Leka their new crowned head; however, a referendum declined the return of the Zogu monarchy. Years later, France ended up expelling the six-foot eight-inch Leka due to his penchant for stockpiling weapons, and mother and son spent time in Spain, where Geraldine became friends with the Queen of Bulgaria. Spain also refused sanctuary due to Leka's vast collection of military grade weaponry, his ten-man guard, and his villa that doubled as an armed fortress. Mother and son accepted South Africa's offer of diplomatic status and moved to the land where apartheid held sway. But the welcome mat disappeared after Leka's arrest for filling his home with landmines and over 14,000 rounds of ammunition.

At the invitation of the Albanian parliament, eleven years after the collapse of its communist regime, Geraldine spent her final months in her adopted country after an absence of sixty-two years. She reclaimed the magnificent family home behind the Hotel Bogner in Tirana from the Greek government, which had been using it as their ambassador's residence. She shared the estate with Leka, Queen Susan, Leka's Austrian born wife, and their son, Crown Prince Leka II, who was to name his own daughter after her grandmother. Geraldine passed away at age eighty-seven from a heart attack while undergoing treatment for lung cancer. Life for the White Rose of Hungary came with the beauty of the flower, along with the sharpest of thorns.

CHAPTER 19

A Pink Pumpkin

— 1919 —

Indian-British writer Rudyard Kipling observed, "Providence had created maharajas to offer mankind a spectacle." And what a spectacle it was: wealth that surpassed that of the Count of Monte Cristo, parties more opulent than the Great Gatsby's, jewels that outshone Marie Antoinette's. Into this milieu of glitter and gold stepped a maharani who left her mark on the exotic Eastern empire.

The cornucopia upended itself on Princess Gayatri Devi, nicknamed Ayesha, after the protagonist in H. Rider Haggard's novel *She* that her mother read while pregnant. Gayatri's father was the Maharaja of Cooch Behar, situated close to the Himalayan foothills, whose reign coincided with the Golden Age of India's princely power. The royal family's personal genies were 400 servants and 120 gardeners who tended their rose gardens. In their palace, trained parrots rode miniature silver bicycles; if injured, servants delivered them on stretchers to physicians. Her mother, Indira, the daughter of the Maharaja of Baroda, owned a pet turtle whose shell held rubies and emeralds that she used as a good luck charm at French casinos. Other indulgences were a gold tongue scraper and more than one hundred pairs of shoes from designer Salvatore Ferragamo. Gayatri's grandfather ordered that his elephant's tusks be embedded with diamonds for his jubilee as ruler of West Bengal. On one occasion, while in London (the city where Gayatri had been born), she went on a shopping spree with the manager of Harrods department store and purchased whatever caught her fancy. Her liberal parents allowed their daughter free rein as a tomboy, and Gayatri participated in duck shooting, horseback riding, and hunting; she shot her first panther at age twelve. Education was a priority, and Gayatri attended schools in England, Switzerland, and India. A second nickname was *"pagh rajkumari"* "mad princess" due to her concern over the palace servants.

Another twelve-year-old first was when Gayatri became infatuated with Sir Sawai Man Singh Bahadur, the Maharaja of Jaipur (Jai), nine years her senior. Six years later, after the princess had blossomed into what *Vogue* magazine described as "a dream in sari and jewels" and *Life* magazine had pronounced her one of the world's most beautiful women, despite Jai's two wives (First Her Highness and Second Her Highness), he eyed Gayatri as his Third. He had first wed at age nine when he married the Maharaja of Jodhpur's sister, an arrangement that gifted the groom several of Jodhpur's famed polo horses. Jai proposed to Gayatri in the back seat of his Bentley as a chauffeur circled London's Hyde Park. The princess accepted with the stipulation she would never be bound by the custom of "purdah" that dictated that blue-blood women had to be veiled in public. After Jai agreed, there were still marital obstacles from Gayatri's parents, who wanted her to marry a bachelor, and from her brother, who warned her that Jai was a serial philanderer.

The couple wed in 1940, and Gayatri's new life as the Maharani of Jaipur was even more dazzling than life as the Princess of Cooch Behar. Her new residence was Rambagh Palace, an eighty-room cream-colored castle near the famed Pink City of Jaipur that she described as the "setting for some fabulous and imagined fairy tale." The Pink City was so christened as a former Maharajah had painted its white buildings pink, and the kingdom's eminence rested on the legend their rulers traced their ancestry back to Lord Rama. The royal's fiefdom consisted of two million peasants; in contrast to their poverty, Gayatri took the Jaipur Dakota plane to Delhi for hairdresser appointments. The royals enjoyed traveling to elegant European resorts and often visited Manhattan, where an assailant robbed the Maharani of $40,000 of jewelry as she exited her limousine. Jai was a staunch supporter of English-controlled India (the Raj), and a photograph shows Jai and Gayatri in the company of Prince Philip and Queen Elizabeth II, a dead tiger at their feet. (The fact that Elizabeth is holding a purse makes it clear she was not the one who had pulled the trigger.) In 1962, the royal couple feted Jacqueline Kennedy; an international magazine reported that the Indian blue blood made the American First Lady appear frumpish. Despite the splendor, Gayatri was displeased that Jai spent a great deal of time on the polo field, leaving her in the company of his other wives. She soon found her niche as mother to her only son, Prince Jagat Singh, founded the renowned Maharani Gayatri Devi Girls School for the cloistered daughters of aristocratic families, and fought for female emancipation. Gayatri also made an appearance in *The Guinness Book of World Records* for her inclusion in her stepdaughter's wedding, the world's most expensive. Her second entry occurred when she entered politics in the Swatantra, "freedom party," and won the most votes (175,000) of any candidate in a democratic country.

The event that shook the foundation of Gayatri's world occurred in 1947 when India declared its independence from Britain and the Raj drew its last breath. In the early 1970s, Prime Minister Indira Gandhi abolished the sovereignty of the maharajas, their right to collect taxes, and their thirteen-gun salutes, an act filmmaker James Ivory described as the French Revolution without the guillotine. While reeling from that blow, a month later, Jai passed away at a polo match in Cirencester, England. Prince Philip wrote a letter in which he shared his memories of "playing polo or shooting or just sitting and chatting under the moon in Jaipur or in a country house in England." This loss caused the widow "to retreat into stricken seclusion, overpowered by grief," for a time.

The Rajmata, her unofficial title of Queen Mother, maintained her political career, where she proved an irritant to Prime Minister Indira Gandhi. Although they shared the commonality of both having attended Patha Bhavana, a school founded by Rabindranath Tagore, Indira despised Gayatri's hereditary wealth, her beauty, and her relationship with dignitaries such as the Mountbattens. Government agents raided the palaces of the Jaipur dynasty, where they unearthed treasure valued at $17,000,000. In a gesture made to prove her innocence, Gayatri voluntarily surrendered her passport. At the same time, Gandhi declared "a state of emergency due to internal chaos," and a month later police arrested Gayatri on the charge of tax evasion while she was attending Parliament in New Delhi as the representative of Jaipur. Mrs. Gayatri Devi spent five months in the notorious Tihar Jail, held behind bars along with prostitutes, a fall from grace for the woman who had been described as "a little queen of a fairy-tale land." In vain, Earl Mountbatten of Burma telephoned Gandhi to protest the incarceration. During her imprisonment, Gayatri gave lessons to the prisoners' children and refused to surrender her dignity. Incarceration took a toll on her health, and after a stay in a hospital, officials released her on parole. Despite ill treatment, when Gandhi's son, Sanjay, died in an airplane accident, Gayatri telephoned to offer condolences, a call not accepted.

The former Maharani, who had steel under her sari, following in the footsteps of other deposed royals who had lost their ancestral fortunes, transformed Rambagh Palace into a luxury hotel where guests could experience a bygone grandeur in settings such as sipping tea on a marble veranda. Her none-too-shabby new residence was Lily Pool, which shared the grounds with her former home. In a nod to the heyday of her yesteryear, on a table she displayed polo trophies alongside a signed photograph of Prince Charles. Initially, she viewed the visitors as interlopers, but eventually adapted to the new paradigm, saying, "You can't be static in your mind." The hotel sent over lists of VIPs, and she invited them to Lily Pool for champagne. The ones she did not care for received bills for their drinks. She split her time between summers in England and the United States and winters in Jaipur.

The golden years were far from "the setting for some fabulous and imagined fairy tale." Her son, Prince Jagat, divorced his wife, who took the children to live in her native Thailand. To add to Gayatri's sorrow,

Jagat passed away from alcoholism in 1997, perishing of the same disease that had claimed her father. A further source of pain was the royal soap opera that raged over his estimated $400 million estate, pitting Gayatri against her stepson, Bhawani Singh, whose English nanny had nicknamed him "Bubbles" due to the amount of champagne consumed to celebrate his birth. Bhawani contended that as the firstborn son, he was entitled to his entire father's fortune under the centuries old law of primogeniture, while other family members felt they should share in the spoils under the more modern Hindu law. With such a storied life, Gayatri published *A Princess Remembers: The Memoirs of the Maharani of Jaipur.* Upon its London debut, she set out for a day of shopping, and her chauffeur later revealed that "shopping" had resulted in a purchase of a large Surrey house.

The last maharani passed away at age ninety, and her country honored her with a state funeral. Bhawani lit her funeral pyre, one that symbolically marked the demise of the old order. Most telling was the last page of the memoir where Gayatri imagined her return to Rambagh Palace, accompanied by her beloved Jai and Jagat, in the days before her fairy tale transformed into a pink pumpkin.

👑

CHAPTER 20

Of Grandeur and Glory

— 1919 —

The most memorable line of the 1978 film *An Unmarried Woman* was Jill Clayburgh's comment, " 'Balls,' said the queen, 'If I had them, I'd be king!' " Although royal women were not born to rule, they could still be a power behind the throne and manipulate the strings of the marionette.

Historically, the siblings of sires have received short shrift. The tragedy that befell Tsar Nicholas II is well known, but what was the fate of his sisters, the Grand Duchesses Olga and Xenia? The Shah of Iran changed the history of the Middle East, and his reign played out on the world's stage. And yet, the decades have drawn the curtain on the Pahlavi siblings.

Princess Ashraf was born five hours after her brother Mohammed, the daughter of Reza Pahlavi, a military commander, and the second of his four wives, the short but fierce Tadjol-Molouk, a Russian-Azerbaijani immigrant who had escaped after the Bolshevik Revolution. In a coup orchestrated by Britain, Reza vanquished the Qajar dynasty that had ruled Iran since 1789. The new shah changed his country's name from Persia to Iran, and Princess Ashraf became Her Imperial Highness. A childhood source of pain was she felt she was always in the shadow of both her twin—the heir to the Pahlavi throne—and her older sister, Shams. Ashraf described her father as "awesome and frightening," and as a child, she fled when she saw the flash of his uniform. Modeling himself on Turkey's Ataturk, Reza sought to free his kingdom from its feudal mindset and urged women to trade the medieval chador for Western garb. The teenaged Pahlavi sisters were the first to appear in public with uncovered hair in defiance of the traditional norm of the Shia country. After a priest had prevented Tad jol-Molouk from entering a mosque while wearing a French dress, the shah publicly beat him with his riding crop. Nevertheless, Reza's liberalism had limits, and his rule was absolute. The autocracy extended to his family; while Mohammad left for school in Le Rosey, Switzerland, the shah did not allow his daughters to attend university. The girls remained in the women's quarters of their Tehran home and learned to ride horseback and play tennis.

Anxious to continue the dynasty he had founded, Reza arranged a double wedding for Shams and Ashraf. His choice of husband for the teenaged twin was Mirza Ali Muhammad Khan Ghava, a member of a powerful family from the historical city of Shiraz. Ashraf claimed she needed a tranquilizer to share her husband's bed. In her 1980 memoir, *Faces in a Mirror*, Ashraf wrote that although she wore white as a bride, her dress should have been black. She added, "I am a girl of the East with Western ideas, I like romance. I do not want to be a pawn in a game of human chess." The couple had one child, Prince Shahram Pahlavi, who was not enough salve to camouflage the misery of his parents' marriage; their union ended after five years. Fantastically rich, the adult prince sold D'Arros Island in the Seychelles to the L'Oréal heiress, Liliane Bettencourt. Ashraf's second husband was Ahmed Chafik Bey, the son of an Egyptian minister; Ashraf had a son with him, Shahriar (who was assassinated in Paris), and a daughter, Azadeh (who passed away from leukemia). Ashraf's third trip down the aisle was with Mehdi Bushehri, a French-based Iranian; they remained married but led separate lives. When thrice did not prove the charm, Ashraf told an interviewer, "It's too late for remarriage. I can't even imagine a man in my bed." The mullahs were outraged with Ashraf's marital history and extramarital flings.

In 1941, fearful of the shah's pro-German sympathies, Britain and Russia invaded Iran and forced Reza to abdicate and go into exile. The Allied Powers agreed to let his son, Mohammad, become the next shah, with the caveat he would rule as a democratic sovereign. During the first stage of her twin's reign, Ashraf became the country's self-appointed "super ambassador," and as such, she traveled through Europe, India, and the United States. She wrote that her desire to modernize Iran stemmed from a walk through the streets of Tehran, "I found myself in the slums...I saw people, my people...living like animals, eating dirt, sleeping in holes." As Iran's representative, Ashraf met President Truman, and he played piano for her in the White House. While in London to study its nursing system, she asserted she had tea in Buckingham Palace. As an envoy, she met with Joseph Stalin to discuss the Soviet hold over neighboring Azerbaijan. Impressed, Stalin gifted her a magnificent sable coat. He called her a "true patriot" and said if her brother had ten like her, he would have no worries. Upon her return home, Ashraf was disheartened when she saw the influence of the mullahs that had resulted in women reverting to "the mournful black chador their grandmothers had worn." She added, "My God, is this how it ends? To me it was like seeing a child you had nurtured suddenly sicken and die."

In 1953, the United States contacted the shah regarding "Operation Ajax," a plot to remove Prime Minister Mohammad Mosaddegh, who had leftist leanings and was pro Soviet Union. A Persian Prufrock, not "daring to disturb the universe," the shah wavered. In order to force his hand, the operatives approached "the shah's dynamic and forceful twin sister" as they felt she was the key to manipulating her brother. In *All the Shah's Men* (2003), Stephen Kinzer wrote, "Ashraf's tongue-lashings of her brother were legendary, including one in the presence of foreign diplomats where she demanded that he prove he was a man or be revealed to all as a mouse." The CIA Agent Assadollah Rashidian paid her a call; when she did not prove receptive, the next day, a delegation of American and British agents tried their luck. Norman Darbyshire had the foresight to bring along a mink coat and a packet of cash. He later reported that when the princess saw the incentives, "Her eyes lit up and her resistance crumbled." Pressured by Ashraf, whom he trusted implicitly, the shah acquiesced. Despite the high level of planning, the coup initially failed, causing Mohammad to flee first to Baghdad, and then to Rome, where Ashraf joined him. She convinced him to return to Iran, where the shah wrested back power from the Peacock throne with an iron hand.

During her brother's reign, Ashraf used her privileged position as princess to advocate for women's rights and was a member of the United Nations Human Rights Commission, the head of the Iranian Delegation to the UN Human Rights, and a member of the Commission on the Status of Women. In her memoir, she recounted how on one occasion, while leaving Iran by helicopter, she saw the streets clogged with demonstrators protesting the Pahlavi regime. While some considered Ashraf a humanitarian, others viewed her as a Lady Macbeth as she turned a blind eye to the 4,000 women incarcerated as political dissidents during Mohammad's dictatorship. When confronted with accusations that the SAVAK, her brother's secret police, employed torture, Princess Ashraf claimed they were no worse than their Israeli, French, or British counterparts. At the close of the 1960s, Ashraf had attained sterling accolades: She was awarded a fellowship from Wadham College, Oxford, and the Grand Cross of the Royal Victorian Order by Queen Elizabeth II; and she was the subject of an Andy Warhol portrait. The artist depicted her with bright red lips, blue-lined eyes, and raven black hair.

The "playgirl princess," became a fixture at the casinos in the French Riviera. The European press dubbed her "*La Panthère Noire*," "The Black Panther" (after her painted nails), as well as "the Persian Marie Antoinette." In the 1970s, with the Mideast oil boom at an unparalleled high, the Pahlavi coffers overflowed; the princess described her financial situation as comfortable. In New York City, she owned a townhouse in Beekman Place and a triplex on Park Avenue; in Paris, her residence was an apartment on Avenue Montaigne. On the Riviera, a seaside villa. But as King Damocles had discovered, royal privilege comes with a price.

In 1977, two hooded gunmen fired ten shots at Ashraf's Rolls Royce on the French Riviera coast after she spent an evening of gambling at the fashionable Palm Beach Casino in nearby Cannes. While the assassins killed her lady-in-waiting, Kahainouri Forough, and Ashraf's chauffeur sustained injuries, the fifty-seven-year-old princess was unharmed. The police said the act was politically motivated by opponents of the Pahlavi reign of terror. Shaken, Ashraf took refuge at her third husband's luxurious villa in Juan-les-Pins.

Ashraf's house of cards fell when mullahs replaced the monarchy during the Islamic Revolution, forcing the entire Pahlavi family to flee from Iran. Her beloved twin succumbed to cancer in Cairo, a tragic echo of their brother Ali, who had perished in a 1954 plane crash. Her enduring mission was the resurrection of her twin's reputation, "I would marry more than once. I would have children. I would work for my country in ways unheard of for a woman of my generation. But always the center of my existence was, and is, Mohammad Reza Pahlavi. Some people worship God. I worship my brother." In her later years, Ashraf retreated from public life, though she did attend President Richard Nixon's funeral. The majority of the time, she passed her days in her well-guarded Right Bank apartment in Paris watching old footage from the pre-revolution days.

The princess without a country passed away in Monte Carlo at age ninety-six. Once, when asked by the Associated Press what she would change if she could, Ashraf replied, "I would want to do the same thing. It's passed now, only memories. But there were fifty years of grandeur and glory."

♛

CHAPTER 21

"Bury You All"

— 1926 —

To be labeled eccentric—rather than crazy—used to be a prerogative of those with blood blue enough to allow them the privilege of straying from the straight and narrow. As writer Edith Sitwell explained, "The genius and the aristocrat are frequently regarded as eccentrics because genius and aristocrat are entirely unafraid of and uninfluenced by the opinions and vagaries of the crowd." If you were posh enough, you could get a pass for any shenanigans. Spain's last duchess took full advantage of her highborn station to do whatever the hell she pleased.

Known as Cayetana—short for María del Rosario Cayetana Alfonsa Victoria Eugenia Francisca Fitz-James Stuart y de Silva, to provide but a few of her twenty-three names—the Duchess was among the most intriguing and unorthodox of Europe's royals. Cayetana was born in her family's neoclassical Palacio de Liria in Madrid—the home where her ancestor had served as Goya's muse—the only child of Don Jacobo Fitz-James Stuart y Falcó, seventeenth Duke of Alba. Through paternal lineage, Cayetana was a descendant of King James II of England, making her a distant relative of Winston Churchill and Diana, Princess of Wales. Her mother was Doña Maria del Rosario de Silva y Gurtubay, the ninth Marquesa of San Vincente del Barco. King Alfonso XII and Victoria Eugenie, his English queen, were her godparents. Due to Cayetana's fifty-seven titles—*The Guinness Book of World Records* lists her as holding the greatest number—she was not required to bow to anyone, not even

King Juan Carlos of Spain, Queen Elizabeth II of England, or the pope. Another perk of her pedigree was she had the right to ride a horse into Seville Cathedral.

And yet Cayetana's childhood did not bring her as many joys as the number of her names or titles. She hardly saw her mother, who suffered from tuberculosis and died from the disease when her daughter was eight. Further upheaval followed when Generalissimo Francisco Franco appointed her father ambassador to England, where she socialized with her poor relations, the Churchills, and Princesses Elizabeth and Margaret. In 1943, while Britain was in the grip of wartime austerity, the dazzling duchess made her debut in what the Associated Press described as "the biggest social affair the European Continent has seen in many years." The Anglican sojourn ended after the Duke resigned his ambassadorship in 1945, declaring that Franco was "harmful to the interests of Spain." The Albas returned to Liria Palace, which had been the target of German bombs during the Spanish Civil War as communists commandeered the estate. The Duke had possessed the foresight to store his priceless collections of paintings in the cellars of the Prado; however, half of its literary collection perished.

In 1947, Cayetana wed Luis Martínez de Irujo y Artázcoz, son of the Duke of Sotomayor, in an affair so lavish that it threatened to eclipse Princess Elizabeth's marriage to Philip Mountbatten the following month. Their nuptials took place in Seville Cathedral with a thousand guests in attendance, in an event *The New York Times* heralded as the most expensive wedding in the world. The bride wore a pearl and diamond crown; she patterned her white satin gown after the dress worn by Napoleon III's bride, Empress Eugénie. Post ceremony, the newlyweds drove by dense crowds in a horse-drawn carriage to the bride's Palacio de Las Dueñas in Seville.

The marriage produced five sons and a daughter, each of whom received a separate noble title and their own palace. The Duchess became a fixture of the international jet set, hosting Audrey Hepburn, Jackie Kennedy, and Camilla, wife of Prince Charles, on their visits to

Spain. She turned her Madrid palace over to the French designer Yves Saint Laurent to stage a Dior fashion show. Nevertheless, the democratic duchess also socialized with bullfighters and dancers. Rumor circulated around her fourth son, Fernando, that claimed he was the result of an affair with Sevillan flamenco dancer Antonio el Bailarín, who acknowledged paternity in a posthumously published memoir. When the magazine *Interviú* carried the story, the Duchess sued, and a court awarded her damages of $426,000 for the assault on her honor. In the 1950s, Pablo Picasso wanted to paint her both clothed and nude. The conservative Luis opposed the idea, and the Duchess declined to pose, though she indicated her refusal was not because of her husband's wish. She felt that sitting for a portrait by the communist Picasso would have created a huge scandal under the Franco regime. And as she put it, "I think he would have worn me out."

Luis passed away from leukemia in 1972, but Cayetana did not choose the path of lifelong widowhood. Six years later, the Duchess married Jesús Aguirre y Ortiz de Zárate, an illegitimate, defrocked Catholic priest thirteen years her junior who had once been her confessor, in a union that checked all the boxes for scandalizing staid Spanish society. Their marriage proved happy, so much so that when Jesús sent three love poems he had written for his wife to Julio Iglesias, asking him to set them to music, the singer refused as he considered them "too steamy." In 1988, when the gossip rags reported strains in their marriage, Cayetana, then sixty-two, responded, "We are happy, as happy as before. And, if you must know, we make love every night"—except that "make" and "love" were not the words that the Duchess used. Their relationship flourished until the Duke Consort passed away in 2001.

In her later years, the Duchess went on the same quest as Juan Ponce de León: to discover the Fountain of Youth. Cayetana felt the redemption of her lost beauty lay in cosmetic surgery; but the result was not kind. Countless operations left her with distorted features that made her as much a public spectacle as those of Jocelyn Wildenstein, who went under the knife over and over to make her features appear feline. A website specializing in such matters claimed the Duchess had a facelift, brow lift, nose jobs, and lip and Botox injections. A family friend remarked, "She overdid it, obviously." Her halo of white Afro and waxy skin made her look akin to the aged Baby Jane portrayed by Bette Davis. In her eighties, the paparazzi photographed the Duchess wading in the ocean off the coast of Ibiza in a bikini and wearing fishnet tights with form-hugging dresses. Immune to publicity, she told a gossip magazine, "If they forget you, you're nobody." Cayetana remained an unabashed bohemian, if the possessor of a fortune of $5 billion can be described as such. The public was mesmerized by the question of what-is-she-going-to-do-next; and the Duchess did not disappoint.

After Jesús's passing, many assumed that the Duchess, then in her mid-seventies, would spend her twilight years as a single woman, although she embarked on affairs (such as the one she pursued with the Russian dancer Rudolf Nureyev). However, she became romantically entangled on a long-term basis with Alfonso Díez Carabantes, twenty-four years her junior, a minor civil servant in the department of social security. Her six children feared Alfonso was interested in his own social security and that he was moonlighting as a gold digger. Fearful of losing their biblical "mess of pottage," the Alba heirs were vocal in their opposition of their mother's plan to tie the knot. There was an alleged intervention by King Juan Carlos, who telephoned the Duchess urging her not to wed her Lothario. The Duchess, every inch a Queen Lear, retaliated against her children, who were claiming that she was "emotionally unstable," by posing on the cover of Spanish *Vanity Fair*. She also mocked her offspring for their divorces, pointing out she was a respectable widow. On a radio interview, Cayetana announced, "Alfonso doesn't want anything. All he wants is me." Regardless of anyone's opinion, the Duchess was hell-bent on ordering invitations and announced, "Every great love story should end in marriage." The man in the eye of the storm stated, "Together we have a wonderful time. She's always asking: What shall we do next? She's unstoppable. It often seems that I'm the older of the two."

The impending nuptials put the House of Alba's wealth under scrutiny. She was believed to own the most important private collection of art in Spain, including paintings by Velázquez, Goya, Van Dyck, El Greco, Titian, Rubens, and Rembrandt. Other prize possessions included a family Bible dating from 1430, a first edition of Miguel de Cervantes's seventeenth-century novel *Don Quixote*, Christopher Columbus's first map of America, and the will of Fernando the Catholic, father of Catherine of Aragon. With estates across the country, the Duchess could have traveled across Spain without having to spend a night in a property not her own.

The family feud ended when the Duchess bequeathed her palaces and possessions to her children and left nothing to the man referred to as her "toyboy." However, the Duchess kept control of her vast holdings until her death. Put out by gossipmongers, Cayetana stated, "Spain is still a macho country. If this were a wealthy man marrying a younger woman, no one would blink an eye. But because it's the reverse, they said he must only be doing it for money. Well, now everyone can see that it's not for money, it's love." Touché. At her wedding at her Seville palace, Cayetana took off her shoes, kicked up her heels, and danced the flamenco.

Spain's spirited Duchess passed away at age eighty-eight in her Dueñas Palace. The year before, Cayetana declared, "I confess I am thinking of keeping on living so I can enjoy the expression on people's faces when I point at them and say, 'I'm going to bury you all.' "

👑

CHAPTER 22

The Emerald Castle

— 1926 —

W hen Dorothy journeyed along the yellow brick road, she chanted, "Lions and tigers and bears, oh my!" Twenty-six years later, a contemporary queen treads a path of purple whose chant could well be, "Castles and corgis and crowns, oh my!" This modern monarch has a life that rivals the marvels of Oz.

In an item for the irony file, the world's longest-reigning royal was not originally slated to become Her Most Excellent Majesty Elizabeth the Second, by the Grace of God of the United Kingdom of Great Britain and Northern Ireland and of Her Other Realms and Territories Queen, Head of the Commonwealth, and Defender of the Faith. At the time of Elizabeth Alexandra Mary Windsor's birth, since her father, Prince Albert, was a second son, the mantle of monarchy belonged to her uncle Edward, the Prince of Wales. Because the princess was never supposed to be queen, her childhood, along with younger sister Margaret, was relatively typical, insofar as "typical" entailed having King George V as your grandfather. The calm shattered in 1936 when her uncle Edward VIII repudiated his ermine robes after 325 days to wed divorced American Wallis Simpson. A shocked footman relayed the news to the young princesses. Margaret asked her ten-year-old sister, "Does that mean you will have to be the next queen?" "Yes, someday," Elizabeth replied. "Poor you," Margaret responded. Only the arrival of a baby brother would have altered her fate.

Margaret's negative comment regarding the crown originated with her father, who had sobbed when he and his mother discussed the abdication, partially as he dreaded his stutter would be on public display. Nevertheless, he accepted the role of King George VI, and, along with his wife, Elizabeth the Queen Mother, moved with his family to Buckingham Palace. As any excursion into London resulted in a media frenzy, normalcy was never their norm. In 1933, the king gifted Elizabeth with Dookie, a corgi, helping her cope with the pressures of her station. (She has owned at least thirty of the breed.) Queen Mary, who always wore a tiara to dinner even if she and her husband dined alone, drilled protocol into her granddaughter.

In 1940, with the outbreak of war, the close-knit family were often separated as the king and queen sent their daughters to Windsor Castle, which was about twenty miles away from the capital and therefore not a likely bombing target during the Blitz. The girls remained in their sheltered enclave for five years. A treat during the wartime austerity was a thatched-cottage playhouse, the Y Bwthyn Bach, a present from the people of Wales, that came with perks such as a heated towel rack, an electric fireplace, French dolls, and eight fur coats. In 1945, Elizabeth enlisted in the Women's Auxiliary Territorial Services as No. 230873, second subaltern Elizabeth Windsor. Photographs of her working alongside members of the military became staples in Allied propaganda.

Following Germany's defeat, at Buckingham Palace, Elizabeth became reacquainted with her third cousin, Prince Philip Mountbatten, whom she had first met at age thirteen at the Royal Naval College in Dartmouth. At that time, she had been mainly enthralled by Philip's agility in jumping over tennis nets. Upon their reunion, the seventeen-year-old was still taken with the twenty-two-year-old who had spent the war years as a naval lieutenant on a British destroyer that had been under danger of bombardment by German Stukas. Their match seemed improbable: she was the daughter of King George VI, while he was the nephew of the deposed king of Greece; the Windsors were the lords of majestic castles, while his family was one of exiles. Despite their differences, romance blossomed: Philip's terms of endearment for Elizabeth were Lilibet, Sausage, or Darling.

The prince proposed, and the twenty-year-old princess accepted without consulting mum and dad. At their 1947 wedding, the crowned heads of Europe and the world's most powerful politicians were in attendance. Those not invited to the Westminster Abbey extravaganza were the groom's sisters, due to their Nazi husbands, as well as her disgraced uncle, who after relinquishing the crown, had become the Duke of Windsor. The couple took their vows in front of an estimated 2,000 in-person guests (with 20 million viewing around the world), which lent a ray of light to a world reeling from the atrocities of war. The princess's gown was truly fit for a princess: It consisted of ivory silk, crystals, and 10,000 seed pearls. Her Russian fringe tiara had once belonged to her grandmother, Queen Mary. The newlyweds received 2,500 presents: President Truman gifted a Steuben bowl, while Gandhi sent a piece of lace he had woven by hand. From her parents, she received a nineteenth-century sapphire and diamond necklace and Cartier diamond chandelier earrings. When the crowds cheered their 1947 wedding, neither expected Elizabeth would be crowned anytime soon, but blue bloods are also the playthings of the gods.

In 1952, Elizabeth and Philip were in Kenya in a hotel, perched in a tree from which the princess snapped photographs of elephants. They descended to the devastating news that her beloved father had passed away. Her cousin Lady Pamela Mountbatten, who had accompanied her to Africa, recalled that Elizabeth had "climbed up that ladder as a princess but had climbed down as a queen." Upon her return to London, although harboring misgivings that Elizabeth was only twenty-five, Prime Minister Winston Churchill stated, "Famous have been the reigns of our queens. Some of the greatest periods in our history have unfolded under their scepter." For the coronation—the first to be televised in the Crown's 1,200-year history—Uncle Edward was again left off the guest list, for his abdication as well as his hobnobbing with Hitler. He said of the secondary snub, "What a smug, stinking lot my relations are." A twenty-four-foot-long gold stagecoach carried Elizabeth to the ceremony, and her dress bore the symbols of Great Britain and the Commonwealth nations: a rose, a thistle, a shamrock, a maple leaf, and a fern. The most sacred part of the ceremony was not telecast: A priest anointed the queen with holy oil. Scepter in hand, balancing a five-pound solid gold crown, Elizabeth II accepted her throne and her niche in history. Over the years, one of her sorrows was the sun setting on the British Empire, with events such as the departure of Canada, Hong Kong, and recently Barbados from under the umbrella of the British Empire. Philip, the Duke of Edinburgh, became the royal sidekick, although he initially bristled against his wife's staggering status. As royal consort—not king—protocol dictated he walk two paces behind her in public. Despite rumors he was a serial philanderer, Elizabeth's love never faltered. On the night of their fiftieth wedding anniversary, she stated, "But he has quite simply been my strength and stay all these years." The couple had children Prince Charles, Princess Anne, Prince Andrew, and Prince Edward. The bond remained unbroken until Philip's passing at age ninety-nine.

Elizabeth's main passion seems to be to the role in which destiny cast her. She has kept the faith to the promise she made while on tour with her parents in Cape Town on her twenty-first birthday, "I declare before you that my whole life, whether it be long or short, shall be devoted to your service and the service of the great imperial commonwealth to which we all belong."

From the outside peering in, Elizabeth is the most enviable of women: The possessor of a loving family and mind-boggling wealth, she has pressed the flesh of the famous and traveled the globe. However, even the ancient Windsor armor could not shield her from horror. In 1974, Ian Ball attempted to kidnap Princess Anne at gunpoint; he said he intended to donate the 3-million-pound ransom he demanded for the treatment of psychiatric patients. Five years later, the IRA assassinated Philip's uncle, Lord Mountbatten, along with his grandson. Another terrifying incident occurred when seventeen-year-old Marcus Sarjeant fired six shots, all blanks, during the Trooping of the Colour while Queen Elizabeth was present on horseback. The Queen garnered accolades for her calmness: She did not lose control of Burmese, her startled mount.

Queen Elizabeth stated, "1992 is not a year on which I shall look back with undiluted pleasure." She pronounced it her "annus horribilis," Latin for "horrible year." Some of the sorrows she weathered: the breakdown of the marriages of Andrew, Anne, and Charles, as well as a fire damaged Windsor Castle. More misery lay in wait: in 1997, her former daughter-in-law, Princess Diana, lost her life in a car accident. The public was angered at Elizabeth's initial failure to address the tragedy, an omission they viewed as indifference.

However, two decades later, in 2012, her annus mirabilis arrived. The queen's Diamond Jubilee, commemorating her sixtieth year on the throne, drew an estimated one million people to London for a four-day party filled with pageantry. Aboard a royal barge, the monarch led a 1,000-vessel flotilla down the Thames; 2,012 beacons shone in her honor from the Scottish Highlands to the Channel Islands. Sir Elton John and Sir Paul McCartney serenaded her at a concert outside Buckingham Palace. In the same year, for the opening of the Olympic ceremony, the queen appeared in a Bond movie spoof where she and "Secret Agent 007" seemed to parachute (shades of Pussy Galore) onto a stadium platform. Given Elizabeth's tenacity, it will hopefully be many a year before England employs the code phrase for her passing: "London Bridge is down." On the Queen's Platinum Jubilee (the seventieth anniversary of her accession to the throne), a touching film clip was shared of the Queen having lunch with Paddington Bear, where they bonded over their love of marmalade sandwiches.

The Queen's greatness lies in her devotion to duty, including her avoidance of scandal. Elizabeth understands that it is not wise to let the public see the magician behind the curtain as that would detract from the enchantment of her emerald castle.

CHAPTER 23

Camelot Queen

— 1929 —

Indulging in make-believe is a rite of passage for many a young girl; envisioning a tiara, a coach, a prince. With the passing of the years, reality takes over, but the fantasy remained for the one who became both an American and European princess.

In Alfred Hitchcock's film *Rear Window*, a wheelchair-bound man asks the woman in his Greenwich Village apartment, "Who are you?" People have posed the same question about his costar, Grace Patricia Kelly. The two most prominent Irish American, Catholic families were the Kennedys of Massachusetts and the Kellys of Philadelphia. The patriarchs shared in common the experience of traversing the road from rags to riches—Joseph Kennedy as a bootlegger and Jack Kelly as a construction company owner—and both felt sex did not need to be exclusive to their wives. Jack and Margaret raised four children in a seventeen-room estate in Germantown overlooking the Schuylkill River, in whose depths Jack relived his days of youthful glory when he won three Olympic medals for rowing. One childhood grief for Grace was she felt her father favored her athletic siblings.

Rather than take the debutante route of a Philadelphia prima donna, Grace heeded the siren call of the stage, though this meant butting heads with father Jack, who believed acting "a slim cut above streetwalker." Leaving Germantown in the rearview mirror, Grace headed for Manhattan, where she attended the American Academy of

Dramatic Art. In New York, Grace traded her mansion for a residence in the Barbizon Hotel for Women. What saved her from the role of a struggling actress was the clout of her successful uncles: George Kelly was a Pulitzer-Prize winning playwright, and Walter C. Kelly a famed vaudevillian. Her breakthrough role was as a Quaker wife in the western *High Noon*, in which she costarred with Gary Cooper. However, her role in Metro Goldwyn Mayer's *Mogambo*, directed by John Ford, brought an Academy Award nomination as Best Actress. The film also turned the spotlight on Grace's love life, and rumors flew that on the set Grace Kelly and the movie's star Clark Gable had embarked on an affair, one the press dubbed, "*L'Affaire* Gable." When questioned as to the rumors, Grace replied, "What else is there to do if you're alone in a tent in Africa with Clark Gable?" In an era when laissez-faire sex was scandalous, Grace's other alleged high-profile horizontal partners included Gary Cooper, William Holden, Bing Crosby, Frank Sinatra, and Oleg Cassini. Her greatest screen success was in *The Country Girl*, in a turn with leading man William Holden that garnered her an Oscar as Best Actress; she dazzled in an aquamarine gown by famed designer Edith Head. Emcee Bob Hope announced, "I just wanna say, they should give a special reward for bravery to the producer who produced a movie *without* Grace Kelly." The woman of the hour graced the covers of *Look* and *TIME* magazines, yet public persona masked private pain. In her suite at the Bel Air Hotel, she revealed, it was "just the two of us, Oscar and I. It was the loneliest moment of my life." Grace was not to be lonely for long, as the star of *To Catch a Thief* was imminently to catch a prince.

The American movie star met the Prince of Monaco through a blind date suggested by Olivia de Havilland, of *Gone with the Wind* fame. In 1955, the two actresses were on a train heading from Paris to the eighth Cannes Film Festival when de Havilland and her husband, *Paris-Match* editor Pierre Galante, played matchmakers. Prince Rainier Louis Henri Maxence Bertrand Grimaldi (his surname reflecting Europe's oldest royal family) and Grace met in his 102-room Monte Carlo pink palazzo on the French Riviera, where the royal took her on a tour of his private zoo. One of the animals was a baby Asian tiger, a gift from Emperor Bao Dai of Vietnam. De Havilland reported that the meeting left Grace "in a state of enchantment." The sense of enchantment may have come from Grimaldi as well as the lure of Monaco, a five-mile principality that had once been the domain of the Bourbon and Napoleon dynasties. As they began to appear together, the press went into a feeding frenzy over the romance of the Hollywood beauty queen and the European prince, enacted against the purple and pink Mediterranean sunset. The hint that their relationship was more than a dalliance occurred when Rainier flew to Philadelphia to spend Christmas with the Kelly family. As it transpired, Albert had proposed on the second date. He had done so out of a mixture that was in part romance and part rationality. He believed having America's sweetheart star as his princess would increase tourism for his principality, and he needed an heir: under the terms of a 1918 treaty, Monaco would become the property of France if Rainier died childless.

Grace agreed to become his seaside kingdom's First Lady, a deal cemented with a 10.47-karat diamond engagement ring from Cartier of New York City. Their fairy-tale romance captured the world's imagination, though not everyone was impressed. Upset his leading lady was trading her talents for a tiara, director Alfred Hitchcock dubbed her "dis-Grace." However, he later softened and remarked, "I am glad Grace has found the best role of her life." Jack Kelly, in a nod to his future son-in-law's diminutive stature, told reporters that Rainier was only "tit-high to Gracie." No wonder Grace remarked, "You choose your friends, but your family you're born with." Another hiccup came when Rainier met David Niven and asked the actor who had been his most exciting lover. Niven answered, "Grace, of course," before catching himself and adding, "er, Gracie Fields." Jack eventually came around and ponied up the cost of the $2 million wedding, making it an affair to remember. His connection to royalty helped salve the insult he had received as a young man, when he was deemed ineligible to compete in the famous English Diamond Sculls at the Henley Royal Regatta because he had once worked as a bricklayer. In response, Jack sent his sweaty rowing cap to the king as a souvenir. Although Jack had been at the receiving end of prejudice, he had never hesitated to dismiss Grace's earlier boyfriends in derogatory racist terms.

In 1956, in a nod to art imitating life, after completing the film *High Society*, Grace set sail for Monaco. She recalled her state of mind while on board the *SS Constitution* thus: "When I left New York, our ship was surrounded in fog. What sort of world was awaiting me on the other side of that fog?" Her trepidation stemmed from the fact she was leaving loved ones, career, and country for a place where she knew only her fiancé and did not speak the language (French), a place where ritual ruled. Her new role as a royal was to place her in a gargantuan fishbowl. Furthermore, she understood that in the contingency of a divorce, her husband would retain sole custody of any future children. Regardless of what the crystal ball would reveal, those who knew her had no doubt Grace would play her role to perfection.

Prince Rainier III and Ms. Kelly exchanged vows, *"Oui, je veux,"* in the Cathedral of St. Nicholas in Monte Carlo. The press called the event the wedding of the century, while Grace referred to it as the carnival of the century: 1,500 reporters converged to capture the image of the twenty-six-year-old blonde bride. Crowds were so massive that Prince Rainier summoned the assistance of the French riot police; the newly minted Princess Grace later suggested that she and the prince should have been awarded battle ribbons for all the fighting required to maneuver through the throng of onlookers. Their six hundred guests included European blue bloods, the international jet set, and American movie stars. MGM filmed the event live for an estimated television audience of thirty million. Before boarding her husband's yacht, *Deo Juvante II*, for their honeymoon, Grace remarked, "Thank you, darling, for such a sweet, intimate wedding."

Life in a postcard-perfect castle perched on a cliff overlooking the Mediterranean became the real-life stage setting for Her Serene Highness Princess Grace. Twenty-one guns heralded the birth of

Princess Caroline, and her nativity day became a national holiday where gambling halted and champagne flowed. Crown Prince Albert merited a 101-gun salute, followed by the last-born, Stéphanie. The Grimaldi siblings were the recipients of their mother's beauty and their father's pedigree and served as catnip to the paparazzi with their romantic hijinks, garnering the type of publicity their parents abhorred. While Grace's priority was family, she also dedicated her life to duty on behalf of her adopted homeland and was a staunch supporter of charities and cultural events.

Seen from the outside looking in, the girl from Philadelphia turned princess of the silver screen reigned over a glittery municipality and enjoyed a life lifted from make-belief. However, as Grace remarked, "The idea of my life as a fairy tale is itself a fairy tale." Disney fantasy transformed to the Brothers Grimm variety when Grace and seventeen-year-old Stéphanie were returning home from Roc Agel, the Grimaldis' French estate. Refusing the service of her chauffeur, Grace was driving her British Rover 3500 on a winding road at Cap-d'Ail in the Cote d'Azur region when she suffered a stroke and plunged down a forty-five-foot embankment. The princess sustained multiple fractures and a cerebral hemorrhage, resulting in her death at age fifty-two. Stéphanie spent time in a hospital for shock and non-life-threatening injuries. An estimated worldwide audience of 100 million was present for the interment of Princess Grace in the Grimaldi crypt. The crowned heads of Europe were in attendance, including Diana, Princess of Wales, representing the British royal family. Years later, when asked if he would consider remarriage, the prince responded, "How could I? Everywhere I go, I see Grace."

The Kelly and Kennedy clans shared a final commonality with the tragic deaths of Princess Grace and President Kennedy. After her husband's death, Jacqueline compared her husband's 1,000 days in the White House to King Arthur's kingdom, as both had been dedicated to democratic ideals. Mrs. Kennedy quoted from the Broadway musical, "Don't let it be forgot, that for one brief, shining moment there was Camelot." During a golden era, Princess Grace reigned as Monaco's own Camelot queen.

♔

CHAPTER 24

Second Best

— 1930 —

The system of primogeniture, a royal rule that dictates power is transmitted from firstborn to the next firstborn, leaves younger siblings hanging. Monarchy is a one-person job, and thus the heir wields the scepter while "the spare" is left with less of a spot in the limelight. Birth order is what drove Scar to turn on Simba, as well as what shaped the life of a woman from the House of Windsor.

Long after they left their nursery, Princess Margaret played the role of the naughty younger sister to the duty-bound Queen Elizabeth II. Margaret Rose was born in her mother Elizabeth's ancestral home at Glamis Castle, the legendary site of Macbeth's murder of King Duncan. Hers was the first royal birth in Scotland since Charles I in 1601, and bagpipers led a torchlight procession to proclaim her arrival. Four years and four months younger than her older sister, the girls referred to each other as Lilibet and Margo. They wore matching clothes and sheltered together in Windsor Castle during the Blitz. Deferential servants attended to their every need, and dedicated royalists lingered around their homes in Windsor Castle and Piccadilly Circus.

Although inseparable, they were far different in temperament; Elizabeth was shy, obedient, and happiest in the company of her dogs and horses. In contrast, Margaret was outgoing and prone to tantrums. When World War II erupted, the ten-year-old Margaret groused, "Who is this Hitler, spoiling everything?" Later in life she stated, "Disobedience is my joy." In 1942, while staging a performance of *Cinderella*, the sisters argued over the price of admission. Elizabeth disagreed with Margaret's suggestion that they charge seven shillings. "No one will pay that to look at us!" Her little sis countered, "They'll pay anything to see us." Their father, Albert, the Duke of York, a second-born son, understood the thorns of royal birth order and overindulged his youngest child. He stated that Margaret could "charm the pearl out of an oyster." He also remarked that Elizabeth was his pride, Margaret his joy.

When King George V passed away in 1936, his eldest son became King Edward VIII. However, with Edward's abdication, Margaret's father became the new crowned head. Taken aback at the abrupt upheaval of their lives, the family relocated to London's Buckingham Palace. Of even more importance to Margaret, her sister had become the heir to the throne. With the weight of a future ermine robe on Elizabeth's shoulders, her parents groomed their eldest daughter for her rendezvous with history while Margaret learned to sing, dance, and play the piano. An elderly courier remarked of the little princess as she cartwheeled down a Buckingham Palace corridor, "Thank God the other one was born first." While Elizabeth's coronation elevated Elizabeth to the status of an icon, it set into motion a major shift in the power structure between Margaret and Elizabeth as their respective standing had been forever altered.

With the marriage of her sister to Prince Philip of Greece in 1947, Margaret became the world's most eligible woman. Pablo Picasso was desperate to marry her; Peter Sellers stated he would have settled for an affair. John Fowler fantasized about abducting her and keeping her as his prisoner. Able to choose any man, the princess turned her violet-blue eyes on Captain Peter Townsend of the Royal Air Force, a hero of the Battle of Britain. Part of his appeal was Peter embodied many of the traits of Margaret's adored father, who had recently passed away. As he was a commoner, twice her age, and even more damning, divorced, the couple kept their relationship under wraps. The cat slipped out of the bag on Elizabeth's Coronation Day after Margaret picked lint off

Peter's uniform, a gesture of intimacy that launched a media firestorm. Prime Minister Winston Churchill was Margaret's ally until his wife, Clementine, pointed out that by doing so he was repeating the same mistake he had made with Edward and Mrs. Simpson. When the besotted princess petitioned for permission to marry, Parliament threatened to cut off her royal allowance and the Palace announced Margaret would simply become Mrs. Peter Townsend. Margaret had to weigh love against a life without a title, wealth, and the perks of princess power.

The Firm took matters into its own hands and dispatched Peter to Brussels as an attaché to the British Embassy. At the time, Princess Margaret and her mother were on a tour of Rhodesia. Margaret went on the radio with her decision: "Mindful of the Church's teachings that Christian marriage is dissolvable, and conscious of my duty to the Commonwealth, I have decided to put these considerations before any others." Peter recovered from the rejection, and at age forty, he married nineteen-year-old Marie-Luce Jamagne of Belgium. In a classic rebound, in 1960, Margaret wed magazine photographer Antony Armstrong Jones, who received the title Lord Snowdon. The nuptials took place at Westminster Abbey before a crowd of 2,000. They embarked on a six-week honeymoon on *Britannia* and then returned to their apartment in Kensington Palace. Their son, Lord Linley, was born in 1961, followed by a daughter, Lady Sarah Chatto, in 1964. While Elizabeth surrounded herself with the tweedy and the trusty, the throneless Margaret courted the celebrities of the swinging sixties: Mary Quant, Rudolf Nureyev, and Vidal Sassoon.

Cracks soon appeared in their marriage, and Antony vented by leaving a note on Margaret's desk that began, "Twenty-Four Reasons Why I Hate You." Both had affairs, and the princess embarked on a long-term one with Roddy Llewellyn, seventeen years her junior. Three years later, the *News of the World* published a picture of them in bathing suits on Les Jolies Eaux, her beachfront estate in Mustique in the Caribbean. The press had a feeding frenzy; Elizabeth must have reached for the smelling salts. The marriage ended in a 1978 divorce—the first to take place in the immediate family of a British monarch since 1533, when Henry VIII divorced Catherine of Aragon in order to wed Anne Boleyn. In her later years, Princess Margaret became Cinderella in reverse. Her tragedy was that unlike her sister, she never found a purpose and spent her life in a never-ending haze of Famous Grouse Scotch, cigarettes, and unfulfilling relationships. Stalked by boredom, she often lay in bed until 11:30 in the morning, sometimes having her hair done twice in the same day.

With her prickly personality, she was not suited to perform the royal rounds of duty and did not bother to mask her boredom. When she visited a home for the elderly, the staff served her dinner, only to be told, "This looks like sick." Upon meeting cross-dresser Boy George, she remarked, "England only has room for one queen." Despite her scandal-filled life, during the Duchess of York's divorce from Prince Andrew, Margaret wrote Sarah a scalding note that ironically applied to herself, "Clearly you have never considered the damage you are causing us all... You have done more to bring shame on the family than could ever have been imagined." Margaret had liked Princess Diana until the Duchess of Wales went around Windsor rules (such as by airing palace laundry), at which time she turned her back on her nephew's wife.

Depending on her mood, Princess Margaret could be the life of the party or the death of it. Attracted to those with star quality, she demanded they pay homage to her as the daughter of a king and the sister of the queen and address her as "Ma'am" or "Princess Margaret." Dubbed "the world's most difficult guest," at formal dinners she smoked during the meal and stubbed her cigarette out on a plate, or, on occasion, on someone's hand. She received condemnation for her insisting on receiving motorcycle escorts and government helicopters when traveling in Britain.

As she entered her sixties, Margaret's health deteriorated as a result of years of heavy drinking and a sixty-cigarette-a-day habit. In 1993, she ended up in the hospital with a bout of pneumonia. Five years later, on Mustique, she suffered a stroke that left her with a mild speech impediment. Misfortune again plagued her on her island retreat when she severely burned her feet with scalding-hot bathwater. A further stroke left her sight and mobility impaired, necessitating a wheelchair. The last time she appeared in public was before Christmas for the hundredth birthday party of Princess Alice, the Dowager Duchess of Gloucester. Wearing dark glasses over a pasty and puffy face, her altered appearance served as a bitter blow for the woman who had prided herself on her looks, and who had always been the pretty sister.

In 2002, three days after Elizabeth marked her fiftieth year on the throne, Margaret passed away at age seventy-one, a far cry from the beautiful child who had romped in a fairy-tale castle. The queen announced her sister's death "with great sadness," and Buckingham Palace's flag flew at half-mast. At her interment, art historian Sir Roy Strong observed, "The common touch she had not;" and he was her friend. In contrast, her mother, with whom she had a difficult relationship, died a few weeks later. While Margaret's funeral had been an intimate gathering, the Queen Mother's funeral was a state occasion that entailed 200,000 mourners.

The questions remain: Would Princess Margaret's life not have been a series of downward spirals had she wed Peter, had she not been a member of the House of Windsor, had she not been the younger sister? As Margaret stated of her supporting role, "I guess I'll be second best to my grave."

CHAPTER 25

The Contemporary Cleopatra

— 1933 —

King Farouk presciently proclaimed, "Soon there will be only five Kings—the King of England, the King of Spades, the King of Clubs, the King of Hearts, the King of Diamonds." His prophecy came to pass, at least in regard to his kingdom making his consort the last queen of the Nile.

The Old Testament relates that King David, watching from the roof of his palace, spied Bathsheba bathing. Although she was the wife of Uriah, her husband did not serve as much of an impediment, and David took her to bed. Fast-forward a few millennia, and a similar Mideastern scenario came to pass. Sixteen-year-old Narriman ("vivacious spirit") Sadek was the only child of Assila and Hussein Fahmy Sadek, the Secretary General of the Ministry of Communications. Narriman was the fiancée of Zaki Hachem, a Harvard-educated economist on Egypt's United Nations staff; the society pages referred to their upcoming nuptials as "the marriage of the year." The couple was shopping in a Cairo jewelry store when its owner, Ahmed Nagib Pasha, told them to return the next day when he would have the perfect ring.

King Farouk, whose name translates to "the one who distinguishes between right and wrong," scion to the century-old Egyptian throne, had gathered several "talent scouts" to find his next consort. His first had been Safinaz Zulficar, renamed Farida ("the Peerless One") in accordance with the tradition that all members of the royal family have names beginning with the letter F, a tradition believed to bring good luck. The marriage ended when, after three daughters, Farouk felt his wife would never deliver a male heir. The Shah of Iran had likewise divorced Farouk's sister, Fawzia Fuad, who had not produced a son.

The jeweler phoned the king with the news he had met the lady who satisfied his requirements: a young, attractive Muslim. The following afternoon, King Farouk peered through the blinds of a window, spellbound by "a mouth that held a glint of lively humor, and eyes that danced with gentle friendliness." He drove to the Sadek home to announce Narriman was going to become the Queen of Egypt. Despite having sent out 500 invitations, her parents cancelled the wedding, partially persuaded after Hussein received the title of Bey (governor of a district). In a nod to winning over Narriman, Farouk lavished her with gifts of jewels and flowers that led newspapers to dub her "the Cinderella of the Nile." Infuriated the king had usurped the woman he loved, Zaki was further incensed when imperial agents raided his apartment and confiscated Narriman's photographs and letters. In addition, the secret police had been trailing him. In compensation, the king offered the would-be groom the position of ambassador to Russia, an opportunity Zaki refused. His final comment on the situation was, "A bad dream. I did not think such things could happen in the twentieth century. Now I know better." When the news leaked of the king's amorous blitzkrieg, Farouk tightened his grip on the media. His rationalization was that an obscure diplomat's happiness was less important than that of "Farouk I, King of Mist, Lord of Nubia and the Sudan, Sovereign of Kordofar and Darfur." His sister, Faiza, simply stated, "He was not mad, just bad."

In the role of a Pygmalion, Farouk sent Narriman to the Egyptian embassy in Rome to prepare her for her role as future queen. There she lived under an assumed identity as the niece of the Egyptian ambassador. Tudors instructed her in etiquette, history, music, and four European languages. Staff monitored her weight to conform with Farouk's directive she return to Egypt weighing no more than 110 pounds. Ironically, the king eventually topped the scales at 300 pounds, partially due to his consumption of industrial quantities of oysters and sodas. A world-syndicated memoir (one not penned by Narriman) stated, "His shoulders fascinated me, and his arms and his powerful wrists covered with dark, virile hair... I found love such as I would never have dared to hope for." The king's memoir, also penned by a professional writer, waxed poetic, "Life without her would be lonely indeed...Narriman was the first human being...who really began...to understand the man behind the panoply of royalty."

In a nod to the troubled state of the world and the fact that he had already enjoyed an opulent first wedding, King Farouk promised his second would be more low-key. Nevertheless, 2,500 people gathered in the square outside the suburban palace at Kubbeh. Missing from the number was the seventeen-year-old bride, in accordance with the Muslim tradition that only males be present. With the close of the formalities, cannons released a 101-gun salute, and the guests enjoyed a lavish reception. At Narriman's home, a smaller crowd kept vigil to catch a glimpse of the seventeen-year-old bride. When she emerged, accompanied by the king's oldest sister, they departed in a bright red Rolls Royce with black fenders, followed by a motorcade of five red motorcycles, three red jeeps, two red Cadillacs, and eleven other vehicles. The procession passed under an arch that displayed a pink neon heart with the initials F and N as an estimated 1,000,000 spectators looked on.

Eighteen minutes after leaving her home, Narriman entered Abdeen Palace for a reception that lasted late into the night. The bride wore a white satin gown emblazoned with 20,000 diamonds brilliants, the result of the work of twenty seamstresses who had labored for 4,000 hours. A seven-tier wedding cake in the banquet hall towered over guests such as the Aly Khan; the king cut a piece for his bride with a small saber and presented it on a gold plate. Guests gifted the royal newlyweds extravagant gifts such as a jeweled vase from Haile Selassie and a writing set embossed with Russian gemstones from Stalin. None rivalled the Mercedes-Benz 540K that Adolf Hitler had sent Farouk for his 1938 marriage to Farida. A four-month European honeymoon began aboard the *Mahroussa*, the royal yacht whose crew of sixty wore identical white blazers, white jackets, and yachting caps. By night, the king lost vast sums at the baccarat table. The lavishness of their vacation erased any goodwill that had been generated from Narriman's status as a commoner.

One of their main homes was the opulent 500-room Aberdeen Palace, three times the size of Buckingham Palace, with a gate fashioned in France that enclosed a fountain encircled by statues of Egyptians rulers. The predominant decorating touch was gold, found on the backs of chairs, the frames of paintings, and the surfaces of countless clocks.

In 1953, the thirty-one-year-old King Farouk instructed his government to announce to "both parts of the Nile Valley, north and south, and to the rest of the world the birth of Crown Prince Ahmed Fuad." The king was reported to be "deliriously happy." In honor of his wife, the king ordered the Anglo-Swiss Hospital in Alexandria renamed the Queen Narriman Hospital.

The golden clocks began to wind down; ten days after welcoming Ahmed, there was an outbreak of rioting and demonstrations where the masses vented their fury against their monarch. Part of their anger stemmed from Farouk's defeat in the 1948 Arab-Israeli War that led to the founding of the Jewish homeland. The king, whose philandering had not stopped with his marriage, grew even more distant from Narriman as the threat to his crown intensified. Under duress from his own military officers, who had surrounded the royal palaces with armed forces, Farouk abdicated. The Cabinet proclaimed the seven-month-old Crown Prince as King Fuad II. When the new rulers raided the palace, they found a thousand men's suits, as well as rare stamps, coins, jewels, and watches. They also stumbled upon a huge stash of pornography, some under Farouk's pillow. The king's take on the smut: "They were classical artworks."

The deposed queen now had to contemplate Farouk's powerful, hairy wrists in exile—first on Capri, later in a thirty-room villa replete with eight servants in the Alban Hills outside Rome. Farouk and Narriman's lives were spent at the casinos, racetracks, and European grand hotels; at the opera, Farouk accompanied the orchestra by banging his silverware. Other times they went their own ways, driving his and hers Mercedes; Narriman hung out with fellow teenaged girls, while her husband stepped out with a French blonde or an Italian brunette.

No longer a vivacious spirit, no longer blinded by the bling, Narriman turned her back on her marriage; accompanied by her mother and Jou-Jou, her pet poodle, she boarded a plane to Switzerland. Farouk, who blamed his mother-in-law for the breakdown of his marriage, retained custody of their son, as he did of his three daughters, Princess Ferial, Princess Fadia, and Princess Fawzia. To her great sorrow, Narriman was seldom allowed visitation. When Egypt became a republic, their son Ahmed lost his title. In Geneva, Narriman let it be known she was returning to Egypt and filing for divorce; she received no alimony. After hearing the news, Farouk visited Rome's Club Boite Pigalle, where he sat at his usual table, one furnished with a bottle of mineral water in a champagne bucket, and kept a 2:00 a.m. rendezvous with a blonde.

In 1954, Narriman married an Alexandria surgeon, Dr. Adham al-Naqu, and had a son, Akram. The marriage floundered; in 1967, she wed another physician, Ismail Fahmi. Her final years were spent in Heliopolis, where she died from a brain hemorrhage at seventy-one.

Despite repeated requests, Narriman only granted one interview, in which the journalist was unfortunately only interested in her first husband. The former queen's response, "We have spoken so much about King Farouk. What about Narriman?" She also refused to write her memoir; had she done so, the world would have had an intimate account from the contemporary Cleopatra.

CHAPTER 26

Who Shot J.R.?

—— 1936 ——

*D*ynasty, the 1980s soap opera, reflected the glitz and greed of an oil-rich family from Denver. Catherine Oxenberg, who played the role of Amanda Carrington in *Dynasty*, is a real-life princess. She hails from a nonfictional European dynasty that makes the Carringtons seem like the Waltons.

Catherine's grandfather, Prince Paul of Yugoslavia, while a student at Oxford, was friends with the Duke of Kent, his future brother-in-law; also with the Duke of York, later King George VI, who served as his best man when he married Princess Olga of Greece and Denmark. Along with his studies, Paul indulged in his hobby of acquiring canvases bearing signatures such as Titian, Monet, and van Gogh.

After the Italian dictator, Benito Mussolini, orchestrated the assassination of Paul's first cousin, King Alexander I, in Marseilles, France, the prince served as regent for Peter, King Alexander's eleven-year-old son. Paul erected the Palladian-style White Palace where his youngest and only daughter, Jelisaveta Karađjorđjević, known as Princess Elizabeth of Yugoslavia, was born.

World War II proved the Regent's version of Sophie's choice: Hitler summoned Paul to Berchtesgaden, and during a five-hour meeting, stated that unless the prince signed the Tripartite Pact, a non-aggression pact with Germany, the Nazis would invade Yugoslavia. A damning photograph showed Jelisaveta's parents, elegantly attired, lunching with the Goebbels family. Reluctantly, Prince Paul acquiesced.

Infuriated, the Serbians took to the streets shouting, "Better a grave than a slave!" Peering from the windows of the White Palace, the four-year-old Princess saw tanks and a frenzied mob. Within two weeks, a British-backed coup ended the rule of the regent. Branded a war criminal, Paul's sentence was incarceration in Kenya; the family had four hours to ready themselves for exile. To distract Jelisaveta, her brother read her a story, giving her nurse time to pack. En route, the Karadjordjevićs were permitted a stopover in Athens, where they had a brief respite with maternal grandmother Grand Duchess Elena Vladimirovna of Russia. The reunion was bittersweet since Elena was cold toward her son-in-law, whom she felt had delivered his family and country into the abyss. As Jelisaveta later stated, "I've never been in therapy, but I probably should have—it was all so dramatic and frightening."

The African incarceration was bleak for Jelisaveta; her brothers were in boarding school, and her mother was often in Greece or England, leaving her alone with her deeply depressed father. For three years, the Karadjordjevićs lived in the dilapidated house of the recently murdered Lord Errol. In 1943, General Smut allowed the family to move to the Cape, and Jelisaveta found herself in the novel situation of attending school. At age ten, the Princess struck a classmate for taunting her by saying that her father had been friends with Hitler. Another child, after bullying her for the same reason, held Jelisaveta's head underwater in a swimming pool. In her new locale, the princess remained "dislocated," "I remember thinking if I shut my eyes long enough and tight enough, and walk around a tree, I'll open them and be back home."

After the war, Marshal Tito's communist regime stripped the Karadjordjevićs of their citizenship, forbade them from ever returning to Yugoslavia, and confiscated the White Palace and other real estate holdings worth $2 billion in contemporary currency. The princess without a country later stated, "I didn't represent anything. I had this

stupid name...Who was I?" Four years later, when King George VI and
Queen Elizabeth visited South Africa, over official objections, the royals
showed support for their friend that lessened the family's social pariah
status. At age thirteen, Jelisaveta's parents enrolled her at Tudor Hall,
a "horrible boarding school" in England. The child tried to deflect her
pedigreed background by dropping her title of princess and traded
Jelisaveta for Elizabeth, Karađorđević for George.

In 1949, upon Paul's release, the family moved to Paris. There, the
Karađorđevićs once again became a lightning rod for tragedy; while
a student at Oxford, Nicholas died in a car crash. He had been her
favorite brother, and Jelisaveta was further grief-stricken when her
grandmother and her aunt passed away soon afterwards. She mournfully
recalled, "There was a deep feeling of gloom and doom in our home. No
music was played, and for three years only black was worn. I had no social
life, and in fact I think I had no friends. The future looked bleak." As a
respite, she wanted to attend Oxford, but her father refused. Instead,
she remained in Paris and studied piano and art history, "neither with
much enthusiasm," and grew more and more depressed. Despondent,
Jelisaveta stated, "I was nobody, and nothing. I didn't belong anywhere
and was burdened with a stupid, antiquated title. Every morning when
I woke up, I dreaded having to see and live through another day." The
princess felt she was "headed for the nuthouse."

During a ski trip, Jelisaveta met Howard Oxenberg, seventeen years
her senior, with whom she shared few commonalities: he was American,
Jewish, and a dress manufacturer. They married in 1961, and due to her
title, she associated with Andy Warhol and John F. Kennedy. Jelisaveta
remains close with her firstborn daughter, Catherine, and helped her
through the ordeal when granddaughter India became embroiled in
the NXIVM sex-slave cult. However, she is estranged from her second
child, Christina, who insists she is the love child of JFK. Christina refers
to her mother as "Genghis Khan," and her sister as "a veritable drooling
sinkhole of want"—the latter a jab at Catherine's nine-day marriage
to producer Robert Evans. Their relationship, one that the princess

described as a disaster, imploded after six years. Second husband Neil Balfour was an English banker with whom she had one son, Nicholas. In 1974, after actor Richard Burton's divorce from Elizabeth Taylor, the son of a coal miner and the princess announced their engagement. His alcoholism led to their breakup. Her take on Burton: "He was charming and entertaining but not when he's had an entire bottle of gin." Richard rebounded by remarrying his first Elizabeth. The princess's third husband, a former Peruvian prime minister, Manuel Ulloa Elias, was instrumental in returning a royal to her roots.

Through her connection to Manuel, in 1987, Jelisaveta obtained diplomatic status that allowed her to visit the country of her birth. She said of the occasion, "I felt like a ghost. No one knew I existed. I cried for twenty-four hours. And then we left." Her homeland remained a siren, and she returned, first for three days, and then for two months. What caused her great distress was how the communist regime had erased her family's history and the Serbs only knew her daughter from her *Dynasty* days. During a visit to a monastery at Studenica, a monk exclaimed, "You're Amanda's mother! Please write in the visitors' book that you're Amanda's mother!" The princess added to the anecdote, "The previous night's episode had been particularly raunchy."

Although her relationship with Manuel became "irrelevant," he provided her with her life's raison d'être: to restore the Karađorđević reputation. Her concerted campaign bore fruit; seventy years after Prince Paul's downfall, the Serbian Supreme Court ruled he had not been an enemy of state. Of her twenty-year long crusade, the Princess effused, "I cannot believe it. My father would have been over the moon. I am just sorry I cannot tell him myself." The royal who had lived in Africa, Paris, Greece, England, and the United States moved to an apartment in Belgrade, surrounded by family photographs and decorated with mementoes that bespoke a fascinating history. In 2004, Jelisaveta ran for the presidency of her native country, placing sixth of sixteen candidates.

Further vindication arrived when the Serbian government granted permission for Prince Paul, Princess Olga, and their son to be removed from their graves in Lausanne, Switzerland, for reburial in the land of their ancestors. Accompanied by Catherine and Nicholas, Jelisaveta watched as soldiers, dressed in medieval costumes of red tunics and chain mail, Karadjordjević swords at their hips, bore the coffins, draped in Serbian flags, to Topola, the small town where King Peter I had built a family mausoleum. After their interment in the royal crypt, Jelisaveta said, "After so many years of pain and alienation, I knew that now the three of them would be together for eternity in their home country."

Jelisaveta Karadjordjević, who has lived in far-flung capitals, who has had three husbands and three children, remains the enigmatic Yugoslavian princess. The royal with the storied past remains as mysterious as the one posed in the cliffhanger from season two of *Dallas*, the rival of *Dynasty*, "Who shot J.R.?"

CHAPTER 27
Lost Shangri-La

— 1940 —

Most people tread the prescribed path: marriage, children, job; in contrast, blue bloods oft lead lives that puts the prefix "extra" before the adjective "ordinary." Such was the case with the first American woman to be crowned a queen.

Sikkim, Asia's smallest kingdom, bordered by India, Tibet, Nepal, and China, is a mountainous nation situated 5,000 feet above sea level. The country's Chogyal (king), Palden Thondup Namgyal, had assumed power upon the 1964 death of his father, Sir Tashi Namgyal. The land on the rooftop of the world was to become home to a woman from a world away.

Hope was a New Yorker whose maternal family had arrived on the Mayflower. Her Irish father, John Cooke, a flight instructor, had abandoned his wife after his daughter's birth. At age two, Hope lost her mother when the Piper Cub airplane she was piloting crashed after takeoff. Her mother's parents, Winchester and Helen Noyes, took Hope to a Manhattan apartment where they deposited her with a nanny while they lived across the hall. They disapproved of their daughter's marriage and refused to answer questions regarding her death, one they felt might have been intentional. Her grandfather's main interaction with her was, after his nightcap, to have the five-year-old Hope recite Winston Churchill's speech, "We Shall Fight Them on the Beaches." Her Scottish governess beat the child with a coat hanger when she did not remember the words to the Lord's Prayer and tied her hands to the bedposts to prevent masturbation. When Hope requested a pair of ankle socks, the governess told her that "only nouveaux riches and Jews wore them." Vacations were spent at the Noyes's summer home in Seal Harbor, Maine; on the trip, her grandmother carried stacks of Bergdorf Goodman hatboxes and caged canaries. Helen sent her to dance classes at the Colony Club, where Hope yearned "for the floor to swallow me up." Parents with an eye to prestige wanted their daughters to dance with Arthur MacArthur, the general's son. Her grandfather passed away when she was twelve, followed by his wife, three years later. Her aunt and uncle, Mary and Selden Chapin, became her guardians; as he was the American ambassador to Iran, Hope attended high school in the Middle East.

At Sarah Lawrence College, Hope majored in Asian studies and immersed herself in Eastern mysticism. In her late teens, she toured India with her aunt and became fascinated with the Himalayas. She gushed over her travels, "I've never been so happy...India! My heart explodes...The East is my home...I must stay near India somehow..." She returned on her own, and in the lounge of the Windermere Hotel in Darjeeling, eighteen-year-old Hope met the recently widowed thirty-six-year-old Crown Prince of Sikkim. Despite their age difference and the fact they hailed from vastly different worlds, they shared a spiritual bond. As the future queen recalled, "The second time we met... he proposed to me...I said, 'yes yes yes...' I just fell in love with his sad eyes." One commonality other than wretched childhoods was Hope felt she had lived in Sikkim in a previous life, while Palden was believed to be the reincarnation of an earlier holy Buddhist. Two years later, they announced their engagement. In a nod to her name, she had hope that in her Oriental palace she would be able to divest herself of the ghosts of yesteryear. Palden was pleased he had found a mother for his three children. The government of India (that controlled the kingdom of Sikkim as its protectorate) disapproved of the interfaith union between a Buddhist and an Episcopalian, an Asian and a Caucasian. Palden's sister,

Princess Pema Tsedeun Yapshi Pheunkhang Lacham Kusho (known as Coocoola), was likewise not a fan. She told Hope how unfortunate it would be if anything were to break before her wedding, and then smashed a saucer, scattering its millet seeds, also a bad omen. As Sikkim astrologers warned that 1962 was not an auspicious year for a wedding, they delayed their marriage until the stars aligned.

Sikkim became the object of worldwide attention after news of the betrothal broke, and their storybook relationship shared headlines with the romance between Grace Kelly and Prince Rainier. Although Sikkim's snow-capped mountains were not as lucrative as Monaco's casinos, it provided a setting where lions and pandas roamed. The royal wedding took place in 1963 in a Buddhist monastery in Gangtok, the capital of Sikkim. The bride's dress was a wraparound, white brocade silk held in at the waist by a gold belt, from which dangled a small dagger. After drinking tea laced with yak butter, a red-robed lama in a scarlet-colored hat prayed for the blessings of the snow lions and Sikkimese deities. To ward off evil spirits, Hope pressed her hand into a piece of dough. To seal the marriage contract, the royal couple exchanged twelve-foot-long white silk scarves that they wrapped around each other's necks. The guests reflected the differences between the Chogyal and the Gyalmo: Men in top hats and black suits mingled with those wearing fur-flapped caps and knee-length yak skin boots. Richly robed maharajas stood alongside twelve foreign dignitaries, including John F. Kennedy's ambassador to India, John Kenneth Galbraith. Outside the chapel were presents from Tiffany's and gifts of rank-smelling tiger and leopard skins. The world press covered the exotic nuptial.

The Gyalmo (Queen Consort) cared deeply for her stepchildren, her son, Prince Palden, and her daughter, Princess Hope Leezum, and vowed, "These children will be happy. The wheel of unhappiness that both my husband and I grew up on will not go to this generation." The family's palace in Gangtok (which was provided with fifteen servants) reflected the royal couple's divergent backgrounds: Ancient Buddhist chants played along with Beatles records. Palden determined to bring the twentieth century to his mountain kingdom; under his rule, the literacy rate increased and the per capita income rose by a third to $100 a year, twice as high as neighboring Nepal. Chogyal promised to banish disease and poverty and to "make Sikkim a paradise on earth." The Gyalmo worked to promote Sikkim's cottage industries and arranged for her adopted country's rugs to be sold in the New York department store Lord & Taylor. Having finally found happiness, in her 1980 autobiography, *Time Change*, Hope wrote, "The mountains give me such a secure feeling. I don't feel vulnerable here."

An enlightened ruler, Palden nevertheless proved far from an ideal husband. A heavy drinker, he was prone to temper tantrums and did not let his marriage vows stand in the way of his affair with a married Belgian woman. When Hope was pregnant, he flew to visit his mistress. During a fight, the king tossed Hope's record player—on which his wife endlessly played Joan Baez—out the palace window.

Marital tensions increased as the political situation worsened. India was bent on annexing Sikkim, and Communist-controlled Tibet proved an ever-encroaching danger. While Prime Minister Jawaharlal Nehru had allowed Sikkim to retain autonomy, Indira Gandhi was dedicated to depriving it of any semblance of independence. Feeling like one of her grandmother's caged canaries, Hope turned to whiskey and Valium. On one of her annual trips to New York, she embarked on an affair with a man she had known in her teens.

Tensions between China and India made Sikkim a political pawn; demonstrators burned a picture of the Chogyal and Gyalmo in the public square. An article in *Newsweek* called Hope a "Himalayan Marie Antoinette." The pivotal moment for the mountain kingdom arrived when India invaded Sikkim, defeated the 400 Royal Sikkim Guards, and placed the king on house arrest in the palace. In 1975, a ruling deposed the Chogyal and abolished the 333-year-old monarchy. Hope fled to the States, along with her two children and two stepchildren. She said of her final farewell to her husband, "I embrace Chogyal a final time, and the children touch their foreheads to his."

Upon her arrival in Manhattan, Hope wore a short dress for the first time in eleven years, to the embarrassment of her children, who had never seen her legs. Guilty over abandoning her husband, she ended her affair. She wrote to Palden, though he was not permitted to communicate with her for the first six months. After that, authorities allowed her letters, though they opened them before delivery. When reporters questioned her over a reunion with her husband, Hope replied that Palden, although divested of his throne, would never abandon his country, as he remained the religious leader of his people. A pressing problem was Hope had relinquished her American citizenship— something she needed to do to wear the crown of Sikkim—and was in her home country on borrowed time. To her immense relief, President Ford signed a private bill granting Mrs. Namgyal and her children permanent resident status.

Hope obtained a separation in 1978 and an uncontested divorce in 1980. The former queen's second husband was Michael Wallace, a history professor specializing in criminal justice at John Jay College; their home was an 1878 house on the periphery of Brooklyn Heights. Determined not to be Lot's wife, who transformed to a pillar of salt upon looking back on Sodom, Hope closed her chapter on her lost Shangri-la.

♔

CHAPTER 28

Fractured Fairy Tale

— 1947 —

Alexandre Dumas fils wrote, "The chains of marriage are so heavy that it takes two to bear them, and sometimes three." Infidelity has long shadowed wedding vows, and when the love triangle involves a future king, carnivorous tabloids descend into a feeding frenzy.

Traditionally, the only association of the name Camilla has been with Dumas fils's novel, *La Dame aux Camélias* ("The Lady of the Camellias"), in which the protagonist-courtesan donned a red camellia as a sign to illustrate she was on her cycle, and a white one to signify she was open for business. The contemporary tie-in with the flower is the woman who caused a whirlwind in the House of Windsor. Camilla (Milla), sister to Mark and Annabel, was the eldest child of Major Bruce Shand, a wine merchant, and mother Rosalind Cubitt, and she was granddaughter of the third baron of Ashcombe. The eighteenth-century family home was an *Architectural Digest*-worthy manor nestled in the English countryside, surrounded by stately manners and ancient abbeys. The estate included a tennis court, swimming pool, and a Victorian-styled greenhouse; Camilla remembers it as "perfect in every way." French and Swiss finishing schools equipped Ms. Shand with the skills required of a wealthy British wife: care of husband, children, and dogs, and ability to maneuver the ski slopes of Gstaad. After graduation, Camilla knew how to fence and possessed a £500,000 inheritance, compliments of the Cubitts, who had developed Belgravia, a pricey London zip code.

In the 1970s, the world's most eligible bachelor was Charles Philip Arthur George, the Prince of Wales. President Richard M. Nixon, playing matchmaker in the hope of hooking the future king for his daughter Tricia, sat them beside each other at a White House dinner. The heir refused the bait, declaring the First Daughter "artificial and plastic." Charles met the one he felt was his destiny at a 1970 polo match in Windsor Great Park; an encounter that ended the possibility of Camilla's membership in *The Real Housewives of London*. Her singular pick-up line, "My great-grandmother and your great-grandfather were lovers. So how about it?" The brazen remark referred to their randy relatives: Alice Keppel had been the mistress of King Edward VII. The bawdy rumor appealed to the prince, as did their commonalities of bloodsports (such as the foxhunt), architecture, and tweed. Cupid-pierced Charles described Camilla as a "breath of fresh air."

The couple embarked on an affair, and had the Prince of Wales popped the question, the paparazzi would have lost the crown jewel of sensationalism. Instead, he allowed himself to be swayed by his mum; Queen Elizabeth was not amused her son was dating a girl who had been around the romantic block and put pressure on Charles to wed a virginal princess-bride. Elizabeth felt her son deserved the finest as he had been born in Buckingham Palace, had been baptized with water from the River Jordan by the Archbishop of Canterbury, and wore shoes fashioned from eighteenth-century reindeer skins. A twentieth-century Prince Hamlet, he was torn between heart and duty; and in a move orchestrated by his uncle Lord Mountbatten to separate the lovers, he joined the Royal Navy for an eight-month stint in the West Indies.

Not willing to follow in "Granny" Alice's footsteps as royal mistress, Camilla set her sights on Andrew Parker Bowles, whom she had met at her 1965 debutante ball. They had dated for a few years even though Andrew slept around on occasion with her friends. Torn between the two men she loved, she chose the one who offered commitment and wed Andrew in 1973; together, they had children Laura and Tom (Prince Charles is Tom's godfather). The price of prevarication was Charles lost the woman he adored; devastated, he wrote to his uncle, "I suppose the feeling of emptiness will pass eventually." Priceless Ming vases shatter as easily as those of common clay.

Past age thirty, Charles, feeling obliged to have a wife and children, felt the shy, teenaged Lady Diana Spencer fit the bill. Diana's opening gambit was far different from Camilla's suggestive innuendo; "You looked so sad when you walked up the aisle at the funeral [that of his assassinated uncle]. You're lonely, you should be with someone to look after you." Despite their twelve-year age difference, the fact that they had only met a handful of times, and the verity that his heart resided with Camilla, Charles proposed. Trouble in paradise began even before the tying of the Windsor knot; Diana discovered a bracelet Charles had bought for Camilla engraved with the initials "GF" for Gladys and Fred, the nicknames they had conferred upon one another based on the *Goon Show*. Post-honeymoon, on an official dinner for President Sadat of Egypt aboard the royal yacht *Britannia*, Charles sported new gold cufflinks that bore two interlocking Cs, the reason Diana would never wear Chanel.

The thorn in the rose of the royal marriage remained the shadowy third. Rather than accepting she had the tiara and the title, Diana would not share her husband. Andrew Morton's 2017 biography *Diana: Her True Story* revealed that when the cat was away, the mice played; Camilla spent nights at their Windsor estate in Highgrove when wifey was out of town. What made matters worse, in 1989, Diana's private humiliation became public through the "Tampax Tapes." An eleven-minute phone conversation between Camilla and Charles leaked in which Charles confided he wished to be reincarnated as his lover's tampon. After that tidbit, they discussed the venue for their next rendezvous. "Tampongate," conducted in an intimate tone, proved the Prince of Wales knew what love meant. No doubt the Queen resorted to a liberal supply of smelling salts.

If Diana harbored any hope that the birth of William would mark the close of the adultery chapter, her illusions shattered when, despite the sound of running bathroom tap water, she overheard Charles on the phone telling Camilla, "Whatever happens, I will always love you." Diana knew he was not merely talking to his mirror's reflection. Conjugal relations ended in 1986 after the Windsors returned from visiting King Juan Carlos of Spain; Charles, no longer bothering to keep his affair under wraps, took Camilla for a holiday in Turkey. Marital troubles took their toll, and Diana suffered from bulimia, depression, and suicide attempts. She explained her rancor, "There were three people in the marriage, so it was quite crowded." Diana dubbed her rival "the Rottweiler;" Camilla referred to Diana as "that ridiculous creature." Public opinion was firmly in Camp Diana: Mr. Blackwell, keeper of the annual worst-dressed lists, awarded Mrs. Parker Bowles the number eight spot of 2001 with the explanation that she "packs the stylistic punch of a Yorkshire pudding."

When the prince admitted on a BBC interview that he had committed adultery, it proved the death knell of the Parker Bowles marriage. The queen, tired of the soap opera of the war of the Windsors, agreed her son could also sever his battle-scarred union. The palace embarked on a public relations campaign to convince the public to go along with the Charles-Camilla relationship. The best laid plan of mice and princes went awry with the death of Diana in a Paris car accident, caused by her inebriated chauffeur. The outpouring of grief was equal to the rancor levied against the other woman, who many felt had contributed to the loss of their princess. Irate shoppers pelted Camilla with bread rolls in her local grocery store, and she became a prisoner in her own home. Of her time in the public pillory, Camilla recalled, "It was horrid. It was a deeply unpleasant time, and I wouldn't want to put my worst enemy through it." A sign in Highgrove embodied the prince's stoicism, "Be patient and endure." Time heals, or at least lessens grief, and Brits eventually gave a grudging acceptance to the woman who made a sad man a happy prince.

After thirty-four star-crossed years, decades that witnessed adultery, divorce, death, and risqué pillow talk, Camilla managed to pull off the coup Alice Keppel never managed: She wed her royal. The civil wedding at Guildhall (in which Prince William served as best man) transformed Camilla Parker Bowles into Her Royal Highness, the Duchess of Cornwall. The palace did not confer upon her the title of the Duchess of Wales as that had been Princess Diana's designation. Not so clear-cut is what Camilla's title will be when hubby assumes the throne. The Firm originally announced that instead of becoming Queen Camilla, she would be known as HRH The Princess Consort. However, in 2010, when asked the question, Charles responded, "That's, well... We'll see, won't we?" The juxtaposition of Charles's first and second nuptials was jarring. For the second go at wedlock, the crowd outside Guildhall was 20,000 instead of 600,000; the bride was fifty-seven, not twenty; and the lady of the hour wore a cream-colored suit and broad-brimmed hat, worlds away from Diana's extravaganza of a dress with a train that seemed to go on forever. The greatest contrast, however, was the joy that radiated from the middle-aged newlyweds. Post ceremony, instead of a carriage, the couple rode off in a Rolls Royce borrowed from the queen for the short trip to Windsor Castle. There, 800 high-profile guests awaited; among them was Andrew Parker Bowles, described as "the man who laid down his wife for his country." The Archbishop of Canterbury delivered a formal blessing. Actor Timothy West read an excerpt from Wordsworth's "Ode on Intimations of Immortality" with an apt line regarding "first affections." The groom's feeling of emptiness had finally passed in a fractured fairy tale.

♔

CHAPTER 29

Dawn

—— 1949 ——

The eighteenth-century Trevi Fountain spurts water from the statue of the god Oceanus, who commands a chariot drawn by sea horses. Legend holds that if you toss a coin in its water, you will once again visit Italy. One American teenager who cast her lira not only returned to the Eternal City, but did so as a principessa of a magical, medieval castle.

A mistress of reinvention, Rita was born in San Antonio and grew up in Austin, the daughter of C. Hunt Carpenter, the millionaire founder of the Shamrock Insurance Company, and his wife Reba, heiress to a cattle fortune. Rita's aspiration was to be a Musketeer.

The same day that DC Representative John Jenrette Jr., a Democrat from South Carolina, met Rita, he suggested that they sunbathe *au natural*. Their 1976 marriage came with landmines. The new Mrs. Jenrette felt like a Washington outsider with detractors branding her as "too flashy, too blonde, too outspoken." Another issue was John's serial infidelities and incessant drinking. The death knell of their relationship was Abscam, an FBI sting that led to John's jail term for bribery. Not one to be overshadowed, Rita posed topless for *Playboy* magazine wearing a feather boa while holding a brandy snifter. In the accompanying story, "The Liberation of a Congressional Wife," she revealed that one night, against the Corinthian column of the Capitol building, she and hubby had "made love on the marble steps that overlook the monuments and the city below." Her father called and asked, "Baby, you didn't take off

your clothes, did you?" to which Rita responded, "Well, it's not *Town &
Country*, Daddy." For a brief time, Rita dated Dan Aykroyd, who picked
her up in a car he had kept from *The Blues Brothers*. Her tell-all, *My
Capitol Secrets*, exposed Washington's "drop-your-clothes-at-the-door
orgies, cocaine parties, alcohol bashes, call girls and call boys."

Having sufficiently scandalized the political power players, Rita
moved to Los Angeles, where she capitalized on her notoriety to secure
a Hollywood career. She appeared on the television show *Fantasy Island*
as Nurse Heavenly, on an episode of *Lifestyles of the Rich and Famous*,
and in the film *Zombie Island Massacre*.

After the acting jobs dried up, Rita became a real estate broker
and arranged the $979 million sale of the General Motors building in
Manhattan to Donald Trump. He promptly installed his name in four-
foot-high gold letters above the front entrance.

In 2002, a friend told Rita about an Italian prince who planned to
build a hotel on one of his palatial properties. Skeptical, she replied,
"Oh, for heaven's sake! Everybody in New York calls themselves count
or prince or whatever—they're not." Notwithstanding, Rita flew to
Rome, where she met His Serene Highness Prince Nicolò Boncompagni
Ludovisi, a scion of a noble family that traced their roots to the Holy
Roman Empire. When Nicolò picked her up from the Grand Hotel Flora,
located in Ludovisi, the Roman district that bears his family's name, she
thought he was charming and down-to-earth. Of their romance, Rita
recalled, "He was a brilliant man in every way, and the least important
part about him was being a prince." Nicolò's take on meeting his soulmate
was, "It was probably written in the stars. I said, in the clumsiest way
one can imagine, 'Well, you are not ugly.' She's beautiful, of course, but
she's as beautiful inside. She's candid like a child but shrewd like a fox."

Enamored, Rita ditched her fiancé, and Nicolò separated from his second
wife, Princess Ludmilla of St. Petersburg. A psychic had told Rita that
she would marry a European, a prediction that came to pass in 2009
in a private chapel in Rome. Rita adored her husband's unconditional
acceptance. When someone in Rome expressed disapproval of the

prince marrying the *Playboy* pin-up, Nicolò responded, "Yes, I'm very
proud of it! I think it's great." An appreciative Rita stated, "Now I have
someone who will stand up for me, with a whole thousand-year-lineage
behind him."

When Howard Carter first peered through the grate at the entrance
of King Tut's tomb, he stated, "I see wondrous things," the selfsame
words he would have used to describe the Casino dell'Aurora, built on the
site of Julius Caesar's former home where he canoodled with Cleopatra.
Erected as a hunting lodge in 1570, it was expanded to 32,000 square
feet resting on eighty-nine acres, replete with two elevators and nine
bathrooms. When asked how many rooms the estate held, Rita replied,
"Nicolò used to say, 'We don't count rooms.' It's at least fifty." The villa's
named derived from a 1618 fresco painted on the ceiling by Guercino
that depicted the goddess Aurora tossing flowers from her horse-drawn
chariot as she ushered in a new day. Other treasures of the five-story
property are a front lawn statue of Pan attributed to Michelangelo and
a marble trough that dates from the era of Hadrian. The magnificence
of the Ludovisi Gardens was such that André Le Nôtre, the designer of
the grounds in the palace of Versailles, pronounced them Rome's most
beautiful. The main staircase bears the workmanship of Carlo Maderno,
responsible for the façade of St. Peter's Basilica. Family portraits line the
walls, one of Pope Gregory XIII Bonacompagni, father of the Gregorian
calendar. The home holds a priceless treasure chest of relics such as a
door that once belonged to an ancient Venetian warship and a telescope
that Galileo Galilei had gifted to the Ludovisi family. A desk holds letters
written by popes and Marie Antoinette. The principessa described the
Bourbon queen as "hot to trot" based on some steamy statements.

The crown jewel of the Casino dell'Aurora is a Caravaggio painted
on the ceiling of a room that long-ago resident Cardinal del Monte used
as an alchemist's laboratory. The artist had created the fresco in his
early twenties, before he killed a man in a duel and had to flee Rome.
Underneath the eyes of the gods, Her Serene Highness practices yoga
in the company of her four Bichon Frise dogs—George Washington,

Henry James, M'Lord, and Gioia. The oil-on-plaster displays Jupiter, Neptune, and Pluto, their faces and naked bodies modeled on the artist's own. Gazing at the masterpiece, Rita gushed, "In-your-face sexuality. His penis [Neptune's] and everything else! He [the artist] was courageous. You're talking about post-Reformation, when they were still burning people at the stake!" She reminisced about the time she spied Caravaggio's ghost in a Tarzan-like loin cloth.

Over the centuries, the villa has attracted legendary figures: Galileo is believed to have peered at the stars through his telescope from an upstairs balcony. From the rooftop loggia, Henry James wrote that he enjoyed the sweeping views of Rome "against a sky of faded sapphire." Goethe was so enraptured by a statue of the goddess Juno that he had it replicated for his German home. Those who have strolled in the gardens include Tchaikovsky, Gogol, Hawthorne, and Goethe, as well as more contemporary visitors Annie Leibovitz and Bette Midler. Captivated by the villa's masterpiece, Madonna wrote in the guest book, "Thank you for showing us your erotic Caravaggio. I will dream about it." During a dinner party for Woody Allen, for whom Rita had once auditioned, she delivered the toast, "I didn't win an Oscar, but I won the Oscar in life—I met my Prince." On one occasion, when cultural heritage officials paid a call, Rita overheard them speaking in Italian, calling her "a crazy American." Versed in the language, the princess replied, "I'm not a crazy American. I'm a crazy Texan—and that's much worse."

In a nod to the admonition not to let too much light into the castle, as in traditional fairy tales, dark forces festered. While Nicolò considered his wife a blend of beauty and brains, his three sons (Francesco, Ignazio, and Bante, from his first marriage to Principessa Benedetta Maria Barberini Colonna di Sciarta) viewed her as someone who would eat her young. The prince said of his boys, "When they were small, you would've eaten them up. When they grew up, you sort of regret that you didn't." Bante referred to Rita as a gold digger; she countered that he was a "borderline personality" who had made a pass at her, a charge he denies. The brothers blamed their father's 2018 death on his widow, who they claimed allowed her husband to drink himself to death. Two of the sons were no-shows at Nicolò's funeral; Francesco did not attend because he was in jail. What irked Rita the most is Bante's claim that she is not a real princess—that she was not one of them. By way of rebuttal, Rita referenced the Almanach de Gotha, a directory of Europe's blue bloods. Opening the book to a photograph of her and Nicolò, she asserted, "And there we are."

Nicolò's will delineated that his wife could live in their marital home for the duration of her life; however, after numerous lawsuits by the princes, the Italian court ordered its sale. The asking price: $531 million; bidders: none. The lion's share of the listing was the $350 million Caravaggio. As Rita explained, "Let's say you're buying a Caravaggio with a house thrown in."

Distraction from the sordid mess presented itself with Rita's new love interest, restaurateur Nello Balan, namesake of the Manhattan hot spot, Nello's, known for its $275 tagliolini with butter and white truffle. An alchemist in her own fashion, the menu is something the principessa could well afford.

Rita can take heart in her tussle with her stepsons: the name Aurora is Latin for dawn.

CHAPTER 30

An Unexpected Life

— 1951 —

S ultan Shahrayar, enraged at his first wife's betrayal, married a virgin each night and had her beheaded in the morning so he would never again be deceived. To escape a similar fate, on her wedding night to the king, Scheherazade wove a fantastical tale that ended with a cliffhanger, and then led the story to a new point of suspense each night thereafter. A curious Shahrayar thus postponed her execution. After a thousand and one nights, the king fell in love, and they lived happily ever after. Scheherazade's stories, collectively known as *The Arabian Nights*, included "Aladdin and His Wonderful Lamp," "Ali Baba and the Seven Thieves," and "the Voyages of Sinbad the Sailor." Equally fantastic is the tale of a contemporary Persian princess.

Holding onto high school yearbooks might be a good idea as the photograph next to yours could be of a future celebrity. At least that was the case with Lisa Najeeb Halaby. Her mother, Doris, was of Swedish descent; her father, Najeeb, had Syrian roots. He earned a degree in law, and President Kennedy appointed him the CEO of the United States Civil Aviation Authority; he later became the chairman of Pan Am Airlines. Along with her younger siblings, Christian and Alexa, Lisa spent her childhood in affluent zip codes in California, New York, and Washington, DC, as well as on ski trips to Austria and Switzerland, vacations in Greece, and excursions to the south of France. The peripatetic lifestyle was difficult for Lisa; extremely shy, she always felt like an outsider. The fact that she wore Coke-bottle glasses and felt unable to live up to papa Najeeb's exacting standards worsened her self-esteem. Nevertheless, she admired her father and was incensed with a Washington newspaper column, "What is a Najeeb Elias Halaby: animal, vegetable, or mineral?" Of her childhood legacy, Lisa stated, "To the day I die, I won't feel adequate." Her education included a trio of elite schools: the National Cathedral School in Washington, DC, the Chapin School in New York, and the Concord Academy in Boston. The awkward duckling grew into a statuesque swan whose hobbies included skiing and traveling.

When Princeton first admitted women, Lisa enrolled as an undergraduate, but in her sophomore year dropped out and headed to Aspen, where she worked as a waitress to support her ski bum lifestyle. Several months later, she returned to the university and graduated with a BA in architecture and urban planning. Her career began with a position in Australia, followed by a job in an Iranian company. Lisa toyed with the idea of joining the Peace Corps or enrolling in a master's program in journalism at Columbia University; however, she ended up following in her father's ancestral footsteps in aviation by moving to the Middle East. In Amman, Lisa worked as an interior designer for ALIA, the Royal Jordanian Airline. Her residence was the InterContinental Hotel, where Lisa shocked employees by wearing her cut-off clothing and by greeting her businessman boyfriend with a passionate public embrace.

Najeeb oversaw the delivery of the company's first Boeing 747 jumbo jet, and he brought along his daughter for the official ceremony in which she met King Hussein. The royal took Lisa out for a lunch that lasted several hours, and for the next six weeks, they dined together every evening. Other dates involved watching Peter Sellers videos, riding on his motorcycle, and hanging out at his palace. They made an odd couple: Lisa was several inches taller, sixteen years younger, and an American Christian. Despite their differences, the king proposed to the beautiful blonde Princeton grad.

Although head-over-heels in love, Lisa harbored trepidation that at age twenty-six she would be marrying a palace dwelling playboy with three former wives; his first two marriages had ended in divorce, and his third wife, Alia, had perished in a helicopter crash. Tying the knot would entail becoming a stepmother to eight children, and security guards would be ever present. Hussein had survived several assassination attempts; at age eleven, he had witnessed the murder of his father, King Abdullah. Another impediment would be living in a country where wives walked several steps behind their husbands. Equally daunting, there would be great expectations laid upon her as the consort of Hussein, a Hashemite—a descendant of the prophet Muhammad. King Hussein, a persistent suitor, wooed her by moves such as crooning the Abba lyric, "Take a chance on me." Eighteen days later, Lisa accepted his proposal, and the world viewed her as his future trophy queen.

In 1978, Lisa Halaby wed Hussein bin Talal in an understated ceremony in Zahran Palace, the residence of the king's mother. The bride wore a simple white silk wedding gown by Christian Dior, and her diamond bracelet and diamond earrings sparkled. Noor was the only woman present, as dictated by Koranic law. In their wedding photograph, the couple sits on a damask settee inlaid with mother-of-pearl, flanked by King Hussein's brothers. In contrast, the reception was lavish and included 500 guests who called out *"Mabrouk"* (congratulations). One of the well-wishers was Doris, recently separated from Najeeb—Lisa had begged them to separate a year earlier due to marital tensions. Committed to her new role, Lisa instructed her mother to call her Noor. For the lavish affair, soft drinks were substituted for champagne, also in accordance with Islamic law. The royal couple cut their seventy-tier wedding cake with a golden Hashemite sword. At last on their own— except for their security detail—they drove off in the king's silver Mercedes 600 limousine to the accompaniment of cheers from a crowd of several hundred gathered at the palace gate. King Hussein and Queen Noor spent their honeymoon at the Red Sea resort of Aqaba, Jordan, and they also spent a few days in Scotland.

Just as legend holds King Nebuchadnezzar built the Hanging Gardens of Babylon in his desert kingdom for Queen Amytis, who missed the lush landscape of her homeland, Hussein created for his wife a palace ski lift, replete with artificial snow and an artificial slope. When Hussein returned home from his office at Basman Palace, they would go on spins on one of his BMW motorcycles. Queen Noor rode on the back, and they had helmet radios that allowed them to communicate.

In an era when Western women were fighting for equal rights, Lisa trod another path. She had traded the name Lisa for Noor al-Hussein (Light of Hussein), relinquished her American citizenship for a Jordanian one, and converted from the Protestant faith to Islam. The queen referred to her husband as "Your Majesty" and readily admitted that she adjusted her schedule and habits to suit the king's needs.

Nevertheless, Lisa was not solely a self-effacing royal figurehead, the Queen has championed several causes such as civil rights for women and an end to honor killings. She is staunchly pro-Palestinian, a trait shared with her Jordanian relatives, who refer to the 1948 birth of Israel as the "year of the catastrophe." Her fairy-tale mystique is catnip for cameras, and the press has covered her meetings with celebrities such as Nelson Mandela and Sting. President Carter has included Noor on the White House guest list, and she entertained Queen Elizabeth II and the Sultan of Brunei. An international jetsetter, Noor spends time in her other residences: a ten-acre estate on the Potomac, until its purchase by Dan Snyder, owner of the Washington Redskins, and at her home in Windsor, England. Early on in her marriage, Queen Noor learned to be wary of the press. When an American journalist asked whether she planned to have children, she replied, "If God wills." In response, *People Magazine* entitled an article, "A Blue-Jeaned American in Jordan Says of Her King, 'I'd Be Delighted to Have His Child.' " The couple had two sons, Hamzah, named for the prophet Mohammad's uncle, and Hashem, as well as daughters Iman and Raiyah; the couple raised their children in Bab al Salaam Palace, "the Door of Peace Palace." Their home included a menagerie of pets: a panther, a gazelle, and Jazz, a black Labrador, a gift from the Grand Duke of Luxembourg. In 2020, Princess Raiyah married famous author Roald Dahl's grandson in the

United Kingdom. In a nod to irony, the palace did not always live up to its name of the Door of Peace. Many Jordanians viewed the foreign-born consort as "the king's CIA wife" and were appalled when she posed for a magazine sitting astride one of her husband's Harley-Davidson motorcycles. Critics condemned her lavish spending and called her Jordan's Imelda Marcos. After Hussein forgot her birthday, she "picked up something I hoped would smash" and it crashed against a door. There were also rumors of Hussein's infidelities, one purported with Rana Najem, liaisons he vehemently denied. And outside the palace doors has hovered the ever-present violence of the Middle East.

In 1999, King Hussein passed away from lymphatic cancer, and his grief-stricken widow attended his funeral, although doing so flew in the face of tradition. His death made it certain there would be still less peace in the palace. A feud erupted between King Abdullah and Hamzah, and officials accused Hamzah of "attempting to destabilize Jordan's security." Hamzah released a video claiming he was under house (palace) arrest and maintaining his innocence. The queen, caught in the crossfire between her stepson Abdullah and her son Hamzah, issued a statement that her son was the victim of "wicked slander." Noor's consolation is her husband did not live long enough to witness the Cain and Abel in-fighting. Her decision to become Queen Noor is encapsulated in the title of her autobiography, *Leap of Faith: Memoirs of an Unexpected Life.*

CHAPTER 31

"Just Sarah"

— 1959 —

Tales that begin with the words "once upon a time" lead girls to believe they are princesses-in-waiting, that a handsome prince will whisk them off to a "happily ever after." Alas, with royal paramours in short supply, women must look elsewhere. Hence, when a duchess exposed the reality beyond fairy-tale enchantment, her revelations packed quite the punch.

If one is known by only one name, it is safe to assume the individual has attained major publicity stature: Cher, Madonna, Adele, Oprah, Barbie, and a British blue blood known as Fergie (birth name: Sarah). Burke's *Peerage* states the latter is a direct descendant of Charles II and his mistress, Lucy Walters. She was the second daughter of Susan and Major Ronald Ferguson, who raised Sarah and her older sister, Jane, in Dummer, a well-heeled hamlet southwest of London. At a local polo match, Sarah met Prince Andrew, the second son of Queen Elizabeth II. Sarah's father played the sport with Andrew's father, Prince Philip, on the grounds of Great Park at Windsor Castle, and served as the polo manager for his brother, Prince Charles. A further commonality: they could both trace their families back 400 years to their common ancestor, King James I. When Sarah was twelve, Susan announced she was moving to Argentina to live with her Latin lover, Héctor Barrantes. Sarah recalled, "I didn't want her to go, but I didn't want to upset her, so I told her I understood and then I ate." In 1975, while in Italy, Sarah received horrific news: Her mother Susan had been decapitated in a car accident in the Argentina pampas near her ranch where she raised polo ponies.

Ronald enrolled Sarah as a weekly boarder at Hurst Lodge School in Ascot, whose teachers and students remember her for her pranks, such as sliding down the broad stairway on a down-filled comforter and leading food fights with dinner rolls in the dining hall.

In 1982, Sarah fell for Paddy McNally, a wealthy widower twenty-two years her senior. Their relationship entailed fabulous vacations and ended after three years when Paddy did not take Sarah up on her ultimatum: Present her with a ring or she would bid him "cheerio."

Princess Diana arranged for her friend, Sarah, to meet her brother-in-law, Prince Andrew. The matchmaker royal added Sarah's name to the guest list for a house party the queen traditionally hosts at Windsor Castle during the week of the Royal Ascot. Seated next to one another, the playful prince tried to force Sarah to eat profiteroles—a chocolate stuffed pastry—over her objections that she was on a diet.

Andrew, a naval lieutenant, left for sea duty, and Sarah returned to the apartment she shared with her friend. Then flowers arrived, accompanied by cards from the prince. The royal upgraded their relationship when Andrew invited Sarah to be his guest at his family's New Year's Eve holiday at Sandringham. Subsequently, they were spotted holding hands in public. Romance rumors spread when Sarah and Diana went on a tour of Andrew's ship, the HMS *Brazen*, docked at the Thames River. Ten days later, after the *Brazen*'s departure, Sarah went skiing in Klosters with Charles and Diana; reporters followed on the scent of a palace romance. When asked if she were dating the prince, Sarah responded in the voice of a British soap opera character, "Cor blimey, darling, you must be joking." The couple secretly rendezvoused in Floors Castle, Scotland, where they had shared their first kiss, and on bended knee, Andrew popped the question. On their engagement day interview, the prince explained he had fallen for Sarah's red hair; his fiancée added, "And the good looks." With a custom ring that consisted of an oval-cut Burmese ruby surrounded by ten diamonds, Sarah moved into her own room in Buckingham Palace. They gushed that they were "over the moon with happiness."

The press could not get enough of the woman who had captured the heart of the world's most eligible bachelor, and they scrutinized every aspect of the freckle-faced, titian-haired, Rubenesque-figured future bride. Although Sarah handled the media frenzy far better than had the shy Diana, she resented the attention focused on her generous proportions. When Madame Tussaud's unveiled her wax figure, a photographer jumped across the barrier and wrapped a measuring tape around its hips. "Forty-two inches" was the pronouncement. Britain went into Fergie-frenzy, and her likeness stared back from T-shirts, wristwatches, and perfume.

The Windsors welcomed Sarah into their fold, relieved that the prince, dubbed "Randy Andy," had chosen an aristocratic girl as opposed to his previous relationship with Koo Stark, notorious for her soft-porn films. Buckingham Palace described the wedding as "essentially a family affair," a nod to English understatement as 1,800 guests received invitations to the Westminster Abbey ceremony, while the worldwide television audience was estimated at 500 million from fifty countries. Sarah wore an embroidered ivory silk wedding dress with a seventeen-foot train which had the letter "A" and "S" sewn into the fabric in silver beads, along with a twenty-foot veil. Miss Ferguson decided to include the promise to "obey," in contrast to Princess Diana, who was the first royal bride to drop the word. The queen gave the newlyweds, both twenty-six years of age, their titles: the Duke and Duchess of York.

To borrow from Ms. Austen, "it is a truth generally acknowledged that" when Sarah Ferguson entered the House of Windsor, she was not in possession of the book on palace etiquette. Living in the castle was not the fairy tale it appeared from the outside. Soon after the wedding bells pealed, the prince left for his job at the Royal Navy, leaving Sarah to fend for herself in a palace that enforced stringent protocol and stiff upper lips. She fretted that she had to spend her entire first pregnancy without her husband, who had only ten days of shore leave to bond with his baby, Princess Beatrice. After his departure, Sarah broke down in tears, only to be told, "Grow up and get a grip." Prince Charming also seemed less charmed by his bride than before the tying of the knot. While Andrew had liked her outfits before they were married, as her husband, he chastised her for wearing flimsy skirts that flew up in the presence of hundreds of photographers. The press also turned on the woman who had once been their media darling: After her weight increased, they pronounced her Frumpy Fergie and constantly compared her to Diana, her rail-thin sister-in-law.

Despite their obvious regard for one another and the arrival of their second daughter, Eugenie, the couple, no longer over the moon, separated. In 1992, an infamous tabloid photo surfaced of the Duchess, sans top, with Texas millionaire John Bryant sucking her toe at a villa near Saint-Tropez. When the scandal hit, Sarah was holidaying with her in-laws at Balmoral Castle. In her memoir, *My Story,* she wrote how excruciating it was to show up for breakfast as the unamused Queen perused headlines such as "Fergie in Conference With Her Financial Adviser." Her response may have been along the line of, "Cor blimey, darling, you must be joking," with a synonym replacing darling. Prince Philip never forgave "toegate." Fergie in flagrante cast the Windsors in the role of a dysfunctional family—the Simpsons in tiaras. A downcast Sarah (who epitomized the name of Andrew's ship) stated, "I'm just not flavor of month right now." The hoopla put the kibosh on a reconciliation, and the couple divorced in 1996. The Windsor clan stripped Fergie of the title "Her Royal Highness" as well as her twenty attendants, including six ladies-in-waiting. As the second son, Andrew technically subsisted on his military salary, which never paid more than $50,000 annually. The new financial reality was a wrecking-ball situation for Fergie, who explains she suffers from "overspending disease" and had accrued millions of dollars of debt. Her monetary woes led to the British version of Watergate.

In 2010, Sarah was in the eye of the storm of an undercover journalism exposé when an "international business tycoon" recorded her offering access to Prince Andrew—a trade envoy for Britain—in exchange for $820,000. The *News of the World* had orchestrated the sting, and to demonstrate even more how much of a royal pariah she was, Sarah did not receive an invitation to the 2011 wedding of William and Kate. To help lessen the slight, Sarah vacationed in Thailand. An emotional eater—she scarfs down Skittles—her weight ballooned to 220 pounds. The press referred to her as the Duchess of Pork; a headline stated, "82 Percent Rather Sleep With Goat Than Fergie."

A bop bag that keeps getting back up, Sarah refused to disappear. In a masterful move designed to both lose weight and earn money, she signed a deal with Weight Watchers that earned her $1.7 million a year. In the doghouse with the Queen, she turned for help to the queen across the pond. Oprah made Ferguson the subject of a six-part documentary, "Finding Sarah: From Royalty to the Real World."

Despite their divorce, Andrew and Sarah's romantic spark was never snuffed. The prince allowed her to live rent-free on the grounds of his residence, the Royal Lodge in Windsor Great Park. For her part, Sarah is standing by her man during his involvement in the Jeffrey Epstein sex scandal. Sarah stated, "We are the most contented divorced couple in the world."

Perhaps more revealing than the Oprah interview or her memoir is a moment that occurred during a Canadian interview. On that occasion, Sarah handed out her business card, where she had drawn a line through the title, "The Duchess of York," and replaced it—in red ink—with "Just Sarah."

👑

CHAPTER 32

England's Rose

—— 1961 ——

The British national anthem ends with the words, "Long to reign over us / God save the Queen." One princess never had the opportunity to sit on the throne, yet forever rules as an immortal icon.

In Greek mythology, Diana was the goddess of the hunt; ironically, she shared her name with the world's most hunted. The girl who would be queen began her storied life as Diana Frances Spencer in Park House, on the Queen's royal estate of Sandringham, Norfolk. Her father, Edward John Spencer, Viscount Althorp, was a descendant of King Henry VII; her mother, Frances Ruth Burke Roche, was the child of the fourth Baron Fermoy. Her parents were disappointed at the birth of a third daughter; they wanted a son to carry on the four-century-old Spencer name. Three years later, they rejoiced at the arrival of their son, Charles. As members of the upper English crust, play dates were with Prince Andrew and Prince Edward.

Blue blood and wealth were not armor against family troubles: After fourteen years of marriage, Frances was the "other woman" in wallpaper heir Peter Shand Kydd's divorce, which then led to her own. To add to the drama, Diana's maternal grandmother, Lady Fermoy, sided with her son-in-law. When the six-year-old Diana fell from a horse while staying with her mother, the court awarded custody of the siblings to the Viscount. Among her lifelong memories were the crunch of gravel as her mother left Althorp and later, the sound of her and her brother crying themselves to sleep.

Upon the 1975 passing of her grandfather, Charles became Viscount Althorp, while his three sisters received the title of Lady. The Spencers relocated to Althorp, the ancestral seat in Northamptonshire, situated on 1,500 acres of forest and meadows, a great house on whose walls hung paintings by old masters, with priceless antiques adorning the home. Two years later, her father married Raine, Countess of Dartmouth, the daughter of romantic novelist Barbara Cartland. His four children resented their stepmother and christened her "Acid Raine."

Diana's education ended at age sixteen at a finishing school in Switzerland where she learned how to ski. On her eighteenth birthday, equipped with family funds, Diana purchased a flat in London and went to work as an assistant at the Young England Kindergarten.

The heir to the British throne became interested in Diana in 1977 at a grouse shooting party; at the time, he was romantically involved with Lady Sarah, Diana's sister. When Sarah admitted she would not marry the prince "if he were the dustman or the King of England," Charles's response was that she had done something incredibly stupid. While Diana recalled her first impression of Charles was, "God, what a sad man," he waxed effusive about his initial encounter with her: "I remember thinking what a very jolly and amusing and attractive sixteen-year-old she was. I mean, great fun, and bouncy and full of life and everything." Three years later, they reconnected at a weekend barbeque at Philip de Pass's house in Sussex. After expressing empathy over the assassination of his uncle, Lord Mountbatten, Diana claimed Charles was all over her and followed her around like a puppy.

The press was hungry for any news of this preschool teacher, the love interest of the heir to the British throne. Reporters besieged the teenager who had been so shy she had only taken nonspeaking parts in school plays. On one occasion, surprised by photographers as she sat at the wheel of her red Mini Metro, she burst into tears. She stated, "I know it's just a job they have to do, but sometimes I do wish they wouldn't."

Thirteen dates later, Charles popped the question over a private dinner in his third-floor apartment in Buckingham Palace just before Diana departed for an Australian vacation. He stated, "I wanted to give her a chance to think about it—to think if it was all going to be too awful." Diana quickly interjected that she would never have entertained any doubts. The Prince of Wales sealed the deal with a twelve-carat Sri Lankan diamond in an engagement ring set off by fourteen white diamonds. Amidst the excitement, one unsettling incident sent off an alarm bell. Asked by a reporter if they were in love, Diana gushed, "Yes, of course we are." The prince responded, "Whatever love is." Diana said the remark traumatized her and increased her prenuptial jitters. Her sisters told her she could not back out as the souvenir tea towels were already on sale.

The 1981 marriage focused on the nineteen-year-old blushing bride, who wore a voluminous gown with puffy sleeves and a twenty-five-foot-long train. Hidden in its depths was a golden horseshoe studded with diamonds. The wedding took place at St. Paul's Cathedral in a scene that was an ode to pageantry. In attendance were Europe's crowned heads and dignitaries such as President Mitterrand of France, First Lady Nancy Reagan, and the King of Tonga. Along with the 2,700 guests, a television audience of 750 million watched from around the world. The Prince and Princess of Wales sailed off to their Mediterranean honeymoon aboard the royal yacht *Britannia*.

The couple's first child was Prince William, called "Wills," and their second was Prince Harry. Diana found her fashion niche, and her dazzling outfits added to her aura of glamor. On her first outing with Charles, she arrived in a décolleté black taffeta dress that caused the octogenarian Lady Diana Cooper to quip, "Wasn't that a mighty feast to set before the king?" The public's taste for the breathtaking princess proved insatiable. On a visit to Canada, there was an outbreak of "Di-mania;" in Norway, the country dubbed her "The Snow Princess;" and during a White House visit, the Princess electrified as she danced with John Travolta to the *Grease* song, "You're the One that I Want."

Although the princess captivated the public, her popularity cast her husband in a supporting role, one he found off-putting. After delivering a speech on a serious issue, Charles fumed when the news only reported on his wife's outfit. In addition, Diana captivated hearts when she crossed royal protocol with gestures such as kissing a child in a crowd. In contrast, the Prince of Wales, who seemed not to have a nonserious bone in his body, was perceived as aloof and eccentric. Their union proved the falsity of the saying "opposites attract." Charles loved horses, gardening, and architecture; Diana loved fashion, pop music, and dancing. Photographs began to appear that captured the couple with faces that mirrored masks of misery. A variation on the song from *Grease* seemed applicable: "You're the one I *don't* want."

Another reason the marriage turned unto an unhappily ever after was because Charles had resumed his affair with Camilla Parker Bowles, the woman with whom he shared the commonalities of age and interests. At a party, Diana confronted Camilla (whom she referred to as "the Rottweiler") about their affair. Camilla responded, "You've got all the men in the world falling in love with you. What more could you want?" Diana's answer: "I want my husband."

The fissure in the royal relationship became manifest on their 1992 trip to Europe and India, where a photograph showed a forlorn princess sitting alone in front of the Taj Mahal, a famed shrine to a husband's conjugal devotion. Visiting Korea soon after, the press dubbed the Prince and Princess of Wales "The Glums." The public release of a phone call between the princess and his mistress fanned the flames of marital tension. After Charles admitted to his adultery in a television interview, Diana, whose clothes were indicators of her emotional weathervane, wore what became known as her "revenge dress," a form-fitting, off-the-shoulder dress in black. The following year, in a nod to what's good for the prince is good for the princess, Diana appeared on a BBC episode to air her own grievances. Referencing the other woman, Diana stated, "There were three of us in this marriage, so it was a bit crowded." In 1996, the royal relationship formally ended when Queen Elizabeth II sanctioned the divorce, thus ending the War of Wales. Diana was no longer to be addressed as Her Royal Highness, though she kept the title of the Princess of Wales. As part of the settlement, she received $22.5 million plus an annual payment of $4,600,000 and kept her five-bedroom apartment in Kensington Palace.

Diana had often compared herself to another blond and glamorous icon, Marilyn Monroe. She related to the star as both were haunted and hunted. In a nod to tragic irony, the princess and the starlet both passed away at age thirty-six. Diana was in Paris with her boyfriend, Emad Mohammed-al-Fayed, nicknamed Dodi; they were staying in the City of Lights after cruising the Mediterranean on his father's yacht. In an attempt to outrace the paparazzi, Henri Paul, the chauffeur of their black Mercedes, crashed in the Pont de l'Alma tunnel. So great was the outcry at the death of the princess that many people forever remember the moment they learned of her tragic end in 1997.

Six weeks earlier, Elton John and Diana had consoled one another at the Milan funeral of their mutual friend, murder victim Gianni Versace. When the royal family asked Elton to perform as part of Diana's Westminster Abbey eulogy, he chose a song that had originally been a tribute for Marilyn. He altered its opening life from, "Goodbye, Norma Jean," to "Goodbye, England's rose."

CHAPTER 33

The Peacock Princess

— 1970 —

I f the Western world played "I Spy," no doubt it would register Disney princesses holding *Little Mermaid* lunchboxes, wearing *Cinderella* couture, sporting *Snow White* backpacks. Girls have long fantasized about an alternate reality with bragging rights to royal roots where they can hang out in a castle until the arrival of Prince Charming. The dark side of the fantasy appeared in the tale of a real-life Persian princess, testimony that a tiara is not a panacea for pain.

The woman who in appearance, ethnicity, and wealth could have served as the model for Princess Jasmine was Leila, though the similarities ended with their respective sultan fathers. The ruler of Agrabah was affable and beloved; his only flaw gullibility regarding his vizier, Jafar. In contrast, the Shah of Iran, Mohammad Reza Pahlavi II, was an absolute autocrat, known as "H.I.M.," short for "His Imperial Majesty." While he was the family's beloved patriarch, he was a dreaded dictator who used SAVAK, his secret police, to torture and murder dissidents. Shabana Farah Pahlavi, his third wife, was beautiful and accomplished, and the foreign press referred to her as the Jacqueline Kennedy of the Middle East. Their daughter Leila was the youngest sister of Crown Prince Reza, Prince Ali-Reza, and Princess Farahnaz. The baby's birth in the military hospital in Tehran was such an honor that it subsequently assumed her name. The year of Leila's birth coincided with the release of a Simon and Garfunkel album whose title could serve as a metaphor for her life, "Bridge Over Troubled Water."

The first couple of Iran brought Leila home, which in their case was the Niavaran Palace, featuring Persian carpets, mammoth chandeliers, and paintings by Chagall, Modigliani, and Calder. The vast compound made bunking with her sister unnecessary as Leila had the run of six rooms. On one wall hung a photograph of First Lady Rosalynn Carter and her daughter, Amy. President Carter was a firm supporter of the shah as his oil-rich kingdom was pro-America.

The Pahlavi princess enjoyed an enchanted childhood in which she lived in unimaginable splendor with her close-knit family. Even when the shah was in a palace meeting with a foreign head of state, Leila was always welcome to sit on his lap, even if doing so rumpled his $6,000 custom-made suits. While Princess Jasmine had her pet tiger, Rajah, Leila and her siblings had a private zoo on the grounds of the palace that included a lion, monkeys, deer, antelope, and an elephant from India, a present from Indira Gandhi.

A modern-day King Midas, the shah threw memorable parties. In 1971, to commemorate the 250th anniversary of the Peacock Throne (the ruling seat of one of the world's first empires), Mohammad and Farah hosted a gala for sixty million at Persepolis, the ancient seat of the Persian dynasty. For the occasion, the hostess with the mostest arranged for 165 chefs to arrive from Paris, and the menu consisted of Imperial Caspian caviar, partridge stuffed with foie gras, and truffles from Maxim's de Paris. Mohammad and Farah made quite the entrance; they arrived forty-five minutes late in their blue-and-white helicopter, piloted by the shah. Mohammad, in full military uniform awash with medals and gold braid, greeted his guests, switching easily from German to French and English to Persian. His shabana wore a green-and-white silk ball gown and long white gloves; the emeralds in her ten-pound crown were the size of golf balls, her diamonds only slightly smaller.

While the opulence of the ruling family might have awed the assembled dignitaries, the over-the-top conspicuous consumption infuriated Iran's communists and religious fundamentalists. In the late 1970s, the country's discontent with the ruling elite was evident: Tens of thousands of black-clad protestors led by mullahs marched down the streets of Tehran, shouting, "Marg bar shah!" "Death to the shah!" By the close of the decade, Iran was caught in the crosshairs of civil war. As the empress wrote in a letter, "The storm clouds are gathering;" in 1979, the storm clouds broke. The shah, gravely ill with leukemia, was desperate to find a safe haven.

The outbreak of the Iranian Revolution sounded the death knell of the Peacock Throne. Mohammad, accompanied by his wife, flew his personal Boeing 70 into exile in Egypt. Nine-year-old Leila, along with her grandmother and other family members, boarded a military jet bound for a Texan air force base to unite with eldest brother Reza, who was in training to be a pilot.

Whenever possible, they flew to visit their parents. Often, for security reasons, Mohammad and Farah had to take off in the middle of the night while their children slept. In a stopover in Panama, during a family reunion, Leila was so traumatized that if her parents left the room, she became hysterical. The Pahlavis were destined to live as royal refugees as the new Iranian government had ordered the execution of the shah and the shabana. HIM had become a king without a kingdom, yet he still possessed a king's ransom of wealth. Although the Pahlavis had left behind an art collection valued at three billion, jaw-dropping crown jewels, and opulent palaces, they had secured a fortune of hundreds of millions (some estimates place it at ten billion) in offshore accounts. Princess Leila was relieved their governess had brought along a photo album, her family frozen forever in images of the enchanted years.

After fleeing Iran, the Pahlavis embarked on a desperate odyssey for sanctuary; however, country after country rescinded their invitations under a barrage of threats from enraged Islamic radicals. Mohammad offered the government of the Bahamas $425 million to purchase Paradise Island; fearful of terrorist retaliation, they declined. The following year, the increasingly desperate family arrived in the United

States for treatment for Mohammad's cancer. In fury at the shah being received in the US, thirteen days later, militant Muslims invaded the US Embassy in Tehran, where they took hostages and demanded Pahlavi's extradition, as well as the return of the plundered wealth. Upon his release from the hospital, the Pahlavis left for Cairo where Mohammad passed away at age sixty. After his death, President Sadat granted the widow asylum and a residence in the Koubbeh palace; however, the assassination of Egyptian President Sadat destroyed this hope. Ultimately, with the shah's death, President Reagan offered sanctuary, and the family settled in Williamstown, Massachusetts, to be near Reza's college. In 1984, home was in upscale Greenwich Village, Connecticut.

The 1,001 Pahlavi tales were not yet at an end, however. Leila attended Brown University, where she studied literature, anthropology, and German philosophy, and the raven-haired beauty modeled for Valentino on the catwalks of Paris. However, never able to find a meaningful career, the princess spent her time hanging out in the fashionable haunts of Manhattan and London; she also spent time in Paris, where her mother lived in a lavish home overlooking the River Seine. With unlimited leisure and funds, the princess was a presence at ambassadorial parties, Swiss skiing trips, and Parisian dinners. In London, she frequented the Tramp, a nightclub favored by wealthy Middle Easterners. As part of the international jet set, she had friends with Ferraris and surnames that bespoke royal lineage.

Nevertheless, beneath the lavish lifestyle, the princess was desperately unhappy. She was unable to recover from the childhood trauma of her family's exodus from their homeland and their desperate quest for stability. Leila also never got over her feeling of being a stranger in a strange land. On one occasion, she stated, "There's one dream [that's] as scary as hell. I'm in the palace, and I'm not supposed to be there. If someone catches me, I could have my head cut off." Another permanent scar was the loss of her father and the final chapter of his once charmed life. A bust of Mohammad dominated her living room, and every year she made a pilgrimage to Cairo for his memorial service. Lonely, Leila never found her Aladdin.

The princess suffered from depression, mood swings, insomnia, anorexia, and bulimia. To blunt the edge of despair, she self-medicated with painkillers, antidepressants, and illegal drugs. In an attempt at regaining control of her life, Leila checked into rehabilitation clinics including the Priory, a London rehab for celebrities, which provided only temporary respite. Ever more reliant on opiates, Leila stole prescriptions from the desk of her doctor.

When in London, Leila stayed at the exclusive eighteenth-century Leonard Hotel, Marble Arch, in a £1,300-a-week suite. The manager said the princess was always unaccompanied and told staff she came "to chill out." Empress Farah, extremely anxious about her daughter, asked her friend Hourieh Dallas to check on Leila. When there was no answer from Room 15, the manager opened the door. Thirty-one-year-old Leila had died from an overdose of prescription drugs and cocaine, her body emaciated from years of anorexia and bulimia. In the room was an undated scrap of paper with some words of scribbled poetry. In the drawer of the nightstand was a photograph of her family, in which Leila is sitting on her father's lap watching television in their Tehran palace. On Farah Pahlavi's website is a tribute to the Peacock Princess:

> *In the garden*
> *By the roses,*
> *Is written*
> *"Please don't pick up the flowers"*
> *But...*
> *The wind doesn't know how to read*

CHAPTER 34

A Mirage

— 1974 —

A fantasy proved a royal woman's reality: She was a princess who married one of the richest rulers in the world. And yet she discovered that a royal tiara could dissolve into a crown of thorns.

A runaway princess-bride who created a tempest in a Middle Eastern teapot was Princess Haya Bint Al Hussein, born in Amman, the capital of Jordan. The family's residence was opposite the Basman Palace, built on the ruins of the ancient city of Philadelphia, which experienced its heyday at the time of Christ's birth. She was the daughter of the staunchly pro-Western King Hussein and his third wife, Queen Alia. The couple's first child was Princess Abir; the royal couple adopted her after her Palestinian parents, who had been living in a refugee camp, perished in a plane crash. Their only son was their youngest, Prince Ali.

At age two, Princess Haya lost her twenty-eight-year-old mother in a military helicopter that crashed in stormy weather as she was returning home after inspecting a hospital at Tafileh. King Hussein proved a loving father who encouraged Haya's independent streak and was always available to his eleven children, whom he shared with his four wives. From her earliest years, Princess Haya adored horses, and she used an ingenious ploy to obtain one of her own. Her convincing argument was if she owned one, she would name it Scandal, saying, "Daddy, every princess has a scandal, and if you want mine to come with four legs rather than two, you'd better buy it for me."

For secondary education, Haya boarded at Bryanston School in Bristol, then studied philosophy, politics, and economics at Oxford University; during her years abroad, she became fluent in five languages. After graduation, Haya became a professional show jumper and spent a decade training horses in Ireland and Germany. Less typically for an Arab princess, at age nineteen, Haya became the only female in Jordan licensed to drive trucks and regularly transported her horses across Europe in a custom tractor-trailer. In the year 2000, the princess became the first Arab woman to compete at the Olympic level when she represented Jordan at the equestrian event at the Sydney games and carried her country's flag in the opening ceremony. She served as the president of the International Federation for Equestrian Sports. Another groundbreaking role was Haya became the first Arab and the first woman to be a Goodwill Ambassador for the United Nations World Food Program.

Haya claimed marriage was not her priority and that she would wait "to meet a man who doesn't feel he has to mold me." Despite her claim, after the 1999 death of her beloved father, she was searching for a Middle Eastern man who held a position of power and would allow her to maintain her autonomy. While attending the World Equestrian Games at Jerez de la Frontera in Spain, Princess Haya met Sheikh Mohammed bin Rashid Al Maktoum, the ruler of Dubai (known as the Las Vegas of the Middle East) and vice president and prime minister of the United Arab Emirates. She said of the sheikh, with whom she had fallen head over heels, "It was wonderful to understand someone without the need for words."

Despite describing herself as educated and empowered, the Princess agreed to marry the polygamous powerhouse, thereby becoming his sixth and most "junior wife." Her explanation for accepting a multi-bigamous relationship was: "Falling in love can eclipse a lot of things. I went into this marriage with my eyes open, and certainly I'm very happy." Other factors may have been he penned poetry and possessed a fortune of $4.5 billion. Some of his trappings of wealth: a

530-foot yacht accommodating forty-eight guests and a staff of eighty-eight; Dardley Stud, a horse breeding farm in Suffolk, England; and a fifty-eight-room hunting estate in Scotland that had once belonged to diamond magnate Cecil Rhodes. The sheikh was happy to wed the quarter-century-younger princess, who came with sterling credentials as the daughter of King Hussein, the half-sister of King Abdullah II of Jordan, and a royal bloodline that made her a descendant of the Prophet. In contrast, Mohammed himself had been born in Dubai when it was a backwater sheikdom under British dominion.

The sheikh and the princess wed in a 2004 ceremony in Amman where the bride was resplendent in a white-and-gold embroidered gown and a sheer white veil, complemented by a necklace with an emerald pendant. The event was low-key in contrast to Mohammed's first marriage ceremony, which included one hundred camel races; his first wife has not since been photographed in forty years. Mohammed and his princess-bride became the It couple of the Middle East, regularly appearing at international social events. The *Emirates Woman* magazine wrote an entry entitled, "11 Moments Sheikh Mohammed and Princess Haya Were the Perfect Couple." The article chronicled their visits to Royal Ascot, Britain's most famous annual horse-racing event, where Mohammed, the Emir of Dubai, as well as owner of the prestigious racing stable Godolphin, is a regular. Unlike the sheikh's five other spouses, Princess Haya did not remain out of the public eye and was actively involved in humanitarian relief projects in Palestine, Haiti, and Liberia. In a *Tatler* interview, she shared that growing up, she had worn rose-tinted glasses and had been sheltered from the realities of the repression of Middle Eastern women but was now a fiery feminist. Always dressed in impeccable Western garb, in a photograph at an equestrian event, she is standing beside Queen Elizabeth II, with the British royal the only one wearing a headscarf. In an interview, Princess Haya spoke highly of her husband, whom she always referred to by his full title. "I've been brought up in a very privileged situation, and equally, I've been given all the chances by His Highness Sheikh Mohammed and by Dubai and the UAE to take the responsibility to help others, and it's an honor to be able to do it."

A busy life became even more so with the birth of her son, Sheikh Zayed, and her daughter, Sheikha Al Jalila. Haya lived with her children in her own lavish compound—all Mohammed's wives (along with his approximately thirty children) maintained their own households, but she was his only spouse to have visitation rights to Zabeel Palace, the massive, walled-off mansion in the center of Dubai. She told an interviewer, "His Highness feels very, very strongly about making sure that the children have a normal childhood, that they can enjoy themselves and have their privacy. Of course, they've got to learn about what they've got to do later in life as royals, but having that childhood and that normality is key to who they are; playing football, getting bruises, and eating ten pounds of dirt." Soon the children, rather than playing in dirt, would be buried in it. The custody case where the Sheikh and the princess battled over their son and daughter became the most infamous since the fight over Gloria Vanderbilt.

What led Haya to sever ties after fifteen years of marriage was her discovery of Mohammed's mistreatment of his daughters, Sheikha Shamsa and her younger sister, Sheika Latifa, with his Algerian wife. Both women had fled their kingdom in a bid for freedom only to be kidnapped and returned on the orders of their father. The sisters' gilded cage—a forty-room seaside villa near Zabeel Palace that maintained a staff of one hundred—was not adequate compensation for lives devoid of freedom.

Princess Haya once more removed her rose-colored glasses and fled with her children and an estimated $40 to $50 million—first to Germany, and then to London. Her bolthole is a $113 million mansion in ultra-exclusive Kensington Palace Gardens, where neighbors include Russian oligarchs, Indian steel magnates, and Saudi royals. She filed for divorce and sole custody; her attorney was Baroness Fiona Shackleton, who had represented Prince Charles, Prince Andrew, ex-Beatle Sir Paul McCartney, and Formula One heiress Petra Ecclestone in their divorces.

What also crawled out of the desert: Haya had embarked on a two-year affair with her similarly married British bodyguard, Russell Flowers, whom she lavished with gifts such as a $16,000 watch and a $66,000 vintage shotgun. She had also paid other bodyguards $1.6 million in hush money. Haya did not keep her promise to her father about limiting scandal to the four-footed. The exposure of the affair resulted in the end of her lover's four-year marriage and Mohammed subjecting her to a "campaign of fear and intimidation." The "sheikh scorned" published his romantic anguish in English and Arabic on his website, saying, "You let the reins of your horse go slack." The princess said she was terrified when a helicopter landed and the pilot told her he had come to take her to a remote desert prison. Mohammed divorced her without her knowledge on the twentieth anniversary of the death of her father. Her husband left a note in her bedroom, "We will take your son—your daughter is ours—your life is over." While the princess appeared each day of the trial—accompanied by two bodyguards—the sheikh was a no-show, even when he was in England. Instead, he visited the Tattersalls auction in Suffolk, where he paid $4.8 million for a horse. The court ruled in favor of Haya, who received $730 million, the largest divorce settlement in British history. No doubt the citizens of Dubai ducked for cover.

For the Jordanian Princess, the desert sands of Dubai, rather than bringing endless romantic Arabian nights at an oasis, were in the end merely a mirage.

CHAPTER 35

State of Grace

—— 1978 ——

I f one were to free-associate with the name "South Africa," images would appear of the horror of apartheid, the heroism of Nelson Mandela, and the music of Paul Simon's *Graceland*. A current litmus test of the country would likely conjure a South African woman who became the princess of a seaside principality that Somerset Maugham described as, "a sunny place for shady people."

On occasion, gold medal winners receive post-game laurels: Tommie Smith and John Carlos are immortalized in a sculpture, Mary Lou Retton graced a Wheaties box, and Caitlyn Jenner made a bid for the post of California's governor. Another athlete—in a variation on medieval alchemy—turned Olympian gold into another type of gold.

The future Serene Highness of Monaco, Charlene Lynette Wittstock, was the daughter of Lynette, a former swimming coach and competitive diver, and Michael, a salesman. The couple raised Charlene and her two younger brothers in Bulawayo, Rhodesia (now Zimbabwe) before relocating to Benoni, South Africa. Michael recalled Charlene as a fearless tomboy who had jumped off a tree with the aim of landing on a horse. In the attempt, she broke her arm in three places. He added, "She was not scared of anything."

A non-little mermaid (she is just shy of six feet), Charlene's passion was swimming, and after winning the national championship, she competed in the Sydney Olympic Games. Two years later, she garnered three World Cup gold medals and a silver medal in the women's 4 x 100-meter relay at the Commonwealth Games. She eyed the 2008 China Olympics as her swan song, but an injury ended her aspirations. Out of the water, Charlene worked as a teacher.

The first time the billionaire bachelor, Prince Albert II, laid eyes on Charlene was in 2000 when he presided over the Mare Nostrum, an international swimming meet in Monaco. While Botticelli's Venus had emerged naked from the sea, the South African swimmer emerged from the pool sheathed in spandex. Albert was taken with the blonde beauty, who bore a strong resemblance to his late mother, Princess Grace. The prince asked her out, a request Charlene said "was incredibly flattering." They bonded over their love of sports; Albert had been a member of his country's bobsled team in five Olympic seasons. The following morning, Charlene headed back to South Africa.

Five years later, following the death of Prince Rainier II, Charlene phoned Albert to offer her condolences, and they reconnected in Cape Town. Their first public appearance was a few months later at the Turin Winter Olympics. The paparazzi went into a feeding frenzy, with a photograph of the royal dubbed "the Party Prince" and his comely companion making international front-page headlines. Although shy with a tendency to stutter, Albert had kept company with a bevy of beauties such as Brooke Shields, Gwyneth Paltrow, Claudia Schiffer, and Naomi Campbell. Albert invited Charlene to move to his enchanted kingdom.

Monaco's ruling family, the Grimaldis, had started off as pirates whose stronghold was a Mediterranean fortress that remains the foundation of the country's royal palace. After the French Revolution, France took control over the rocky enclave. Sixty years later, Napoleon III returned it to the Grimaldis, although he kept eighty-five percent of the territory. In compensation for the acquisition, the French King gave Monaco's monarch, Charles III, four million francs that Charles used to build a casino on a hill he christened Monte Carlo. The gambling mecca drew the well-heeled from the French and Italian Rivieras, where gambling was illegal. However, Prince Rainier was the driving force behind transforming his less than one-square-mile realm (the world's smallest state after the Vatican) from a disreputable gambling den into a tax-free haven for the world's wealthy. Garages and luxury hotels hold Ferraris, Rolls-Royces, and Bentleys; Lady Moura, a 344-foot-long Saudi-owned yacht replete with a helicopter, dominates its small harbor.

Charlene lived in her own apartment in the rarified zip code, waiting for her indecisive prince to propose. Although once fearless enough to try to land on a horse from a tree, her situation at that point required another brand of courage. Ms. Wittstock was devoid of friends or family and without knowledge of French, a college degree, or a career; her only role was to appear at the side of the prince when summoned, where she smiled a lot and said very little. The idle rich of Monaco gossiped about the woman they disliked due to her middle-class upbringing, her foreign roots, and her Protestant religion. Charlene admitted to a reporter that since moving to Monaco, she had only made two friends, revealing, "It was sometimes overwhelming. I was trying too hard to please too many people and at times was at risk of losing my sense of myself." To add to Charlene's stress, news circulated that Albert had fathered son Alexandre with Nicole Coste, an Air France flight attendant from Togo, and a daughter, Jazmin Grace, with a California tourist, Tamara Rotolo. One Monaco resident admitted, "Rumor and malice are held up as a national sport."

Persistence paid off, and the prince presented Charlene with a three-carat pear-shaped diamond engagement ring. Her role as the new princess was daunting as she would be stepping into the shoes of the legendary Princess Grace. As news of their wedding circulated, a Brazilian woman came out of the proverbial woodwork, claiming she was the mother of Albert's daughter. She stated that she had traveled the world with the prince and that they had met with Russian president Vladimir Putin. What made this especially troublesome for Charlene— who had learned of the bombshell in Paris while being fitted for her wedding dress, which took the Giorgio Armani house over 2,500 hours to fashion and held 40,000 Swarovski crystals—was the math. If the baby was Albert's, conception would have taken place while he was involved with his fiancée. The media began circulating articles on the runaway bride, who had attempted to flee to the Nice airport with a one-way ticket to South Africa. The press reported that Monaco officials confiscated her passport and strong-armed her to continue with her marriage. The palace vehemently denied the salacious stories, claiming they had originated from jealousy aimed at spoiling a "happy event." The hoopla led French newspapers to revive the fabled thirteenth-century curse of the Grimaldis. The legend holds that the Genovese noble Francesco Grimaldi captured the Rock of Monaco. He had achieved his first conquest when, disguised as a monk, he had sought sanctuary and returned the favor by slaughtering his defenders. A further conquest was of a Flemish girl who, after Francesco ravished her, cursed him with the words, "Never will a Grimaldi find true happiness in marriage."

Charlene and Albert first said their "I dos" in a civil ceremony in the throne room of the medieval palace. While the devil wore Prada, the newly minted Serene Highness wore a powder blue blazer and silk trousers. After Philippe Narmino asked in French if Charlene would marry Albert, the groom's sister, Princess Stéphanie, raised her eyes to the ceiling art depicting the history of Alexander the Great, as if invoking his aid. When the bride responded, "*oui*," Stéphanie let out her breath. The following day, when Ms. Wittstock walked down the aisle, she had something old (a groom twenty years her senior) and something new (her designer gown), and the something blue could have been the bride. As she dabbed at her tears, the prince's expression displayed his displeasure. A spectator stated Her Serene Highness looked more like "Her Miserable Highness." Whether her crying jag was from emotion or trepidation, the ceremony continued with the exchange of eighteen-carat rings from the House of Cartier. Albert later toasted his bride, "Charlene, thank you for putting up—er—with my busy schedule, with my—uh—absences sometimes, with my—er, uh—inconsistencies and my idiosyncrasies."

Regardless of Charlene's psychological state, the three-day wedding—reportedly one with a cost estimated at $55 million—was an affair to remember. Couturier-clad guests encompassed forty heads of state, including the kings of Belgium, Sweden, and Spain and the presidents of Ireland, Iceland, and France. Proud papa Mike beamed about the event, effusing, "It feels like we've won the World Cup." The American rock band the Eagles belted out hits like "Hotel California." French chef extraordinaire Alain Ducasse provided the 650-person banquet. As an infusion of adorableness, seven flower girls were dressed in traditional Monegasque outfits. The extravaganza ended with a ball at Monaco's Opera Garnier, where European royalty wore splendid gowns and jaw-dropping jewels. For their honeymoon, the royals flew to South Africa, where they stayed at the $7,000-a-night Oyster Box Hotel in Durban.

In 2014, Charlene gave birth to twins: Prince Jacques Honoré and Princess Gabriella Thérèse Marie, young fashionistas who rock designer duds. In accordance with Monaco's law, Jacques is the Crown Prince of the 700-year-old House of Grimaldi, although his sister was the firstborn. Hopefully, the princess, who recently left a treatment center, will defy the ancient curse and will ultimately enjoy her royal role in a state of grace.

♛

CHAPTER 36

A Mermaid

— 1981 —

R oyal weddings are the stuff of which fairy tales are made, as well as media magnets for millions. As for the happily ever after, a contemporary royal has rewritten the traditional Disney trope.

The genesis of the saga that sent shock waves into an ancient regime a continent away began on the Hollywood set of the television soap opera *General Hospital*, where Emmy-award-winning lighting director Thomas Markle fell for makeup artist Doria Ragland. They raised their daughter, Rachel Meghan, in predominantly white Woodland Hills, Los Angeles; residents assumed the African American Doria was the young girl's nanny. Though Meghan's parents divorced when she was a child, both remained committed to her upbringing. A memorable accomplishment for the eleven-year-old occurred when she wrote to the then First Lady Hillary Clinton regarding a sexist television commercial for liquid detergent that carried the tagline, "Women all over America are fighting greasy pots and pans." In subsequent airings, due to her intervention, the word "people" replaced the word "women." At her all-girls private school, Immaculate Heart High, Meghan presciently starred in a production of *The Princess Bride*. Afternoons were spent on the set of the sitcom *Married with Children*, waiting for her dad to finish work.

At age eighteen, Meghan attended Northwestern University with a double major in international relations and theater; she was the first college graduate in her family. A feminist, she used the quotation, "It's time to focus less on glass slippers and more on glass ceilings."

Determined to break into acting, Meghan joined the cast of the television game show *Deal or No Deal*, where she carried a suitcase packed with cash (hers was number twenty-four) while wearing short dresses and sky-high stilettoes. She traded the suitcase in for a briefcase in her subsequent role as paralegal, then attorney Rachel Zane in the legal series *Suits*. For the production, Meghan moved to Toronto, where she shared her home with rescue dogs Guy and Bogart and her husband, film producer Trevor Engelson, when he visited from their second home in Los Angeles. The couple, who had wed on a Jamaican beach in 2011, ended their marriage two years later. The salve for her wound: "I was born and raised in Los Angeles, a California girl who lives by the ethos that most things can be cured with either yoga, the beach, or a few avocados."

The event that put Markle on the media radar transpired in 2016 when Prince Harry met Meghan. The matchmaker extraordinaire is speculated to have been a baron's daughter, Violet von Westenholz. While most blind dates make one grateful for therapy, Meghan's evening made her the love interest of HRH Harry, Prince Charles's younger son. The prince whisked Meghan away on a romantic getaway to Botswana, where they celebrated her thirty-sixth birthday under the African stars. After the media discovered that Meghan was wild about Harry and Harry was wild about her, the Internet ignited. Romantics were enthralled that an American woman had bagged a British prince; others sprinkled poison in the fairy dust. The British *Daily Mail* reported, "Harry's girl is (almost) straight outta Compton." Prince Philip, Harry's grandfather, cautioned him, "One steps out with actresses, one doesn't marry them." A royal rift ensued when Prince William told his brother that things "were moving too fast with this girl." The greatest vitriol came from Samantha Markle, who made a cottage industry of bashing her half-sister, such as in her book *The Diary of the Princess of Pushy's Sister*. On Twitter, Samantha referred to her stepsibling as "duchASS." Meghan's only preparation for her transition from Ms. to Duchess was her agility in wearing heels, acting experience, and carrying a hefty amount of cash.

Although Meghan gained unimaginable wealth, prestige, and privilege, in exchange she had to surrender her role on *Suits*, as well as her prerogatives of dressing to her own preferences and speaking her mind. Accordingly, she pulled the plug on her Twitter and Instagram accounts. Another casualty was her lifestyle website, Tig, the abbreviation for the red wine Tignanello. Meghan said the first time she tasted it, she got what the fuss was about the Italian wine. Tig became her code name for an *aha* moment: "The TIG is my nickname for me getting it. Not just wine, but everything." In her final post, she told her followers, "Don't ever forget your worth—as I've told you time and time again: You, my sweet friend, you are enough."

In 2018, the thousand-year-old St. George's Chapel brushed off centuries of tradition; Prince Charles walked Meghan down the aisle as both Hollywood and British royalty looked on. Except for Doria, Meghan had no other relatives in attendance. A gospel choir sang "Stand by Me," and the couple exited the church to the accompaniment of the civil rights anthem "This Little Light of Mine." The television audience of two billion tuned in to watch the latest forty-five-million-dollar episode of the world's most storied soap opera.

The Windsors, taken together with Prince William and Princess Kate, and the Duke and Duchess of Sussex, were dubbed the Fabulous Four and starred as Britain's power players. The public enthusiastically welcomed the 2019 birth of the couple's firstborn, Archibald Harrison Mountbatten-Windsor, "Archie." (Harry is also a nickname; his legal one: Henry Charles Albert David.) What prevented the family from living happily ever after in seventeenth-century Frogmore Cottage was that behind Meghan's megawatt smile lay a sea of misery. She claimed that her life was wretched because of in-laws who gave her the cold shoulder, not to mention constant vilification in the press.

What further chipped at her soul were the inevitable comparisons to Princess Kate, who never has a bad hair day or an excess pound.

Tabloids reported on Thomas Markle, who, bankrupt, had moved to Mexico, where he was always available for comment if he smelled the scent of money. Rumors abounded that the Duchess had been a bridezilla on steroids who had a temper tantrum when Queen Elizabeth had not allowed her to wear an emerald studded tiara, reduced Kate to tears, and bullied the palace staff. Accusations also flew that she had stolen Eugenie's wedding-day thunder with news she and Harry were expecting, as well as engaging in out-of-control spending while failing to assist her financially strapped father. Another faux paus: For a formal dinner in Fiji, Meghan wore earrings that had been a wedding present from Crown Prince Mohammed Bin Salman of Saudi Arabia, who three weeks earlier had approved the assassination of journalist Jamal Khashoggi. Harry was frantic the press would hound his wife as it had his mother. The situation showed there were some things that cannot be cured by yoga, the beach, or avocadoes.

The chill of the castle led to Harry and Meghan's TIG moment: Their lives as senior royals were no longer a deal. Britons spilled their collective tea upon learning of the Duke and Duchess of Sussex's decision to exit Britain, stage West, a move referred to as "Megxit." Comparisons arose likening the Duchess of Sussex to Wallis Simpson, the Duchess of Windsor, also an American divorcee who had removed a royal from his birthright. Madame Tussauds in London separated its wax figures of the duo from the rest of the Windsors.

After a stint in Canada, and then a stay in tycoon Tyler Perry's $18 million Los Angeles mansion, the couple purchased an 18,000-square-foot, $14.65 million home in Montecito, near Santa Barbara, California, whose celebrity neighbors include Ellen DeGeneres, Oprah Winfrey, and Gwyneth Paltrow. Pregnant with Lilibet Diana, rather than observing the Queen Mother's mantra of "Never complain, never explain," the Duke and Duchess were guests on Oprah. With an audience of 17.1 million, the couple levied a *"J'accuse!"* against the Windsors, dropping bombshells such as their failure to provide psychological support to a suicidal Meghan, and reporting that Princess Kate had actually reduced her to tears.

The most shocking segment was the Duchess's claim that a member of the royal household had expressed concern about whether their baby would be dark-skinned; Oprah responded, "Whoa." Despite the airing of the Windsor dirty laundry, the couple did not reveal who had made the comment (they later stated it was not the queen or Prince Philip). Prince William hotly denied the grenade his brother had lobbed, declaring, "We are very much not a racist family." The public exposé of the royal rupture severed the bond between the brothers. The segment proved controversial: Was Meghan more sinned against than sinner? Detractors cited the insensitivity of giving a warts-and-all show-and-tell while the ninety-nine-year-old Prince Philip was hospitalized. Another dagger aimed at the couple is in their quest to "finding freedom" (also the title of a 2020 biography of the Windsors), they made a deal with Netflix that earned an estimated $100 million that would never have been possible had Harry not been the British prince. A romantic note amidst the vitriol was when Meghan shared that her love story with Prince Harry was "greater than any fairy tale you've ever read."

In the interview, Meghan made a reference to Disney's *The Little Mermaid* who traded her tail for legs (and, by implication, what lies between them) as well as sacrificing her voice in order to be with the prince. Meghan made it clear she would no longer be silenced.

In 2019, Meghan helped edit an edition of *Vogue* in which she shared that erotica writer Anaïs Nin had inspired her to be different from Disney's Ariel: "I must be a mermaid...I have no fear of depths and a great fear of shallow living."

CHAPTER 37

Jewel in the Crown

— 1982 —

I f the Grimm brothers had championed morganatic marriages, Cinderella would still be sweeping cinders, Rapunzel would remain trapped in her tower, Snow White would yet slumber. Similarly, if the English monarchy had harkened to the matrimonial rule of yesteryear, a throne would not have beckoned for a coal miner's "daughter."

The British national anthem uses the adjectives "gracious" and "noble" to describe the queen, words that aptly applied to a woman not to the manor born. Carole and Michael Middleton met at British Airways where she worked as a flight attendant, he as a dispatcher. In 1984, the company transferred him to Amman, Jordan, where the Middletons, along with their daughters, Catherine Elizabeth (Kate) and Philippa (Pippa), lived for two and a half years. Their son, James, arrived upon their return. The couple shed their middle-class roots when they founded their Internet site, Party Pieces. Carole came up with the idea on Kate's fifth birthday; outfitting girls in princess pink proved so lucrative that the Middletons purchased a five-bedroom wisteria-covered brick house in Bucklebury, Berkshire, and a second in Chelsea, as well as skiing trips and private education becoming part of their lives.

Kate attended St. Andrews Preparatory School in West Berkshire, where at age eleven, she starred in the role of Eliza Doolittle in a production of *My Fair Lady*. A natural athlete, Kate broke a high jump record at prestigious Marlborough boarding school. After graduation,

Kate left for Florence to study art, but it was in Scotland where she had her rendezvous with royalty.

In 2001, the University of St. Andrews doubled as matchmaker when Prince William Arthur Philip Louis of Wales, third in line to the British throne, met Kate, a fellow art history major. William had an advantage in his field of study as the walls of his palaces display Vermeers, Rembrandts, and Turners. Initially, they shared a platonic friendship: Handsome, wealthy, and royal, the prince had his pick of dates, from princesses to porn stars. What made their relationship something more is when Kate modeled something less—a see-through black dress—for a 2002 charity fashion show at St. Andrews Bay Hotel. Sitting in the front row, complements of his 200-pound ticket, the prince suddenly viewed Ms. Middleton in a new light. He told his chum, "Wow, Fergus, Kate's hot!" Nine years later, the leave-nothing-to-the-imagination garment that bagged a billionaire went up for auction and sold for $125,884.

A 2004 photograph taken on a ski trip in Klosters, Switzerland, captured the couple against the backdrop of the snow-capped Alps. *The Sun*'s headline proclaimed, "FINALLY...WILLS gets a girl." In truth, they had each other for months. The lovers had shed dorm life for residence at Balgove House, an estate surrounded by two acres of wild grassland hidden behind a six-foot stone wall. Renovations included bombproof windows; unmarked police cars served as sentries. *The Sun*'s photograph launched thousands more, and Kate-sightings proved irresistible catnip.

Although educated, poised, and cultured, because of her pedestrian roots, Kate had detractors. Carole's great-grandfather had labored in a coal mine, one that belonged to the Bowles-Lyon family, whose descendants became British royalty. Feeling her background made her an unworthy love interest for the prince, William's friends mimicked the flight attendant phrase, "doors to manual," in reference to her mother's airline stewardess days. The upper crust scoffed at Carole, who had committed the royal faux pas of chewing gum in the presence of the queen. In the same vein, various media outlets derisively dubbed Kate "Middle-class Middleton." The press called Pippa and Kate "the wisteria sisters," as they were "highly decorative, terribly fragrant, and have a ferocious ability to climb."

Even more hurtful, in 2007, the prince, claiming he felt claustrophobic, broke up with Kate. Along with friends, he visited Mahiki, a Polynesian-themed club in Mayfair, where he jumped on a table yelling, "I'm free!" He also ran up an $18,000 bar bill in less than a week. Hounded to dish Windsor dirt, Kate remained mum, immune to the dollar signs journalists dangled. The woman scorned put on a brave face—along with a thigh-skimming minidress—and the paparazzi snapped pictures of her emerging from limousines and nightclubs looking knock-'em-dead gorgeous. As bachelor status wore thin, William resumed his relationship with Kate, although after years of dating, he still did not offer the four coveted words, "Will you marry me?" Will's failure to make her his future queen earned Middleton the nickname of "Waity Katie." The derogatory epithet became obsolete when Will whisked Kate away to Kenya, where they stayed at the 1,500-pounds-a-night, Masai-owned Il Ngwesi Lodge in the Mukogodo Hills. In Africa, William presented Kate with Princess Diana's sapphire and diamond ring. He said of his gift, "It's very special to me. As Kate's very special to me now, it was right to put the two together." The announcement resurrected royal romances that had gone from regal to rancid due to the Charles-Diana-Camilla triangle, Prince Andrew's divorce, Prince Harry's shenanigans. The bride-to-be was over the moon. William described himself as, "massively excited."

The 2011 day when Kate entered the Firm, receiving the title of Duchess of Cambridge, was as greatly anticipated as the day William's parents had cemented their alliance with each other and the Firm thirty years before. The magnificent gala was an over-the-top display of pageantry, romance, and outrageous hats. While most brides have the jitters, Kate's nerves were even more frazzled as she was tying the knot with an audience of 100 million. For those not in possession of the golden ticket in-person invitation, thousands lined the route of the royal procession as it wound its way to Westminster Abbey. Crowds congregated in front of Buckingham Palace to watch as the newlyweds kissed, twice, on the palace balcony. Shakespeare wrote, "A touch of nature makes the whole world kin," and the same holds true to a world event: People in Hong Kong wore Kate and William masks, Australians held bouquet-throwing competitions, crowned heads assembled in London. The bride dazzled in a dress that came with a price tag of $434,000; the "something borrowed" was the 1936 Cartier diamond tiara loaned by the Queen; the "something blue" was the color of her late mother-in-law's engagement ring. In a bid for privacy, after a wedding enacted in a gargantuan fish tank, the Duke and Duchess of Cambridge spent a ten-day honeymoon in the Indian Ocean paradise of Seychelles.

Two years later, the press went into a fresh frenzy with the news of the Duchess of Cambridge's pregnancy. The world was as fixated on the arrival of the royal baby as it would have been with the second coming. Hundreds of people camped outside St. Mary's Hospital in order to catch a glimpse of the new Windsor, Prince George Alexander Louis, and the proud parents. To mark the occasion, the king's Troupe Royal Horse artillery delivered a forty-one-gun salute. In 2015, Britain welcomed his sister, Princess Charlotte; to celebrate her arrival, famous landmarks such as the Tower of London and the Trafalgar Square fountains were awash in pink lights. Prince Louis came along in 2016, as genetically and financially blessed as his siblings. For each delivery, when the Duchess left the hospital, she looked as if she had stepped out of a photo op rather than undergone labor: auburn hair in lustrous waves, almost prepregnancy figure, feet encased in heels.

The Duchess, who must belong to some more evolved species, has hardly had a misstep since stepping onto the international stage. Nevertheless, since she had become a future queen and a member of the most headline-worthy family anywhere, scandal intruded. In 2012, the royal couple were vacationing in Luberon, Provence, where they stayed at Viscount Linley's secluded 640-acre nineteenth-century château. A hidden photographer using a long-range lens snapped a picture of Kate sunbathing topless on the terrace. The British press refused to run the image; however, not all publications were so scrupulous. An infuriated William condemned the action and took legal action. A judge ordered the French magazine, *Closer*, to pay 100,000 euros in damages. However, as the future queen and king of England, expectations of privacy are a luxury they cannot command.

The dust settled on scandal until 2019, when the Brit headlines ignited with the rumor of an affair between Prince William and the Marchioness of Cholmondeley, Rose Hanbury, allegedly conducted while his duchess suffered from a severe case of hyperemesis gravitas, an illness that beset her three pregnancies. Kate allegedly demanded Rose be "phased out" even though David Rocksavage, the Marquis of Cholmondeley, was a friend of William, and the couple had often gone on double dinner dates. Kate had no comment.

A river of ink followed in the wake of news of a feline fight between the Duchess of Cambridge and the Duchess of Sussex that supposedly ended the reign of the Fab Four (the two princes and their wives), thereby casting Meghan as a modern version of Yoko Ono.

Rising above the sordid, hurling all high jumps, the Duchess has traversed the road from Waity Katie to Kate the Great, the Windsors' jewel in the crown.

Damocles's Sword

When my editor approached me with the idea of writing a book on royal women, I harkened to my first memory of the queen, who stared out from Canadian postage stamps, coins, and bills, although Elizabeth II lived far afield from my Toronto home. In 1965, the principal of West Prep, my elementary school, summoned students and staff to the courtyard at the back of the building. With much ado, he lowered the Union Jack and hoisted the Canadian Maple Leaf. I had no idea why he had swapped one flag for another; the event only stayed in my mind as it was out of the ordinary to leave class. When I became a teacher in the 1980s, another wave of goodbye to the Windsors occurred when the students substituted "Oh, Canada" for "God Save the Queen."

Currently, while some Canadians still have an allegiance to the crown, others feel the country should follow the example of Barbados, which recently declared independence from its former colonial ruler. Popular opinion still varies as to whether there should be "Canex," severing the last of the royal strings. Dedicated Anglophiles cling to the crown as it offers pageantry and pomp, as well as a sense of tradition. On the other end of the spectrum, there is the belief that there is no longer a need for a ceremonial figurehead from across the ocean, especially as some Windsors are examples of royals behaving badly. Those of the latter mindset want native-born Canadians on the stamps and on the currency, with the honor deriving from accomplishment rather than a hereditary birthright. A step in this direction occurred in 2018, when Viola Desmond became the first woman other than a British queen to appear on a Canadian ten-dollar bill. Viola's ninety-year-old sister was present at the ceremony for the bill's unveiling, at which time she stated of the historic event, "It's unbelievable to think that my sister—a Black woman—is on the $10 bill. The Queen is in good company."

After researching royal women of different eras and from far-flung kingdoms, a lingering question hovers: Do blue bloods dwell in a vastly better sphere far removed from the travails of the common folk? Initially, from the outside looking in, the answer would be a resounding yes (or a sarcastic "Duh"). Those born to sit on a gilded throne, whose names bespeak power and privilege, seem to glisten with fairy dust. Their extreme wealth makes them enjoy existences lifted from *The Lifestyles of the Rich and the Famous* as opposed to the lifestyles of the poor and the desperate. Money, a soul-sucking concern for most, seldom enters the radar of those who hold the key to royal coffers. Their homes are nonfictional Xanadus, and they serve as the stars of glittering galas. While Everyman's destiny is to be as insignificant in the grand scheme of things as grains of sand, those born on the pinnacle of the social hierarchy oftentimes shape history. Desperate to make an honest woman of Anne Boleyn, King Henry VIII changed the religion of England from Roman Catholicism to Protestantism; Marie Antoinette helped usher in the French Revolution; and Tsarina Alexandra closed the curtain on the reign of the Romanovs.

However, after researching the blue-blooded women profiled in *Royal Women,* I perceived them in a different prism. Yes, they were born with silver spoons, but privilege comes with a price. In some cases, the ultimate price: Anne Boleyn, Lady Jane Grey, Mary, Queen of Scots, Marie Antoinette, Empress Sisi, and Tsarina Alexandra met their ends through execution. Catherine the Great had to share her bedroom with the king she despised; dynastic ambitions destroyed the relationship of Joséphine and Napoleon.

Another burn that arises from holding the scepter is having to dwell in an aquarium-sized fishbowl that magnifies every misstep, every foible. The chief opponents of privacy are the paparazzi, dedicated hunters of the royals: Fergie experienced the pain of headlines that proclaimed her the Princess of Pork; Meghan said vilification by the

British tabloids led to suicidal thoughts; Princess Diana's death resulted from her chauffeur attempting to evade reporters. The Windsors (at least most of them) only reply to rumors with a terse "No comment." In contrast, Thailand's lèse-majesté law makes it illegal to defame, insult, or criticize its king, queen, heir, or regent. The punishment for violation, delineated in Section 112, is three to fifteen years imprisonment. Even minor infractions are not tolerated. A woman who wore black on the birthday of then-King Bhumibol Adulyadej, as well as a man who wrote a sarcastic Internet post about the king's dog, fell afoul of the authorities.

The New Testament, Luke 12: 48, places a heavy load on royals—who are in essence celebrities on steroids: "For unto whomsoever much is given, of him shall be much required." And woe to those who do not heed the biblical injunction. One who did so was Princess Margaret, who attempted to double dip: She wanted the Windsor robes but not to be required to shoulder Windsor responsibilities.

Cicero, in the fourth century BCE, examined the wisdom of desiring to trade places with those of kingly lineage. In the Latin writer's account, he relayed the legend of Dionysius I of Syracuse. One of his couriers, Damocles, lamented that he had been born to a lowly station and could never dwell in the lap of luxury. As the two men bore a strong resemblance, the king suggested Damocles dress in his regal robes and impersonate him for the night. A delighted Damocles ate a sumptuous feast; women danced for his pleasure, and men paid homage. During the enchanted evening, Damocles looked up and saw a sword suspended by a single thread above his head. The pleasure of the banquet disappeared. When Dionysius returned and asked if he had enjoyed the evening, the look on his courier's face was all the answer he needed. Intermingled with royal perks is the ever-present threat of Damocles's Sword.

Acknowledgments

After writing about those who dwell in a world far removed from my own, here on this page is the time to thank those whose orbits have crossed my own. The genesis of *Royal Women* came from my editor, Brenda Knight, who suggested I follow *Women of Means* with other wealthy women, those who additionally carried the mantle of royalty. The research was a labor of love, and I am endlessly indebted for the wonderful opportunities you have afforded me. Even nonroyal women deserve their knights in shining armor, and since 2014, mine has been Roger Williams. Together we have birthed eleven books, and more await. How extraordinarily fortunate I am that my path crossed yours.

Through happenstance, I met Jamie Lovett when she wrote me several years ago regarding my first book, *Once Again to Zelda*. Jamie is an example of how strangers can morph into best friends. Publishing is the joy that delivers unimaginable gifts, and she is certainly one of my most cherished.

Lastly, I want to send a collective hug to those who have supported my writing journey, as you are the wind beneath my wings. I appreciate you emailing me, posting Amazon and Goodreads reviews, and inviting me to speak at your book clubs. You are the reason I write, the reason I have a passion that transforms the black-and-white of everyday existence into Technicolor.

Hearing from my readers means so much; please contact me through:

wagmangeller@hotmail.com
https://www.facebook.com/marlene.wagman.5/
marlenewagmangeller.com

Happy reading trails,
Marlene Wagman-Geller
San Diego, California (2021)

About the Author

Marlene Wagman-Geller received her Bachelor of Arts from York
University and her teaching credentials from the University
of Toronto and San Diego State University. She recently retired after
teaching high school English and history for thirty-one years. The author
shares her home with her husband, Joel, daughter, Jordanna, and dog,
Harley. Reviews from her books have appeared in *The New York Times*
and dozens of other newspapers such as *The Washington Post, The
Chicago Tribune,* and *The Huffington Post.*

Bibliography

Chapter 1: Queen Anne Boleyn

Alberge, Dalya. "Chilling Find Shows How Henry VIII Planned Every Detail of Boleyn Beheading." *The Guardian*, October 25, 2020. https://www.theguardian.com/uk-news/2020/oct/25/chilling-find-shows-how-henry-viii-planned-every-detail-of-boleyn-beheading.

"Ambitious Anne Boleyn." *The Washington Post*, June 23, 1984. https://www.washingtonpost.com/archive/lifestyle/1984/06/23/ambitious-anne-boleyn/12a10c79-659e-47b2-a27d-e429138fc7d5/.

Farquhar, Michael. " 'Forgive Me': The Brutal Execution of Mary, Queen of Scots." *The Washington Post*, December 17, 2018. https://www.washingtonpost.com/history/2018/12/16/forgive-me-brutal-execution-mary-queen-scots/.

Lisle, Leanda de. "Seductress or Scholar—the Real Anne Boleyn." *Newsweek*, March 14, 2016. https://www.newsweek.com/2015/01/30/seductress-or-scholar-real-anne-boleyn-300764.html.

Mantel, Hilary. "Anne Boleyn: Witch, Bitch, Temptress, Feminist." *The Guardian*, May 11, 2012. https://www.theguardian.com/books/2012/may/11/hilary-mantel-on-anne-boleyn.

Chapter 2: Queen Elizabeth I

"**Elizabeth I.**" *Tudor Times*, May 6, 2017. https://tudortimes.co.uk/
     people/elizabeth-i.

Harrison, Kathryn. "The Body Politic." *The New York Times*, Feb-
     ruary 7, 2014. https://www.nytimes.com/2014/02/09/books/
     review/the-queens-bed-by-anna-whitelock.html.

McGeary, Johanna. "16th Century: Queen Elizabeth I (1533–1603)."
     TIME, December 31, 1999. http://content.time.com/time/sub-
     scriber/article/0,33009,993034,00.html.

Quilligan, Maureen. "Married to England." *The New York Times*,
     April 3, 1983. https://www.nytimes.com/1983/04/03/books/
     married-to-england.html.

Stewart, Doug. "Reign On." *Smithsonian Magazine*, June
     2003. https://www.smithsonianmag.com/history/reign-
     on-82958484/.

Chapter 3: Lady Jane Grey

Kaufman, Joanne. "The Noble Virgin." *The New York Times*, Sep-
     tember 21, 1986. https://www.nytimes.com/1986/09/21/books/
     the-noble-virgin.html.

"**Lady Jane Grey.**" Historic Royal Palaces. Accessed January 7, 2022.
     https://www.hrp.org.uk/tower-of-london/history-and-stories/
     lady-jane-grey/#gs.b8rq2o.

Selwood, Dominic. "On This Day in 1554: Unwilling Pretender to
     the Tudor Throne Lady Jane Grey Was Beheaded, Aged 16." *The
     Telegraph*, February 12, 2018. https://www.telegraph.co.uk/

news/2018/02/12/day-1554-unwilling-pretender-tudor-throne-lady-jane-grey-beheaded/.

Weir, Alison. *Innocent Traitor: A Novel of Lady Jane Grey*. New York: Ballantine Books, 2008.

Zarin, Cynthia. "Teen Queen." *The New Yorker*, October 8, 2007. https://www.newyorker.com/magazine/2007/10/15/teen-queen.

Chapter 4: Mary, Queen of Scots

Collin, Robbie. "Mary Queen of Scots Review: Margot Robbie and Saoirse Ronan Butt Heads in a Thrilling Drama of 16th Century Statecraft." *The Telegraph*, November 16, 2018. https://www.telegraph.co.uk/films/0/mary-queen-scots-review-margot-robbie-andsaoirse-ronan-butt/.

Dockterman, Eliana. "The True Story Behind the Movie Mary Queen of Scots." *TIME*, April 30, 2021. https://time.com/5473365/mary-queen-of-scots-true-story/.

Farquhar, Michael. " 'Forgive Me': The Brutal Execution of Mary, Queen of Scots." *The Washington Post*, December 17, 2018. https://www.washingtonpost.com/history/2018/12/16/forgive-me-brutal-execution-mary-queen-scots/.

Fraser, Antonia. *Mary, Queen of Scots*. New York: Delta Trade Paperbacks, 2001.

"Killer Queen: The True Story of Mary, Queen of Scots." *Independent*. Accessed January 7, 2022. https://www.independent.ie/entertainment/movies/killer-queen-the-true-story-of-mary-queen-of-scots-37681522.html.

Kilroy, Gerard. "Mary Stuart Living." *The New York Times*, April 11, 2004. https://www.nytimes.com/2004/04/11/books/mary-stuart-living.html.

Solly, Meilan. "The True Story of Mary, Queen of Scots, and Elizabeth I." *Smithsonian Magazine*, December 6, 2018. https://www.smithsonianmag.com/history/true-story-mary-queen-scots-and-elizabeth-i-180970960/.

Chapter 5: Empress Catherine the Great

Harrison, Kathryn. "Empress of All the Russias." *The New York Times*, November 16, 2011. https://www.nytimes.com/2011/11/20/books/review/catherine-the-great-portrait-of-a-woman-by-robert-k-massie-book-review.html.

Lally, Kathy. " 'Catherine the Great: Portrait of a Woman by Robert K. Massie." *The Washington Post*, November 18, 2011. https://www.washingtonpost.com/entertainment/books/catherine-the-great-portrait-of-a-woman-by-robert-k-massie/2011/10/31/gIQApvKLZN_story.html.

Massie, Robert K. *Catherine the Great: Portrait of a Woman.* New York: Random House Trade Paperbacks, 2012.

Pipes, Richard. "Catherine the Great." *The New York Times*, March 27, 1977. https://www.nytimes.com/1977/03/27/archives/catherine-the-great-catherine.html.

Wilson, Frances. "Catherine the Great by Robert K Massie: Review." *The Telegraph*, July 3, 2012. https://www.telegraph.co.uk/culture/books/historybookreviews/9364528/Catherine-the-Great-by-Robert-K-Massie-review.html.

Chapter 6: Queen Marie Antoinette

Covington, Richard. "Marie Antoinette." *Smithsonian Magazine*, November 1, 2006. https://www.smithsonianmag.com/history/marie-antoinette-134629573/.

Dargis, Manohla, and A. O. Scott. " 'Marie Antoinette': Best or Worst of Times?" *The New York Times*, May 25, 2006. https://www.nytimes.com/2006/05/25/movies/25fest.html.

Foreman, Amanda. "Enfant Terrible." *The New York Times*, July 16, 2000. https://www.nytimes.com/2000/07/16/books/enfant-terrible.html.

Fraser, Antonia. *Marie Antoinette: The Journey*. New York: Anchor Books, 2020.

—-. "Review: Marie Antoinette by Antonia Fraser." *The Guardian*, July 14, 2001. https://www.theguardian.com/books/2001/jul/14/biography.highereducation.

Plessix, Francine Du. "It's Not so Good to Be the Queen." *The New York Times*, September 23, 2001. https://www.nytimes.com/2001/09/23/books/it-s-not-so-good-to-be-the-queen.html.

Roosevelt, Selwa. "Caught in the Deluge." *The Washington Post*, October 7, 2001. https://www.washingtonpost.com/archive/entertainment/books/2001/10/07/caught-in-the-deluge/81d2d759-dbba-4241-a5be-b1893402c02f/.

Schillinger, Liesl. "The Queen's Wardrobe." *The New York Times*, October 15, 2006. https://www.nytimes.com/2006/10/15/books/review/the-queens-wardrobe.html.

Thurman, Judith. "Dressed for Excess." *The New Yorker*, September 18, 2006. https://www.newyorker.com/magazine/2006/09/25/dressed-for-excess.

Willsher, Kim. "From Hated Queen to 21st-Century Icon: Paris Exhibition Celebrates Life of Marie-Antoinette." *The Guardian*, October 15, 2019. https://www.theguardian. com/artanddesign/2019/oct/15/marie-antoinette-from-hated-queen-to-21st-century-icon-paris-exhibition.

Chapter 7: Empress Joséphine

Rounding, Virginia. "Josephine: Desire, Ambition, Napoleon, by Kate Williams, Review." *The Telegraph*, October 26, 2013. https://www.telegraph.co.uk/culture/books/history-bookreviews/10402795/Josephine-Desire-Ambition-Napoleon-by-Kate-Williams-review.html.

"Scent of a Woman." *The Washington Post*, August 8, 2004. https://www.washingtonpost.com/archive/entertainment/books/2004/08/08/scent-of-a-woman/4ed84d94-2a83-4114-b847-9bdb4a10521e/.

Wagman-Geller, Marlene. *And the Rest Is History: The Famous (and Infamous) First Meetings of the World's Most Passionate Couples.* London: Penguin, 2011.

Weber, Caroline. " 'Ambition and Desire: The Dangerous Life of Josephine Bonaparte,' by Kate Williams." *The New York Times*, December 5, 2014. https://www.nytimes.com/2014/12/07/books/review/ambition-and-desire-the-dangerous-life-of-josephine-bonaparte-by-kate-williams.html.

Williams, Kate. "Life Story: Napolean's [sic] Secret Weapon—Joséphine Bonaparte." *Daily Mail Online*, October 28, 2013. https://www.dailymail.co.uk/home/you/article-2473426/Life-story-Napoleans-secret-weapon—Jos-phine-Bonaparte.html.

Chapter 8: Queen Victoria

Baird, Julia. *Victoria the Queen: An Intimate Biography of the Woman Who Ruled an Empire.* New York: Random House, 2017.

Blakemore, Erin. "How Queen Victoria Remade the British Monarchy." *National Geographic*, May 4, 2021. https://www.national-geographic.com/history/article/history-queen-victoria-british-monarchy.

Miller, Julie. "How 20-Year-Old Queen Victoria Forever Changed Wedding Fashion." *Vanity Fair*, April 3, 2018. https://www.vanityfair.com/style/2018/04/queen-victoria-royal-wedding.

Price, Leah. " 'Victoria: A Life,' by A. N. Wilson." *The New York Times*, December 12, 2014. https://www.nytimes.com/2014/12/14/books/review/victoria-a-life-by-a-n-wilson.html.

Yardley, Jonathan. "Queen for Many a Day." *The Washington Post*, November 14, 2014. https://www.washingtonpost.com/opinions/2014/11/14/e5dfcfbc-5f77-11e4-8b9e-2ccdac31a031_story.html.

Chapter 9: Empress Elisabeth "Sisi"

Emmet, Kathleen. "Elisabeth: The Unhappy Empress of the Hapsburgs." *The Washington Post*, December 28, 1986. https://www.washingtonpost.com/archive/entertainment/books/1986/12/28/elisabeth-the-unhappy-empress-of-the-hapsburgs/fcd10912-65a8-4e75-bbac-e335f0a066ad/.

Fremantle, Anne. "Nothing Brought Happiness; *The Lonely Empress. A Biography of Elizabeth of Austria by Joan Haslip.*" *The New York Times*, September 5, 1965. https://www.nytimes.com/1965/09/05/archives/nothing-brought-happi-ness-the-lonely-empress-a-biography-of.html.

Hadley Meares. "The Tragic Austrian Empress Who Was Murdered by Anarchists." *History*, August 22, 2018. https://www.history.com/news/the-tragic-austrian-empress-who-was-murdered-by-anarchists.

Pataki, Allison. *The Accidental Empress: A Novel.* New York: Howard Books, 2015.

Chapter 10: Queen Liliuokalani

Boyd, Malia. "The Other Side of Paradise." *The New York Times*, March 9, 2012. https://www.nytimes.com/2012/03/11/books/review/lost-kingdom-a-history-of-hawaii.html.

Goo, Sara Kehaulani. " 'Lost Kingdom: Hawaii's Last Queen, the Sugar Kings, and America's First Imperial Adventure' by Julia Flynn Siler" January 20, 2012. *The Washington Post*, https://www.washingtonpost.com/entertainment/books/lost-kingdom-hawaiis-last-queen-the-sugar-kings-and-americas-first-imperial-adventure-by-julia-flynn-siler/2011/12/29/gIQAj8kUEQ_story.html.

Lewis, Peter. " 'Lost Kingdom,' by Julia Flynn Siler: Review." *San Francisco Chronicle*, January 7, 2012. https://www.sfgate.com/books/article/Lost-Kingdom-by-Julia-Flynn-Siler-review-2446729.php.

Siler, Julia Flynn. *Lost Kingdom: Hawaii's Last Queen, the Sugar Kings, and America's First Imperial Adventure.* New York: Atlantic Monthly Press, 2012. Kindle.

Smith, Wendy. "Review: 'Lost Kingdom' by Julia Flynn Siler." *Los Angeles Times*, February 5, 2012. https://www.latimes.com/

entertainment/la-xpm-2012-feb-05-la-ca-julia-flynn-siler-20120205-story.html.

Chapter 11: Tsarina Alexandra

Finder, Joseph. "Blood Will Tell." *The Washington Post*, October 22, 1995. https://www.washingtonpost.com/wp-srv/style/longterm/books/reviews/fall.htm.

Fitzpatrick, Sheila. "The Last of the Tsars by Robert Service: Review—Dispelling the Myths." *The Guardian*, February 15, 2017. https://www.theguardian.com/books/2017/feb/15/the-last-of-the-tsars-by-robert-service-review.

"The Romanovs—a Long Reign of Blood, Sex and Tears." *Independent*, February 8, 2016. https://www.independent.ie/entertainment/books/book-reviews/the-romanovs-a-long-reign-of-blood-sex-and-tears-34424756.html.

Chapter 12: Queen Marie of Romania

Dennison, Matthew. "What Becomes of the 'Spare's Spare'?" *The Telegraph*, June 6, 2021. https://www.telegraph.co.uk/royal-family/2021/06/06/becomes-spares-spare/.

France-Presse, Agence. "Heart of Queen Victoria's Granddaughter Finally to Be Laid to Rest after 70 Years." *The Guardian*, September 25, 2015. https://www.theguardian.com/world/2015/sep/25/heart-of-queen-victorias-granddaughter-finally-laid-to-rest-after-70-years.

Gillet, Kit. "Romania Places the Heart of a Queen in Her Castle." *The New York Times*, November 3, 2015. https://www.nytimes.

com/2015/11/04/world/europe/romania-places-the-heart-of-a-queen-in-her-castle.html.

Gross, John. "*The Last Romantic: A Biography of Queen Marie of Roumania* by Hannah Pakula." *The New York Times*, March 19, 1985. https://www.nytimes.com/1985/03/19/books/books-of-the-times-by-john-gross.html.

Kenyon, Paul. "From Windsor to Castle Dracula: A New Book Charts the Making of a Dazzling Romanian Queen." *Tatler*, August 16, 2021. https://www.tatler.com/article/queen-marie-of-romania-who-was-she.

Pakula, Hannah. *The Last Romantic: A Biography of Queen Marie of Roumania.* New York: Simon & Schuster, 2017.

Chapter 13: Princess Alice of Battenberg

Devaney, Susan. "Who Was Princess Alice, the Most Enigmatic Royal in 'The Crown' Season 3?" *British Vogue*, November 25, 2019. https://www.vogue.co.uk/arts-and-lifestyle/article/princess-alice-the-crown-real-life.

Foussianes, Chloe. "How Princess Alice of Battenberg, Prince Philip's Mother, Became the Royal Family's Black Sheep." *Town & Country*. November 2, 2021. https://www.townandcountry-mag.com/society/tradition/a29310694/who-is-princess-alice-prince-philip-mother-the-crown-facts/.

Holmes, Oliver. "How Princess Alice Saved an Entire Family from the Nazis." *The Guardian*, December 1, 2019. https://www.theguardian.com/uk-news/2019/dec/01/princess-alice—saved—my-famils-from-nazis-in-wartime-greece.

Mackelden, Amy. "The Incredible True Story of Prince Philip's Mother, Princess Alice of Battenberg." *Harper's Bazaar*, November 17, 2019. https://www.harpersbazaar.com/celebrity/latest/a29796667/who-is-prince-philip-mother-alice-battenberg/.

Miller, Julie. "The Crown: The Extraordinary Story of Prince Philip's Mother Princess Alice." *Vanity Fair*, November 18, 2019. https://www.vanityfair.com/hollywood/2019/11/the-crown-season-3-prince-philip-mother-princess-alice.

Paunescu, Delia. "Princess Alice's Life Was Even More Dramatic than 'The Crown' Depicts." *Elle*, November 29, 2021. https://www.elle.com/culture/movies-tv/a29849010/princess-alice-battenberg-the-crown-real-life/.

Rosenwald, Michael S. "Fact-Checking 'The Crown': Did Sigmund Freud Mistreat Prince Philip's Mother After a Mental Breakdown?" *The Washington Post*, November 23, 2019. https://www.washingtonpost.com/history/2019/11/23/fact-checking-crown-did-sigmund-freud-mistreat-prince-philips-mother-after-mental-breakdown/.

Vincent, Alice. "Exile, Schizophrenic, Nun: The Truth about Prince Philip's Mother, Princess Alice." *The Telegraph*, November 18, 2019. https://www.telegraph.co.uk/tv/0/crown-episode-4-accurate-prince-philip-mother-bubbikins-fact/.

Chapter 14: Wallis Simpson, The Duchess of Windsor

Carmody, Deirdre. "Duchess of Windsor, 89, Dies in France; Woman Who Won a King." *The New York Times*, April 25, 1986. https://www.nytimes.com/1986/04/25/obituaries/duchess-of-windsor-89-dies-in-france-woman-who-won-a-king.html.

Halzack, Sarah. " 'That Woman: The Life of Wallis Simpson, Duchess of Windsor' by Anne Sebba." *The Washington Post*, March 30, 2012. https://www.washingtonpost.com/entertainment/books/that-woman-the-life-of-wallis-simpson-duchess-of-windsor-by-anne-sebba/2012/03/30/gIQAFUk1lS_story.html.

Smith, J.Y. "The Duchess of Windsor Dies at 89." *The Washington Post*, April 25, 1986. https://www.washingtonpost.com/archive/politics/1986/04/25/the-duchess-of-windsor-dies-at-89/527355f5-b283-441c-b892-a5d35c0a341f/.

Wagman-Geller, Marlene. *And the Rest Is History: The Famous (and Infamous) First Meetings of the World's Most Passionate Couples*. London: Penguin, 2011.

Weintraub, Stanley. "The Love Letters of the Duchess of Windsor." *The Washington Post*, June 8, 1986. https://www.washingtonpost.com/archive/entertainment/books/1986/06/08/the-love-letters-of-the-duchess-of-windsor/01e274ba-f337-49df-ab63-1bbd0dde6615.

Chapter 15: Queen Elizabeth, the Queen Mother

Barbash, Fred. "Britain's Queen Mother Is Dead at 101." *The Washington Post*, March 31, 2002. https://www.washingtonpost.com/archive/politics/2002/03/31/britains-queen-mother-is-dead-at-101/32953720-714d-423c-8ae4-31f94dfc15e0/.

Ezard, John. "Obituary: Queen Elizabeth, the Queen Mother." *The Guardian*, March 30, 2002. https://www.theguardian.com/uk/2002/mar/30/queenmother.monarchy12.

"Her Majesty Queen Elizabeth, the Queen Mother." *The Telegraph*, April 2, 2002. https://www.telegraph.co.uk/news/obituar-

ies/1389435/Her-Majesty-Queen-Elizabeth-the-Queen-Mother.
html.

Lyall, Sarah. "Britain's Beloved 'Queen Mum,' a Symbol of Courage,
Dies at 101." *The New York Times*, March 31, 2002. https://www.
nytimes.com/2002/03/31/world/britain-s-beloved-queen-
mum-a-symbol-of-courage-dies-at-101.html.

Chapter 16: Empress Nagako

Downer, Lesley. "Nagako, Dowager Empress of Japan." *The Guardian*, June 17, 2000. https://www.theguardian.com/news/2000/
jun/17/guardianobituaries.

"Empress Dowager Nagako of Japan Dies, Ending an Era." *The
Washington Post*, June 17, 2000. https://www.washingtonpost.
com/archive/local/2000/06/17/empress-dowager-nagako-
of-japan-dies-ending-an-era/060ecc16-2325-4660-b3f0-
30c1a0bd4411/.

"Japan Empress Nagako Dies at 97." *Deseret News*, June 16, 2000.
https://www.deseret.com/2000/6/16/19513025/japan-empress-
nagako-dies-at-97.

Kristoff, Nicholas D. "Dowager Empress Nagako, Hirohito's Widow,
Dies at 97." *The New York Times*. June 17, 2000. https://www.
nytimes.com/2000/06/17/world/dowager-empress-nagako-hi-
rohito-s-widow-dies-at-97.html.

Murphy, Paul. "Empress Was Longest Living Japanese Royal." *The
Irish Times*, June 17, 2000. https://www.irishtimes.com/news/
empress-was-longest-living-japanese-royal-1.282927.

Oka, Takashi. "Hirohito No Longer a Semi Divine Emperor, but a Secure One." *The New York Times*, August 16, 1970. https://www.

nytimes.com/1970/08/16/archives/hirohito-no-longer-a-semi-divine-emperor-but-a-secure-one.html.

Reitman, Valerie. "Empress Dowager Nagako; Widow of Japan's Hirohito." *Los Angeles Times*, June 17, 2000. https://www.latimes.com/archives/la-xpm-2000-jun-17-me-41849-story.html.

Chapter 17: Queen Marie-José

Elgyar, Raluca. "Marie-José of Belgium—the May Butterfly." *History of Royal Women*, June 14, 2020. https://www.historyofroyal-women.com/marie-jose-of-belgium/marie-jose-last-queen-italy-may-butterfly/.

"Queen Marie José of Italy." *The Telegraph*, January 29, 2001. https://www.telegraph.co.uk/news/obituaries/1320052/Queen-Marie-Jose-of-Italy.html.

Stanley, Alessandra. "Maria José, 94, Queen of Italy for Just 27 Days after the War." *The New York Times*, January 29, 2001. https://www.nytimes.com/2001/01/29/world/maria-jose-94-queen-of-italy-for-just-27-days-after-the-war.html.

Willan, Philip. "Obituary: Queen Marie-José of Italy." *The Guardian*, February 3, 2001. https://www.theguardian.com/news/2001/feb/03/guardianobituaries.philipwillan.

Chapter 18: Queen Geraldine Apponyi de Nagy

"H M Queen Geraldine of the Albanians." *The Telegraph*, October 24, 2002. https://www.telegraph.co.uk/news/obituaries/1411080/H-M-Queen-Geraldine-of-the-Albanians.html.

Martin, Douglas. "Geraldine of Albania, 87, Queen with US Ties, Is Dead." *The New York Times*, October 27, 2002. https://www.nytimes.com/2002/10/27/world/geraldine-of-albania-87-queen-with-us-ties-is-dead.html.

Pettifer, James. "A Life in Focus: Queen Geraldine of the Albanians." *The Independent*, November 30, 2018. https://www.independent.co.uk/news/lifeinfocus/queen-geraldine-of-the-albanians-king-zog-a8614901.html.

Vickers, Miranda. "Obituary: Queen Geraldine of Albania." *The Guardian*, October 30, 2002. https://www.theguardian.com/news/2002/oct/30/guardianobituaries.

"Queen Geraldine of Albania." *The Times*, April 1, 2010. https://www.thetimes.co.uk/article/queen-geraldine-of-albania-cjhv5tswkw0.

Chapter 19 Maharani Gayatri Devi

Buncombe, Andrew. "A Battle of Wills: Gayatri Devi's £250m Legacy." *The Independent*, September 18, 2009. https://www.independent.co.uk/news/world/asia/a-battle-of-wills-gayatri-devi-s-pound-250m-legacy-1790048.html.

Bumiller, Elisabeth. "Family Feud in the House of Jaipur." *The Washington Post*, January 3, 1987. https://www.washingtonpost.com/archive/lifestyle/1987/01/03/family-feud-in-the-house-of-jaipur/07e7c2bd-f830-47bb-a269-8378e7065af0/.

"Gayatri Devi: Indian Princess Who Combined the Life of a Socialite." *The Independent*, August 24, 2009. https://www.independent.co.uk/news/obituaries/gayatri-devi-indian-princess-who-combined-the-life-of-a-socialite-with-an-outspoken-commitment-to-political-action-1776806.html.

Moore, Molly. "From Luxury to Litigation." *The Washington Post*, June 2, 1994. https://www.washingtonpost.com/archive/politics/1994/06/02/from-luxury-to-litigation/d257313a-d9f5-42eb-aad9-3c956e5e0f1e/.

"Rajmata Gayatri Devi." *The Telegraph*, July 29, 2009. https://www.telegraph.co.uk/news/obituaries/royalty-obituaries/5934077/Rajmata-Gayatri-Devi.html.

Seebohm, Caroline. "Fairy Tale with a Dark Ending." *The New York Times*, March 13, 1977. https://www.nytimes.com/1977/03/13/archives/fairy-tale-with-a-dark-ending-a-princess-remembers.html.

Tully, Mark. "Obituary | Gayatri Devi, Indian Princess Turned Politician." *The Guardian*, August 10, 2009. https://www.theguardian.com/global/2009/aug/10/obituary-gayatri-devi.

Weber, Bruce. "Gayatri Devi, 90, a Maharani and a Lawmaker, Dies." *The New York Times*, July 31, 2009. https://www.nytimes.com/2009/07/31/world/asia/31devi.html.

Chapter 20: Her Serene Highness Ashraf Pahlavi

AP in Dubai. "Princess Ashraf, Twin Sister of Iran's Last Shah, Dies at 96." *The Guardian*, January 9, 2016. https://www.theguardian.com/world/2016/jan/09/princess-ashraf-twin-sister-of-irans-last-shah-dies-at-96.

"Ashraf Pahlavi." *The Times*, January 18, 2016. https://www.the-times.co.uk/article/ashraf-pahlavi-2lklm3kx0z3.

De St. Jorre, John. "My Brother and Me." *The Washington Post*, June 8, 1980. https://www.washingtonpost.com/archive/entertainment/books/1980/06/08/my-brother-and-me/c05030e2-fc56-4d9f-b7ac-a9a9121e9a7c/.

Grimes, William. "Ashraf Pahlavi, Twin Sister of Iran's Last Shah, Dies at 96." *The New York Times*, January 8, 2016. https://www.nytimes.com/2016/01/08/world/middleeast/ashraf-pahlavi-sister-of-irans-last-shah-defender-and-diplomat-dies-at-96.html.

"Gunmen Try to Kill Shah's Sister." *The Washington Post*, September 14, 1977. https://www.washingtonpost.com/archive/politics/1977/09/14/gunmen-try-to-kill-shahs-sister/a7b4f15d-a720-434b-a86e-a1b0e361d945/.

McGuinness, Mark. "Diminutive Iranian Princess Dubbed the 'Black Panther' Loved Luxury." *The Sydney Morning Herald*, January 27, 2016. https://www.smh.com.au/national/diminutive-iranian-princess-dubbed-the-black-panther-loved-luxury-20160127-gmes96.html.

Murphy, Brian. "Ashraf Pahlavi, Twin Sister of Iran's Late Shah, Dies at 96." *The Washington Post*, January 8, 2016. https://www.washingtonpost.com/world/middle_east/ashraf-pahlavi-twin-sister-of-irans-late-shah-dies-at-96/2016/01/08/e5df0e32-b5b7-11e5-9388-466021d971de_story.html.

Chapter 21: Cayetana de Silva, The Duchess of Alba

Callahan, Maureen. "The Last Duchess." *New York Post*, October 2, 2011. https://nypost.com/2011/10/02/the-last-duchess/.

"The Duchess of Alba—Obituary." *The Telegraph*, November 20, 2014. https://www.telegraph.co.uk/news/obituaries/11243062/The-Duchess-of-Alba-obituary.html.

Eaude, Michael. "The Duchess of Alba Obituary." *The Guardian*, November 20, 2014. https://www.theguardian.com/global/2014/nov/20/duchess-of-alba.

Langer, Emily. "Spain's Duchess of Alba, Noblewoman with Flair, Dies in Seville at 88." *The Washington Post*, November 22, 2014. https://www.washingtonpost.com/world/europe/spains-duchess-of-alba-noblewoman-with-flair-dies-in-seville-at-88/2014/11/20/c11d407a-70c9-11e4-8808-afaa1e3a33ef_story.html.

McDonald, Soraya Nadia. "Spain's Charmingly Eccentric Duchess of Alba Has Died." *The Washington Post*, October 26, 2021. https://www.washingtonpost.com/news/morning-mix/wp/2014/11/20/spains-charmingly-eccentric-duchess-of-alba-has-die

Chapter 22: Queen Elizabeth II

Davies, Caroline. "The Queen at 90: Across the Decades." *The Guardian*, April 21, 2016. https://www.theguardian.com/uk-news/2016/apr/21/the-queen-at-90-across-the-decades.

Dockterman, Eliana. "When Queen Elizabeth Was a Princess." *TIME*, June 1, 2018. https://time.com/5298945/queen-elizabeth-princess/.

Schillinger, Liesl. "Lighting the Shadows behind the Queen and Her Consort." *The New York Times*, January 20, 2012. https://www.nytimes.com/2012/01/22/fashion/queen-elizabeth-and-prince-philip-books-of-style.html.

Chapter 23: Princess Grace Kelly

Haberman, Clyde. "Princess Grace Is Dead after Riviera Car Crash." *The New York Times*, September 15, 1982. https://www.nytimes.com/1982/09/15/world/princess-grace-is-dead-after-riviera-car-crash.html.

Jacobs, Laura. "Grace Kelly's Forever Look." *Vanity Fair*, March 30, 2010. https://www.vanityfair.com/news/2010/05/grace-kelly-201005.

Smith, J.Y. "Princess Grace of Monaco, Academy Award-Winning Star, Dies." *The Washington Post*, September 15, 1982. https://www.washingtonpost.com/archive/local/1982/09/15/princess-grace-of-monaco-academy-award-winning-star-dies/8863badb-5ee3-48c8-b338-494c230ad309/.

Wagman-Geller, Marlene. *And the Rest Is History: The Famous (and Infamous) First Meetings of the World's Most Passionate Couples.* London: Penguin, 2011.

Chapter 24: Princess Margaret

Brown, Craig. *Ninety-Nine Glimpses of Princess Margaret.* New York: Farrar, Straus and Giroux, 2019.

Burchard, Henry. "Princess Margaret Dies at 71." *The Washington Post*, February 10, 2002. https://www.washingtonpost.com/archive/local/2002/02/10/princess-margaret-dies-at-71/9bd2a9d4-e23c-4077-a5fb-7a04f1c3c6b2/.

Gregory, Joseph R. "Britain's Princess Margaret Dies at 71." *The New York Times*, February 10, 2002. https://www.nytimes.com/2002/02/09/obituaries/britains-princess-margaret-dies-at-71.html.

"Princess Margaret Obituary." *The Guardian*, February 11, 2002. https://www.theguardian.com/news/2002/feb/11/guardianobituaries.princessmargaret.

Chapter 25: Queen Narriman

"Egypt: Life without Narriman." *TIME*, March 23, 1953. http://content.time.com/time/subscriber/article/0,33009,806609,00.html.

"Egypt: Simple Affair." *TIME*, May 14, 1951. http://content.time.com/time/subscriber/article/0,33009,935234,00.html.

Elgyar, Raluca. "Queen Narriman of Egypt—Coping with a Royal Past." History of Royal Women, March 19, 2021. https://www.historyofroyalwomen.com/the-royal-women/queen-narriman-egypt-coping-royal-past/.

Graham, Roy. "The King Who Gets What He Wants: Maclean's: March 1, 1950." *Maclean's*, March 1, 1950. https://archive.macleans.ca/article/1950/03/01/the-king-who-gets-what-he-wants.

"Narriman Sadek." *The Telegraph*, March 1, 2005. https://www.telegraph.co.uk/news/obituaries/1484617/Narriman-Sadek.html.

Chapter 26: Princess Jelisaveta

"Prince Paul of Yugoslavia Exonerated of War Crimes." *The Times*, January 24, 2012. https://www.thetimes.co.uk/article/prince-paul-of-yugoslavia-exonerated-of-war-crimes-v3fwp7w5mbr.

Weinraub, Judith. "The Princess's Awakening." *The Washington Post*, July 12, 1991. https://www.washingtonpost.com/archive/

lifestyle/1991/07/12/the-princesss-awakening/863696cb-2983-
499c-b330-3a4661f520cb/.

Williams, Emma. "A Royal Quest." *The Economist*, March 13, 2013.
https://www.economist.com/1843/2013/03/13/a-royal-quest.

Chapter 27: Gyalmo Hope

Cooke, Hope. *Time Change, an Autobiography*. New York: Simon &
Schuster, 1980.

Darling, Lynn. "Finale of a Fairy Tale." *The Washington Post*, March
6, 1981. https://www.washingtonpost.com/archive/life-
style/1981/03/06/finale-of-a-fairy-tale/c9f569f5-58c8-4cfe-b281-
a90d30cfba2f/.

Kaufman, Michael T. "When East Met West and Walking Around Led
to Brooklyn." *The New York Times*, February 24, 1993. https://
www.nytimes.com/1993/02/24/nyregion/about-new-york-when-
east-met-west-and-walking-around-led-to-brooklyn.html.

Kennedy, Shawn G. "Hope Cooke: From Queen of Sikkim to 'Regular' New Yorker." *The New York Times*, June 18, 1976. https://
www.nytimes.com/1976/06/18/archives/hope-cooke-from-
queen-of-sikkim-to-regular-new-yorker.html.

Krebs, Albin. "Palden Thondup Namgyal, Deposed Sikkim King,
Dies." *The New York Times*, January 30, 1982. https://www.
nytimes.com/1982/01/30/obituaries/palden-thondup-namgyal-
deposed-sikkim-king-dies.html.

Plessix, Francine Du. "The Fairy Tale That Turned Nightmare?"
The New York Times, March 8, 1981. https://www.nytimes.
com/1981/03/08/books/the-fairy-tale-that-turned-night-
mare.html.

Prial, Frank J. "Hope Cooke, Separated from the King of Sikkim, Is Living On the East Side." *The New York Times*, May 16, 1974. https://www.nytimes.com/1974/05/16/archives/hope-cooke-separated-from-the-king-of-sikkim-is-living-on-the-east.html.

"Sikkim: Where There's Hope." *TIME*, March 29, 1963. http://content.time.com/time/subscriber/article/0,33009,896732,00.html.

Chapter 28: Camilla, The Duchess of Cornwall

Lyall, Sarah. "Charles Calls End to the Affair: He'll Happily Wed His Camilla." *The New York Times*, February 11, 2005. https://www.nytimes.com/2005/02/11/world/europe/charles-calls-end-to-the-affair-hell-happily-wed-his-camilla.html.

McLellan, Diana. "Book World." *The Washington Post*, December 5, 1994. https://www.washingtonpost.com/archive/lifestyle/1994/12/05/book-world/5cd8888a-45e3-4a5f-acd9-8904b6b85912/.

Roberts, Roxanne. "A Fairy Tale for Grownups." *The Washington Post*, February 11, 2005. https://www.washingtonpost.com/archive/lifestyle/2005/02/11/a-fairy-tale-for-grownups/056e1d7d-6149-4bfa-b88d-c8ce5c08d325/.

—. "Prince Charles Is Sad and Sexy and Maybe Too Nice to Be King." *The Washington Post*, April 3, 2017. https://www.washingtonpost.com/lifestyle/style/prince-charles-is-sad-and-sexy-and-maybe-too-nice-to-be-king/2017/04/03/9039942a-160f-11e7-833c-503e1f6394c9_story.html.

Timmons, Heather. "The Once and Future Camilla." *The New York Times*, April 3, 2005. https://www.nytimes.com/2005/04/03/fashion/the-once-and-future-camilla.html.

Wagman-Geller, Marlene. *And the Rest Is History: The Famous (and Infamous) First Meetings of the World's Most Passionate Couples*. London: Penguin, 2011.

Chapter 29: Principessa Rita

Cavallier, Andrea. "Texas-born Italian princess, 72, who once modeled for Playboy will be kicked out of her $538M Rome villa when it goes up for auction next week after inheritance battle with her stepsons: World's priciest property contains $354M Caravaggio mural." *Daily Mail*, January 14, 2022. https://www.dailymail.co.uk/news/article-10403857/Texas-born-Italian-princess-kicked-Rome-villa-goes-auction-week.html.

Conradi, Peter. "Princess and her stepsons feud over £400m Villa Aurora—the world's most expensive home decor by Caravaggio." *The Sunday Times*, January 16, 2022. https://www.thetimes.co.uk/article/princess-and-her-stepsons-feud-over-400m-villa-aurora-the-worlds-most-expensive-home-decor-by-caravaggio-xht382fr2.

Giuffrida, Angela. "The princess and the Caravaggio: bitter dispute rages over Roman villa." *The Guardian*, January 14, 2022.https://www.theguardian.com/world/2022/jan/14/the-princess-and-the-caravaggio-bitter-dispute-rages-over-roman-villa.

Hervieux, Linda. "US-Born Princess Opens Historic Villa to the Public." *The New York Times*, July 15, 2010. https://www.nytimes.com/2010/07/16/greathomesanddestinations/16iht-rerome.html.

Horowitz, Jason. "In a Run-down Roman Villa, a Princess from Texas Awaits Her Next Act." *The New York Times*, March 4, 2022. https://www.nytimes.com/2022/03/04/world/europe/italy-princess-rita-boncompagni-ludovisi-jenrette.html.

Levy, Ariel. "The Renovation." *The New Yorker,* November 20, 2011. https://www.newyorker.com/magazine/2011/11/28/the-renovation.

Porterfield, Carlie. "Meet The Texas-Born Italian Princess Who's Selling A $532 Million Roman Villa With A Caravaggio Ceiling." *Forbes,* December 12, 2021. https://www.forbes.com/sites/carlieporterfield/2021/12/12/meet-the-texas-born-italian-princess-whos-selling-a-532-million-roman-villa-with-a-caravaggio-ceiling/?sh=2d6b70d16374.

Squires, Nick. "Preserve my €400m Caravaggio palace as a museum, urges ex-Playboy princess forced to sell." *The Telegraph,* January 22, 2022. https://www.telegraph.co.uk/world-news/2022/01/22/preserve-400m-caravaggio-palace-museum-urges-ex-playboy-princess/.

Chapter 30: Queen Noor

Jehl, Douglas. "Once Derided, Noor Is Likely to Remain a Power at the Palace." *The New York Times,* February 8, 1999. https://www.nytimes.com/1999/02/08/world/death-king-royal-widow-once-derided-noor-likely-remain-power-palace.html.

Khouri, Rami G. "Royal Wedding in Amman." *The Washington Post,* June 16, 1978. https://www.washingtonpost.com/archive/lifestyle/1978/06/16/royal-wedding-in-amman/28767ced-576d-4ee8-82a7-6183e0018fdf/.

"Light of Hussein." *The Irish Times,* February 13, 2013. https://www.irishtimes.com/news/light-of-hussein-1.45800.

McGinn, Daniel. "The Light of His Life." *Newsweek,* March 14, 2010. https://www.newsweek.com/light-his-life-169048.

Miller, Judith. "After 5 Months as Queen Noor, Life as Lisa Is Ancient History." *The New York Times*, November 19, 1978. https://www.nytimes.com/1978/11/19/archives/after-5-months-as-queen-noor-life-as-lisa-is-ancient-history.html.

Noor, Queen. *Leap of Faith: Memoirs of an Unexpected Life*. New York: Hyperion, 2003.

Roberts, Roxanne. "After the Reign." *The Washington Post*, March 2, 2004. https://www.washingtonpost.com/archive/lifestyle/2004/03/02/after-the-reign/ac9c1808-efba-4f0a-8627-5357b922a469/.

Schneider, Howard. "Queen Noor, Standing Alone." *The Washington Post*, June 19, 1999. https://www.washingtonpost.com/archive/lifestyle/1999/06/19/queen-noor-standing-alone/92023010-a7c7-4169-a958-00b9b920f402/.

Shlaim, Avi. "Review: Leap of Faith by Queen Noor." *The Guardian*, May 31, 2003. https://www.theguardian.com/books/2003/may/31/featuresreviews.guardianreview.

Wen, Christopher S. "Hussein Marries American and Proclaims Her Queen." *The New York Times*, June 16, 1978. https://www.nytimes.com/1978/06/16/archives/new-jersey-pages-hussein-marries-american-and-proclaims-her-queen.html.

Chapter 31: Sarah, The Duchess of York

Ferguson, Sarah. *Finding Sarah: A Duchess's Journey to Find Herself*. New York: Atria Books, 2011.

Hampson, Laura. "Sarah Ferguson Says Being Married to Prince Andrew Was 'Happiest' Time in Her Life." *The Independent*, December 16, 2021. https://www.independent.co.uk/

life-style/royal-family/sarah-ferguson-prince-andrew-mar-
riage-b1977386.html.

Holson, Laura. "Saving Sarah from Herself, Oprah Style." *The New
York Times*, June 3, 2011. https://www.nytimes.com/2011/06/05/
fashion/sarah-fergusons-transformation.html.

Robinson, Eugene. "Zooming in on Fergie, in Flagrante." *The Washington Post*, August 21, 1992. https://www.washingtonpost.
com/archive/lifestyle/1992/08/21/zooming-in-on-fergie-in-fla-
grante/bebe6a94-afe6-407b-815b-10b6afa9d077/.

See, Carolyn. "Fergie's Royal Pain." *The Washington Post*, February 28, 1997. https://www.washingtonpost.com/archive/life-
style/1997/02/28/fergies-royal-pain/7ca77b91-6f2c-4bef-9d9b-
c56ac066e551/.

Stanley, Alessandra. "You Can Feel Her Pain (Just Don't Ask Questions)." *The New York Times*, June 9, 2011. https://www.nytimes.
com/2011/06/10/arts/television/finding-sarah-with-sarah-fer-
guson-on-own-review.html.

Stuever, Hank. "On Own's 'Finding Sarah,' Getting to the Roots of a
Royal's Pain." *The Washington Post*, June 10, 2011. https://www.
washingtonpost.com/entertainment/television/on-owns-find-
ing-sarah-getting-to-the-roots-of-a-royals-pain/2011/06/08/
AGModVPH_story.html.

Chapter 32: Princess Diana

Cornwell, Rupert. "Obituary: Diana, Princess of Wales." *The Independent*, August 31, 1997. https://www.independent.co.uk/news/
obituaries/obituary-diana-princess-of-wales-1236982.html.

Morton, Andrew. *Diana: Her True Story—in Her Own Words.* New York: Simon & Schuster, 2017.

Nevin, Charles. "Diana, Princess of Wales: Obituary." *The Guardian,* September 1, 1997. https://www.theguardian.com/news/1997/sep/01/guardianobituaries.monarchy.

"Obituary: Diana, Princess of Wales." *The Times,* April 27, 2010. https://www.thetimes.co.uk/article/obituary-diana-princess-of-wales-05btftp37s0.

Chapter 33: Princess Leila

Burke, Jason. "Profile: Leila Pahlavi." *The Guardian,* October 13, 2001. https://www.theguardian.com/theobserver/2001/oct/14/features.magazine47.

George, Rose. "Leila Pahlavi: The Peacock Princess." *The Independent,* June 12, 2001. https://www.independent.co.uk/news/world/middle-east/leila-pahlavi-peacock-princess-9146076.html.

Reuters. "Leila Pahlavi Is Dead at 31; Youngest Daughter of Shah of Iran." *The New York Times,* June 12, 2001. https://www.nytimes.com/2001/06/12/world/leila-pahlavi-is-dead-at-31-youngest-daughter-of-shah-of-iran.html.

Tweedie, Neil, and Thomas Harding. "Shah's Daughter Found Dead of Overdose in London Hotel." *The Telegraph,* June 12, 2001. https://www.telegraph.co.uk/news/uknews/1308790/Shahs-daughter-found-dead-of-overdose-in-London-hotel.html.

Tweedie, Neil. "Shah's Daughter Stole to Fuel Her Drug Habit." *The Telegraph.* July 26, 2001. https://ssristories.org/shahs-daughter-stole-to-fuel-her-drug-habit-the-telegraph/.

Chapter 34: Princess Haya

Grigoriadis, Vanessa. " 'You're Essentially a Prisoner': Why Do Dubai's Princesses Keep Trying to Escape?" *Vanity Fair*, November 11, 2019. https://www.vanityfair.com/news/2019/11/why-do-dubais-princesses-keep-trying-to-escape.

Hammer, Joshua. "The Runaway Princesses of Dubai." *Town and Country Magazine*. Accessed October 15, 2021. https://www.townandcountrymag.com/society/money-and-power/a29848986/dubai-princess-disappearance-divorce/.

Mellen, Ruby. "Dubai's Princess Haya Wants Protection from the Glitzy City's Ruler. She's Not the First." *The Washington Post*, August 2, 2019. https://www.washingtonpost.com/world/2019/07/31/dubais-princess-haya-wants-protection-glitzy-citys-ruler-shes-not-first/.

Stanford, Peter. "Inside Story: Princess Haya's Divorce and the Gulf Royals Caught between Two Worlds." *The Telegraph*, July 9, 2019. https://www.telegraph.co.uk/women/life/princess-haya-bint-al-hussein/.

Yee, Vivian. "Princess Haya, Wife of Dubai's Ruler, Seeks Refuge in London." *The New York Times*, July 2, 2019. https://www.nytimes.com/2019/07/02/world/middleeast/princess-haya-sheikh-mohammed-bin.html.

Chapter 35: Princess Charlene

Boyle, Katherine. "Style." *The Washington Post*, July 3, 2011. https://www.washingtonpost.com/lifestyle/style/2011/07/03/AGDsex-wH_story.html?_=ddid-4-1621726380.

Chrisafis, Angelique. "Prince Albert of Monaco and Charlene Wittstock Prepare for Wedding." *The Guardian*, June 26, 2011. https://www.theguardian.com/world/2011/jun/26/prince-albert-monaco-charlene-wittstock-wedding.

Cohen, Stefanie. "The Prisoner Princess." *New York Post*, July 7, 2011. https://nypost.com/2011/07/07/the-prisoner-princess/.

Jacobbi, Paola. "Why the Paternity Claim Facing Prince Albert of Monaco Later This Month Is the Strangest Yet." *The Telegraph*, February 7, 2021. https://www.telegraph.co.uk/luxury/society/paternity-claim-facing-prince-albert-monaco-later-month-strangest/.

Sciolino, Elaine. "The Quiet Royal Wedding." *The New York Times*, June 22, 2011. https://www.nytimes.com/2011/06/23/fashion/charlene-wittstock-and-monaco-prepare-for-royal-wedding.html.

Smith, Craig S. "Monaco Adjusts to a Bachelor Prince without Heirs." *The New York Times*, April 10, 2005. https://www.nytimes.com/2005/04/10/world/europe/monaco-adjusts-to-a-bachelor-prince-without-heirs.html.

Chapter 36: Meghan, The Duchess of Sussex

Barry, Ellen. "As Prince Harry and Meghan Markle Wed, a New Era Dawns." *The New York Times*, May 19, 2018. https://www.nytimes.com/2018/05/19/world/europe/meghan-markle-prince-harry-wedding.html.

Magra, Iliana. "Harry, Meghan and Britain: When Did the Fairy Tale Go Sour?" *The New York Times*, January 11, 2020. https://

www.nytimes.com/2020/01/11/world/europe/duchess-sus-sex-prince.html.

Nikkhah, Roya. "How Meghan Became the Unmerry Wife of Windsor." *The Sunday Times*, March 7, 2021. https://www.thetimes. co.uk/article/how-meghan-became-the-unmerry-wife-of-windsor-qotdojs6m.

Scobie, Omid, and Carolyn Durand. *Finding Freedom: Harry and Meghan and the Making of a Modern Royal Family.* New York: Dey Street Books, 2020.

Chapter 37: Kate, The Duchess of Cambridge

Lyall, Sarah. "Diana's Ring Seals Prince William's Marriage Plans." *The New York Times*, November 16, 2010. https://www.nytimes. com/2010/11/17/world/europe/17royal.html.

—. "Fixating on a Future Royal as Elusive as Cinderella." *The New York Times*, April 21, 2011. https://www.nytimes. com/2011/04/21/world/europe/21kate.html.

Nicholl, Katie. "Wills and the Real Girl." *Vanity Fair*, November 4, 2010. https://www.vanityfair.com/news/2010/12/william-and-kate-201012.

Tominey, Camilla. "How the Duchess of Cambridge Became the Monarchy's Greatest Asset." *The Telegraph*, May 30, 2021. https://www.telegraph.co.uk/royal-family/0/duchess-cam-bridge-became-monarchys-greatest-asset/.

Mango Publishing, established in 2014, publishes an eclectic list of books by diverse authors—both new and established voices—on topics ranging from business, personal growth, women's empowerment, LGBTQ+ studies, health, and spirituality to history, popular culture, time management, decluttering, lifestyle, mental wellness, aging, and sustainable living. We were recently named 2019 *and* 2020's #1 fastest-growing independent publisher by *Publishers Weekly*. Our success is driven by our main goal, which is to publish high-quality books that will entertain readers as well as make a positive difference in their lives.

Our readers are our most important resource; we value your input, suggestions, and ideas. We'd love to hear from you—after all, we are publishing books for you!

Please stay in touch with us and follow us at:

Facebook: Mango Publishing
Twitter: @MangoPublishing
Instagram: @MangoPublishing
LinkedIn: Mango Publishing
Pinterest: Mango Publishing
Newsletter: mangopublishinggroup.com/newsletter

Join us on Mango's journey to reinvent publishing, one book at a time.